RESEARCH IN PARAPSYCHOLOGY 1986

Abstracts and Papers from the
Twenty-ninth Annual Convention of the
Parapsychological Association, 1986

DEBRA H. WEINER
and
ROGER D. NELSON
Editors

The Scarecrow Press, Inc.
Metuchen, N.J., & London
1987

Responsibility for the contents of these papers rests with the contributors and not with the Parapsychological Association, Inc.

ISBN 0-8108-2068-4
Manufactured in the United States of America
Library of Congress Catalog Card No. 66-28580
Copyright © 1987 by the Parapsychological Association, Inc.

CONTENTS

Preface: The Twenty-ninth Annual Convention (Roger D. Nelson) ... ix
Editorial Introduction (Debra H. Weiner) ... xi
Note to the Reader ... xiii
Abbreviations ... xv

1. Papers

PSYCHOKINESIS STUDIES

Analysis of Variance of REG Data (Sitha Babu) ... 1
Psi Effects Without Real-Time Feedback Using a PsiLab// Video Game Experiment (Rick E. Berger) ... 6
Psi Effects Without Feedback: Will the Real Psi Source Please Stand Up? (Rick E. Berger) ... 9
Operator-Related Anomalies in a Random Mechanical Cascade Experiment (Roger D. Nelson, Brenda J. Dunne, and Robert G. Jahn) ... 12
Random Event Generator PK in Relation to Task Instructions (John Palmer and James R. Perlstrom) ... 17
Behavioral Response of Microorganisms to Psi Stimulus, Part II: Statistical Analyses of Data from *Dunaliella* (C.M. Pleass and N.D. Dey) ... 20
Infrared Spectra Alteration in Water Proximate to the Palms of Therapeutic Practitioners (Stephan A. Schwartz, Randall J. De Mattei, Edward G. Brame, Jr., and S. James P. Spottiswoode) ... 24
Hypnotic Suggestion and RSPK (Jeannie Lagle Stewart, William G. Roll, and Steve Baumann) ... 30

FREE-RESPONSE ESP STUDIES

Ganzfeld Target Retrieval with an Automated Testing System: A Model for Initial Ganzfeld Success (Charles Honorton and Ephraim I. Schechter) ... 36
Replication of an "Incline" Effect in Blind Judging Scores (Michaeleen Maher) ... 39
Exploring Hypnotizability, Creativity, and Psi: Conscious and Unconscious Components to Psi Success in the Ganzfeld (Nancy Sondow) ... 42

FORCED-CHOICE ESP AND TIMING STUDIES

Successful Performance of a Complex Psi-Mediated Timing Task by Unselected Subjects (William Braud and Donna Shafer) — 48

Children's ESP Scores in Relation to Age (Susan Shargal) — 51

Effects of Electrical Shielding on GESP Performance (Charles T. Tart) — 53

Comment: Electromagnetic Measurements of the Shielded Room at U.C. Davis (G. Scott Hubbard and W.R. Vincent) — 55

Event-Related Brain Potentials as Clairvoyant Indicators in a Single-Subject Design, Forced-Choice Task (Charles A. Warren and Norman S. Don) — 56

DISPLACEMENT EFFECTS IN ESP AND PK

Effects of Cognitive Style and Type of Target on Displacements (James E. Crandall) — 62

Further Evidence of the Relation of Displacement Effects to Favorability of ESP Testing Conditions, with a Discussion of Possible Artifacts (James E. Crandall and H. Kanthamani) — 66

Displacement Effect Revisited (H. Kanthamani and Anjum Khilji) — 69

Missing and Displacement in Two RNG Computer Games (Ephraim I. Schechter) — 73

PSI AND GEOMAGNETIC FACTORS

Persistent Temporal Relationship of Ganzfeld Results to Geomagnetic Activity, Appropriateness of Using Standard Geomagnetic Indices (Marsha H. Adams) — 78

Aspects of the Measurement and Application of Geomagnetic Indices and Extremely Low Frequency Electromagnetic Radiation for Use in Parapsychology (G. Scott Hubbard and Edwin C. May) — 79

Attempted Correlation of Engineering Anomalies with Global Geomagnetic Activity (Roger D. Nelson and Brenda J. Dunne) — 82

Experimental Dream Telepathy-Clairvoyance and Geomagnetic Activity (Michael Persinger and Stanley Krippner) — 85

Geomagnetic Factors in Spontaneous Telepathic, Precognitive, and Postmortem Experiences (Michael A. Persinger and George B. Schaut) — 88

Geomagnetic Effects in a GESP Test Are Altered by Electrical Shielding (Charles T. Tart) — 90

METHODOLOGY

Monte Carlo Methods in Parapsychology (George P. Hansen) — 93

Representation and Performance Evaluation Approaches
   in Psi Free-Response Tasks (A. Jean Maren) 97
Judging Strategies to Improve Scoring in the Ganzfeld
   (Julie Milton) 100
An Ethnographic Approach to the Study of Psi: Method-
   ology and Preliminary Data (Marilyn Schlitz) 103

THEORIES AND TESTS OF THEORIES

Psychology of the OTs: Introduction to the Observational
   Quasi-Motor Model (Brian Millar) 107
Testing the Intuitive Data Sorting Model with Pseudorandom
   Number Generators: A Proposed Method (Dean I. Radin
   and Edwin C. May) 109
The Out-Of-Body Experience as an Imaginal Journey: A
   Study from the Developmental Perspective (Rex G.
   Stanford) 111

2. Symposia

FIFTY YEARS OF THE JOURNAL OF PARAPSYCHOLOGY (Convener: K. Ramakrishna Rao)

Publication Policy and the Journal of Parapsychology
   (Richard S. Broughton) 116
Controversy and the JP (John Palmer) 119
J.B. Rhine in the Journal of Parapsychology (H. Kan-
   thamani) 123

PSI AND SYSTEMS THEORY (Convener: William G. Roll)

Psi and Systems Theory (William G. Roll) 126
Systems Theory: Philosophical Assumptions and Impli-
   cations for Parapsychology (Hoyt L. Edge) 129
Interpersonal Systems and Parapsychology (R. Jeffrey
   Munson) 130

3. Roundtables

IDS VERSUS PK: TESTING DIFFERING INTERPRETATIONS OF THE DATA (Convener: Richard S. Broughton)

Introduction (Richard S. Broughton) 136
Recent Advances in the IDS Model (Edwin C. May, G.
   Scott Hubbard, and Beverly S. Humphrey) 137
Exploratory Test of the IDS Model (Dean I. Radin) 138
Comments on the Intuitive Data Sorting Hypothesis
   (Evan Harris Walker) 139
Striving Toward a Model (George P. Hansen) 140

On Some Statistical Implications of the IDS Hypothesis (Zoltan Vassy) ... 141
An Interactive System Model for Anomalous Data (Roger D. Nelson) ... 142

WHAT RESEARCH SHOULD WE BE DOING? (Convener: Keith Harary)

On the Scientific Study of Other Worlds (Charles T. Tart) ... 145
Questioning Our Assumptions About the Mind (Keith Harary) ... 146
On Miracles and Modern Shamanism (D. Scott Rogo) ... 148
Human Perceptual Modalities and Remote Volitional Interaction (Elizabeth A. Rauscher) ... 149

STUDYING CHANNELING (Convener: Arthur Hastings)

The Study of Channeling (Arthur Hastings) ... 152
The Case of Patience Worth (Stephen E. Braude) ... 153
Statistical Methods for Disputed Authorship Applied to Channeling (Jerry Solfvin) ... 154
Healing Through Spirits: An Experiential Account of Disobsession in the Brazilian Spiritist Tradition (Matthew C. Bronson) ... 156
Early Findings on the Nature of Channeled Discourse (Dan Hawkmoon Alford) ... 157
Psychological Resistance in Research on Channeling: A Discussion of the Channeling Panel (Charles T. Tart) ... 159

PSI AND MENTAL HEALTH (Convener: William G. Roll)

Notes on Clinical Parapsychology (William G. Roll) ... 161
Psi and Therapeutic Insight (Jeannie Lagle Stewart) ... 162
On the Mental Health of Parapsychology and Parapsychologists (Charles T. Tart) ... 164
The Need for a Hermeneutic Methodology in Applied Clinical Parapsychology (Oscar Miro-Quesada S.) ... 165
Resonance and Psychotherapy (Virginia A. Larson) ... 166
Cross-Cultural Approaches to Multiple Personality Disorder: E.C. Mendes and "Psico-Sintese" (Stanley Krippner) ... 168

CLINICAL ETHICS IN PSI RESEARCH (Convener: R. Jeffrey Munson)

Introduction: Ethical Concerns with Clinical Services in Parapsychology (R. Jeffrey Munson) ... 170
Changing Ethical Perspectives and Parapsychology (Hoyt L. Edge) ... 171
The Ethics of Clinically Relevant Situations Encountered in Research (Rex G. Stanford) ... 172

Ethical Structure in Clinical Applications of Parapsychology
(James A. Hall)   173

The Practice of Clinical Parapsychology: Ethical Considerations and Training Issues (Maria Nemeth)   175

DO WE DISCOVER AND/OR CREATE REALITY? (Convener: Elizabeth A. Rauscher)

Exploring Our Limited Perceptions (Keith Harary)   176
Do We Create or Discover Reality? (William C. Gough)   177
Can We Utilize Our Current Research and Experience in Parapsychology and the Physics of Consciousness to Address the Issue, "Do We Discover and/or Create Our Own Reality?" (Elizabeth A. Rauscher)   177
Do We Discover or Create Reality? (Julian Isaacs)   179
Co-Created Reality (Robert-Peter F. Quider)   180

Addendum: STAGE MAGIC: WHAT DO PARAPSYCHOLOGISTS NEED TO KNOW? (Convener: Loyd Auerbach)

Summary (Loyd Auerbach)   182

Examples of a Need for Conjuring Knowledge (George P. Hansen)   185

4. Invited Address

Therapeutic Touch: Report of Research in Progress (Janet F. Quinn)   187

5. Presidential Address

Thoughts on the Role of Meaning in Psi Research (Debra H. Weiner)   203

Name Index (Linda Vann)   225

Subject Index (Linda Vann)   229

PREFACE
THE TWENTY-NINTH ANNUAL CONVENTION

The 29th Annual Convention of the Parapsychological Association, marking also the 50th anniversary of the Journal of Parapsychology, was held at Sonoma State University in Rohnert Park, California, August 5-9, 1986. The Program Committee included Rick Berger, George Hansen, G. Scott Hubbard, and several specialist reviewers. The Arrangements Committee was chaired by Robert-Peter Quider.

A wide spectrum of research was represented at the convention in some 34 contributed papers, six roundtable discussions, two symposia, and four invited addresses. The latter include the Presidential Address by Debra H. Weiner and a multidimensional presentation on healing by Janet F. Quinn; written versions of these can be found in this volume. In other invited talks Joe Kamiya described his philosophy of research and in the J.B. Rhine Banquet Address Stephen LaBerge examined lucid dreaming.

Several sessions in the program were composed of various perspectives on the same issue, with a notable overlap or actual replication of results. A few papers described new areas of exploration, while others described topics that are being reopened for consideration with the aid of new and powerful technologies and analytic strategies. It is to be hoped that such efforts will stir the imagination of replicators, for this field of inquiry clearly continues to demand special patience and unusual dedication to the strict rules of scientific inquiry. The tantalizing glimpses of order in the experimental results are often accompanied by thoroughly mystifying exceptions and sometimes by clearly contradictory indicators.

The difficulties pale before the potential significance of the relationship that seems to be indicated between human consciousness and the environment of experiments, other people, and the physical world. The opportunity to work in the areas described in this volume carries responsibility, and the work excites criticism that is sometimes unfortunately irrational, but it also provides the pleasure of exploration at a frontier. In the words of the Sufi Mullah Hasrudin:

Enjoy yourself, or try to learn; you will annoy someone. If you do not, you will annoy someone!

Roger D. Nelson
Program Chairperson

EDITORIAL INTRODUCTION

This volume of Research in Parapsychology (RIP) introduces two changes which will be continued in future volumes. The first reflects the desire of the Board of Directors of the Parapsychological Association, Inc. (PA) and the RIP staff to clarify the status of RIP abstracts. This issue has been the topic of lively debate, and the Editorial Introductions of at least two volumes (1983 and 1985) have discussed it. While the status of abstracts will change as new convention procedures or philosophies are adopted, it is important for readers to have an accurate perspective on RIP's contents. A Note to the Reader, which briefly summarizes some of the central issues, will be included as part of RIP's front material.

The second change reflects the findings of a recent poll of PA members regarding RIP, which showed that members wanted some means for obtaining complete versions of papers abstracted in RIP. Therefore, for each abstract the address of at least one author whom readers can contact for further information will be printed, when possible.

This volume continues the practice used last year of grouping papers by topic area rather than by the session in which they were presented at the convention. The reason for this is simply that the considerations going into designing the convention program are not always the same as those going into organizing RIP, and a rigid adherence to the convention program would make for a disjointed format here. Because of this arrangement, however, session chairpersons cannot be listed with the abstracts. Therefore, we would like to acknowledge here the following individuals who served as session chairpersons: Loyd Auerbach, Patricia Barker, George P. Hansen, William Keepin, Roger D. Nelson, and Diana Robinson.

Debra H. Weiner
Editor

NOTE TO THE READER

With the exception of the Presidential and Invited Addresses, all papers published in Research in Parapsychology are abridged versions of the authors' convention papers. In many cases length restrictions have required authors to eliminate over half their original reports. Therefore, it should not be assumed that the articles contained herein are complete descriptions of the research being reported. The address of one author per abstract is being included, when possible, so that readers may contact an author for a copy of the complete report.

Readers should also be aware that while the Convention Program Committee does evaluate all submissions to determine their acceptability for presentation, this review process must be conducted within a limited time period. Time constraints are such that the papers cannot receive the level of evaluation enjoyed by papers submitted to journals. Readers interested in a particular paper should consult contemporary issues of refereed parapsychological journals to see if they contain a more developed representation of the work being reported here.

For further comments on some of the issues regarding the status of these abstracts, please see the Editorial Introductions to the 1983 and 1985 volumes of Research in Parapsychology.

ABBREVIATIONS

The following abbreviations are used in reference citations:

EJP	European Journal of Parapsychology
JASPR	Journal of the American Society for Psychical Research
JP	Journal of Parapsychology
JSPR	Journal of the Society for Psychical Research
PASPR	Proceedings of the American Society for Psychical Research
PSPR	Proceedings of the Society for Psychical Research
RIP 19xx	Research in Parapsychology (for the year indicated)

Part 1: Papers

PSYCHOKINESIS STUDIES

ANALYSIS OF VARIANCE OF REG DATA

Sitha Babu (Princeton Engineering Anomalies Research, School of Engineering/Applied Science, Princeton University, Princeton, NJ 08544)

An experiment to explore the effects of the interaction of human consciousness with random physical systems using an electronic random event generator (REG) device has been in operation in the Princeton Engineering Anomalies Research (PEAR) laboratory for the past several years. Briefly, data are generated from a random series of binary samples, or bits, derived either from a commercial electronic noise diode or a pseudorandom shift-register board, sampled at various counting rates and recorded and displayed to the operator as "trials" or counts of 200 bits each. Extensive calibration tests have demonstrated that the output scores distribute normally and closely approximate the theoretically expected mean, standard deviation, and higher moments. The experimental protocol is designed to investigate the effect of the operator's intention on the trial scores, compounded in runs of 50 trials each. Trials are generated under three levels of intention: to raise the value of the run mean (PK^+), to lower the value of the mean (PK^-), or to generate a baseline. The intention of the operator is the primary variable of the experiment, although various secondary parameters are also explored, e.g., whether operator intention is established volitionally or by random instruction; whether each trial in the run is initiated manually or automatically; the sampling rate; and the details of the noise source.

For purposes of the preliminary analysis described herein, data acquired by 29 operators using a microelectronic noise diode source were compounded to a total of 77 series, each consisting of approximately 5000 or 2500 trials per intention and yielding approximately 100 or 50 run means per condition. In addition, 29 series of approximately 2500 trials per intention were acquired by 10 operators using a pseudo-REG source, following the same protocol. These data were analyzed in several different groupings, ranging in size from the total data base to the individual operators' data bases.

Analysis of Variance (ANOVA)

The purpose of the analysis was to confirm and extend the results of earlier partial assessments of primary effects (Nelson, Dunne, Jahn, PEAR Technical Report 84003) and to evaluate quantitatively the effects on the results of certain of the secondary variables, e.g., the automatic/manual, instructed/volitional, and sampling rate options. To accomplish this, a standard analysis of variance (ANOVA) technique was employed, which is capable of comparing in a single analysis the contributions of various experimental factors to the response variable, i.e., the deviation of run means in the direction of effort. Since the experiment in question involves factors with discrete but multiple levels, a full factorial design was applied to both the collective data bases and to the individual data bases, using a computer program known as SAS (SAS Institute, Cary, NC 27511-8000) and the GLM (General Linear Model) procedure on an IBM 3081.

Data Groupings

Although it is possible to combine all variations of the protocol into one comprehensive analysis of variance, for this exploration a simpler approach was taken: examining major subgroups separately. For purposes of this analysis, data were concatenated into the following groups:

Group 1: All data generated on the REG

Group 2: All data generated on the pseudo-REG

Group 3: All data (Groups 1 and 2 combined)

Group 4: All data from operators who completed series on both the REG and the pseudo-REG

Group 5: All data from series generated on the REG that met the t-test one-tailed significance criterion ($t > 1.645$) in the direction of intention

Group 6: All series generated on the pseudo-REG that met the significance criterion in the direction of intention

Group 7: All series that met the significance criterion in the direction of intention (Groups 5 and 6 combined)

In addition, data bases of all individual operators who had explored both options of at least one secondary variable were processed separately.

The factors explored for Groups 1-7 were these:

OP: varying number of levels depending on particular group

IN: level 1 = PK^+; level 2 = PK^-

V: level 1 = Volitional; level 2 = Instructed

A: level 1 = Automatic; level 2 = Manual

NS: level 1 = REG; level 2 = Pseudo-REG
(Groups 3, 4, and 7 only)

(SR was not included as a factor in Groups 1-7 since most operators did not explore this option.)

The main interaction terms explored were OP x IN, OP x V, OP x A, IN x V, IN x A (for Groups 1,2,5,6); and OP x IN, OP x V; OP x A, OP x NS, IN x V, IN x A, IN x NS (for Groups 3,4,7).

The models used for individual operator ANOVA depended on the particular factors prevailing in the given data base.

Discussion of ANOVA Results

Group 1 (All REG): Only the OP factor showed a significant effect (p = .0378), indicating that the individual operator performances are the strongest distinguishing influence on the REG data base.

Group 2 (All Pseudo-REG): Although OP was not significant per se, the interaction terms OP x IN and OP x V were both significant (p = .0035 and .0030, respectively), suggesting that while there were smaller differences in individual operator performance in the pseudo-REG data than in the REG data, individual operators appeared to respond differently to the IN and V variables on the pseudo-REG.

Group 3 (REG + Pseudo-REG): In the combined data base the main effect of OP (p = 0.0029) is stronger than in the REG data base alone, implying that the differences in individual operator performance on the pseudo-REG, while not themselves significant, were sufficient to compound in the overall data base to a highly significant level. On the other hand, the interaction term OP x V (p = 0.0105) decreased in significance. This may be interpreted as an indication that while performance varied strongly from one operator to the next, the effect of the volitional versus instructed mode was less important to some operators on the REG than on the pseudo-REG.

Group 4 (Operators Completing REG and Pseudo-REG Series): Looking only at the data from nine operators who performed experiments on both the REG and the pseudo-REG, once again OP appeared as a significant factor (p = 0.0044). Additionally, A emerged as a significant variable (p = 0.0374), although only two of the nine operators explored the automatic/manual option. The interaction OP x V was strongly significant for this group (p = 0.0007). By comparing these results with those of Group 3, it becomes clear that the importance of this interaction is reflected in the performance of these nine operators on both noise sources, although this was not observable when their data were subsumed in the larger REG data base containing 20 other operators as well.

Group 5 (REG, t > 1.645): In order to provide a clearer picture of the factors contributing to the primary effect of the experiment, this group was composed of only those series where a significant result was obtained in the intended direction of effort (t > 1.645). IN was found to be a significant factor (p = 0.0076), indicative of a strong asymmetry between the overall results of the PK^+ and PK^- intentions. Combined with the findings of a significant IN x V interaction (p = 0.0303), it may be concluded that this asymmetry was influenced by the effect of the secondary variable, V. The interaction term OP x A was also marginally significant (p = .0429), suggesting a differential effect of the secondary variable, A, for some operators in the group.

Group 6 (Pseudo-REG, t > 1.645): A similar analysis of the significant pseudo-REG series displayed a strong effect for the interaction term OP x IN (p = .0045). Since this group represented more than 33% of the entire pseudo-REG data base and 70% of the pseudo-REG operators, it is not surprising that these results were consistent with the findings of Group 2, where the asymmetrical results of the PK^+ and PK^- intentions showed strong operator differences. Such a similarity was not observed in a comparison of Group 5 with Group 1, where Group 5 represents less than 20% of the overall REG data base and approximately 28% of the operators.

Group 7 (REG + Pseudo-REG, t > 1.645): Combining all the significant series regardless of noise source, IN appeared as a significant factor (p = .0100), although less so than in the REG series alone. This implies that this subset of the data displayed a more symmetrical PK^+/PK^- effect in the pseudo-REG series than in the REG series. However, the modest OP x IN interaction (p = .0516) suggests that the strong asymmetry in individual operator PK^+/PK^- results in the pseudo-REG series was not a significant factor in the REG series. IN x V showed a stronger effect in the combined series (p = .0081) than in the REG series alone, indicating that the correlation between intention and mode of instruction, while not a significant feature of the pseudo-REG series, was still a contributing factor.

Note that in none of the groups that combined REG and pseudo-REG did noise source (NS) emerge as a significant primary factor in spite of some apparent differences in secondary aspects of the comparisons. As an independent factor, V also was not significant in any of the groups, although as part of interaction terms it displayed strong correlations with operator and intention, indicating its role as a secondary parameter subject to differences in individual operator performance. IN, on the other hand, appeared independently and in interaction with OP, indicating that individually and collectively the PK^+/PK^- distinction displayed consistent asymmetries.

The data bases of all individual operators who explored at least two secondary parameters were also examined. Wherever appropriate, REG and pseudo-REG data were analyzed separately as well as in combination. Conforming to earlier observations of individual "signatures" of achievement, no systematic pattern of performance across operators was observed. In addition, with the exception of two operators with marginally significant NS x IN interactions, noise source did not appear to be á significant factor in any of the individual results.

Summary

This preliminary analysis of variance of the current REG data base provides some quantitative support for our heretofore qualitative observations of individual operator "signatures," reinforcing the importance of maintaining separate data bases for all operators. On the other hand, the results indicate that the physical variable of noise source is not as influential a factor as some of the more subtle psychological variables. Further examination will be required to substantiate and interpret the various cross-correlations indicated.

Acknowledgments

The author would like to express her indebtedness to her research colleagues S.M. Intner, B.J. Dunne, R.D. Nelson, W.N. Keepin, and R.G. Jahn, and all the operators. The Princeton Engineering Anomalies Research program is supported by The McDonnell Foundation, The John E. Fetzer Foundation, Inc., Helix Investments, Ltd., and The Ohrstrom Foundation.

PSI EFFECTS WITHOUT REAL-TIME FEEDBACK USING A PSILAB// VIDEO GAME EXPERIMENT

Rick E. Berger (Science Unlimited Research Foundation,
   311-D Spencer Lane, San Antonio, TX 78201)

Though it has been rather widely assumed by investigators using random number generators (RNGs) that real-time feedback from the target system is necessary for psi effects to occur, a growing data base of studies has reported putative psi effects in the absence of real-time feedback to subjects. In one series of experiments, for example, subject personality variables were found to correlate with such "silent" (no feedback) data (Berger, Schechter, and Honorton, RIP 1985, 1-3). Silent-data effects suggest that there may be no such thing as a "control" condition in psi research in the traditional meaning of the term.

Method

The Psi Invaders experiment is a module in the PsiLab// standardized psi-testing system produced by the Psychophysical Research Laboratories in which silent-data effects can be explored (Berger and Honorton, RIP 1984, 68-71). Psi Invaders is a video game very similar to the Space Invaders arcade game. When the player attempts to fire the "laser," a hardware RNG is sampled 100 times, the high bit of the sampled 8-bit byte is compared with a binary target which is complemented every trial, and the run score (number of matches between the target and generated bit) determines whether the laser fires or misfires. Above-chance run scores result in both laser fire and special game score and audiovisual bonuses. Date are automatically recorded to computer disk.

In the PsiLab// version of Psi Invaders, each button press yields two data samples. Participants receive trial-by-trial feedback of the output of the feedback sample. With every button press a second matched trial, the silent data sample, is collected for which the subject receives no feedback. Identical RNG sampling parameters are employed for both conditions and the order of feedback/silent samples is pseudorandomly determined.

In the current experiment, a live RNG decision randomizes each game into one of two data observation conditions: In the first condition, each button press yields two data samples (here called feedback with silent saved [FSS], and silent). The second experimental condition is called feedback with silent destroyed (FSD) in which both feedback and silent data are collected as in the normal game; however, at the game's end all silent data are destroyed by zeroing prior to their being saved to computer disk. This insures that the only difference between the FSS and FSD conditions is the availability of silent data for their later observation.

The Psi Invaders system has a mode in which the computer simulates the game playing of a human subject. All auditory and visual feedback is turned off (though the program timing considerations have been retained), and game-player "decisions" (where to point the "laser" and when to press the button) are made with a pseudorandom timing loop which was tailored to simulate actual game-play timing. The same program that administers the experimental games also administers the simulations.

The RNG is a PsiLab// noise-based RNG for the Apple computer. This RNG is in daily use and is periodically verification-tested with long randomness checks. Sampling frequency was approximately 6.7 kHz.

The data base reported here is a subset from a larger ongoing research effort. The current series of experiments is attempting to find "talented" subjects in a pilot series and to continue to collect a large, systematic data base across several studies, varying parameters of the feedback/silent conditions. Each subject's data base will be considered as a separate experiment, and within-subject consistency will be studied both within and across experimental series. The present report documents the performance of the experimenter (who has a long history of silent-data effects across experiments) acting as subject, who completed a planned 600-game experiment (24 series of 25 games each). A report on the data of the other experimental participants can be found elsewhere in this volume (see pp. 9-12).

Two primary hypotheses were tested in this experiment:
(1) In accordance with the subject's past experimental performance, significant scoring would emerge in the silent-data condition and (2) by removing the availability of later observation of the silent data, effects comparable or exceeding the silent-data effects would emerge in the feedback-with-silent-destroyed condition.

Results

Mean game Z-scores were found to be significantly shifted in the positive direction for both data subsets (feedback with silent saved: $M = .126$, $t = 2.3$, 322 df, $p = .02$, two-tailed; silent: $M = .12$, $t = 2.1$, 322 df, $p = .036$), whereas data in the feedback-with-silent-destroyed condition were at chance level ($M = -.068$, $t = -1.14$, 276 df, $p = .25$). Simulation data did not differ from chance expectation.

Over the 24 individual experimental series, t-scores obtained by comparing Cohen's d measures to the expected mean Z-score of zero showed that the FSS+SILENT data showed significant hitting ($M = .55$, $t = 3.14$, 23 df, $p = .004$). The FSD data showed no overall effects ($M = -.27$, $t = -1.41$, 23 df, $p = .17$). Regarding consistency of the effect, 18 of the 24 effect-size measures in the

FSS+SILENT condition were in the positive direction (exact binomial p = .022, two-tailed). The FSD condition showed an opposite and consistent effect with 17 of the 24 series effect-size measures in the negative direction (exact binomial p = .064, two-tailed). Simulation data revealed no such differences: 11/24 positive in FSS+SILENT data; 12/24 positive in FSD data.

When a histogram of simulation run scores for all data was graphed, an interesting anomaly appeared. The mean run score of 50 protruded noticeably above the theoretical curve. In fact, while the distribution of run scores showed a propensity to "hug the curve" too closely, this cell is independently significant (chi-square = 5.17, 1 df, p = .02). What was most striking about this graph was its similarity to data seen elsewhere (Nelson, Dunne, and Jahn, PEAR Technical Note 84003, Princeton University, Princeton Engineering Anomalies Research, 1984). The baseline condition from the Princeton Engineering Anomalies Research (PEAR) group represented data collected while being observed by subjects instructed to generate "baseline" data ("Let the machine perform without your influence"). Indeed, the only deviation from their large data base's run-score histogram occurred around the run score of 100 (the mean), which also occurred at a level significantly greater than chance (chi-square = 5.656, 1 df, p = .017).

In the present data, the simulations were collected in quite a different manner. The experimenter set up the number of games to be generated by the computer, pressed a button on the computer, and left the area. Since there is no real-time feedback available in any condition in the simulations, all three data sets produced by simulations (FSS, FSD, and silent) are functionally similar to the experimental silent-data condition. The primary difference (from an observational standpoint) is that the experimental silent condition allows trial-by-trial initiation of runs whereas in simulations only one button press initiates collection of hundreds or thousands of runs.

Discussion

Though significant apparent psi effects emerged in both feedback-with-silent-saved and silent data samples, contrary to the hypothesis removing the silent data did not enhance feedback performance in the feedback-with-silent-destroyed condition. Though the directional silent effects reported here are consistent with previous performance of the subject, it had been thought that the presence of the silent data might have been "watering down" potential effects in the feedback condition. The emergence of the equal magnitude feedback condition effects at the game score level was unexpected.

The collection, then subsequent destruction, of silent data in the FSD condition was mostly a matter of programming expedience to create a feedback-only condition in which essential program timing was retained. It was not thought that the collection of such silent data could affect its associated feedback data (without the subsequent observation of the silent data). Perhaps it was simply the availability of the silent-data sample in the FSD condition which was responsible for its "effects" (consistent, though nonsignificant, negative scoring).

If it is accepted that it is good methodological procedure to perform simulations that closely approximate experimental conditions, then we must acknowledge the possible (or probable) role of the experimenter in affecting such data. In the present study, a possible influence of this experimenter is seen in both the experimental and "control" condition data. As similar data will be collected in other experiments by this experimenter in which other persons will be serving as "experimental subjects," it must be recognized that the comparison condition intended to serve as a control may indeed be an "experimenter psi" condition.

While the PEAR data seem to indicate the active involvement of subjects in the production of "baseline" data, the present data seem to indicate the active role of the experimenter both in data obtained without real-time feedback and data intended to serve as a control condition. Perhaps it is nearing the time to acknowledge that when interacting with "truly random systems," it may not be possible to "let the machine perform without your influence."

PSI EFFECTS WITHOUT FEEDBACK: WILL THE REAL PSI SOURCE PLEASE STAND UP?

Rick E. Berger (Science Unlimited Research Foundation,
    311-D Spencer Lane, San Antonio, TX 78201)

Data were reported elsewhere (see pp. 6-9) in which apparent psi effects were produced by the experimenter acting as a subject in a video game "micro-PK" random number generator (RNG) psi experiment. The data showed significant effects both in a data set of which the subject received real-time, trial-by-trial feedback and in a yoked data set ("silent" data) of which the only feedback was of a summary nature and occurred months later. This is a preliminary report of the performance of the other eight subjects who have to date performed the same experimental task. Each of the eight subjects has completed the minimum number of games for the series (25). The maximum number of games per subject is 600 for this series. To date, 5 subjects have contributed 25 games each, one has contributed 50, one has contributed 61 games, and two have contributed 100 (though one game was lost due to a computer malfunction).

Method

The Psi Invaders experiment (developed by Charles Honorton and the present author) is a module in the PsiLab// standardized psi-testing system produced by the Psychophysical Research Laboratories. (A more complete detailing of this experiment's method and rationale can be found on pp. 6-7.) In the current experiment, a live RNG decision randomized each game into one of two data observation conditions: In the first condition, each button press yields two data samples (here called feedback with silent saved [FSS] and silent). The second experimental condition is called feedback with silent destroyed (FSD). In this condition, both feedback and silent data are collected as in the normal game; however, at the game's end all silent data are destroyed by zeroing prior to their being saved to computer disk. This insures that the only difference between FSS and FSD conditions is the availability of silent data for their later observation. Five of the eight participants were completely unaware of the presence of the silent-data sample and no subjects were given feedback of their silent-data performance.

Simulations. The Psi Invaders system has a mode in which the computer simulates the game playing of a human subject. In this mode, all auditory and visual feedback is turned off (though the program timing considerations have been retained), and game-player "decisions" (where to point the "laser" and when to press the button) are made with a pseudorandom timing loop which was tailored to simulate actual game-play timing.

Subjects. Five females and 3 males with ages ranging from 13 to 38 are participating in the ongoing series. Four of the participants are working in some capacity as parapsychologists. All participants are strong believers in the existence of psi. All four parapsychologists rated their belief in psi as "6" on a 7-point scale where 7 indicated "believe very strongly." All nonparapsychologists rated their belief as "7."

Results

Collapsed across the experimental data of all participants, run-score (individual button press) distributions were shown by chi-square analyses to be normal for both feedback-with-silent-saved and feedback-with-silent-destroyed samples (FSS: chi-square = 38.8, 36 df, p = .34; FSD: chi-square = 31.6, 36 df, p = .68). There was a significant deviation in the run-score distribution of the silent-data sample (chi-square = 58.50, 36 df, p = .01). This group effect mirrors those produced by the experimenter serving as subject (see pp. 7-8) which comprise a large portion of the present data base. If we parse out the experimenter's contribution to the overall data base, the residual data show an even stronger deviation of silent run scores from the theoretical distribution (chi-square = 68.11, 36 df, p < .001). A significant deficit of run scores at the theoretical mean run-score value (chi-square = 11.23, 1 df, p = .0008) also contributed to the significant deviation in the data of the eight subjects. All simulation data showed normal chi-square values.

If we look closer to see how these results were derived (bearing in mind that only the experimenter ever observed these data), it appears that the experimenter-as-subject and other subjects arrived at their significant deviations by different paths. The experimenter-as-subject produced a small but consistent shift of the run-score mean (silent mean = 50.06, Z = 2.18, p = .03). No such shift was seen in the other subjects as a group (mean = 49.99, Z = -.36, p = .72). The experimenter-as-subject had a slight deficiency of run scores in the +3.6 standard deviation and higher range (Z = -.64, p = .26, one-tailed), whereas the other eight subjects, as a group, produced a significant excess of these extreme run scores (Z = 3.01, p = .0013, one-tailed). The overall "silent effect" is being contributed to by six of the eight participants.

Discussion

As most of the subjects were unaware of the silent-data sampling and never received any feedback of these data, observational theorists might argue that the effects seen in the data represent an experimenter (observational) effect. Though this interpretation cannot be ruled out, especially in light of the experimenter-as-subject's own significant silent-data effects in the present experiment, the "operating characteristics" of the two data sets (experimenter-as-subject vs. other subjects) seem to have been achieved by quite different means (no pun intended). The experimenter showed a small but consistent mean shift of run scores and no excess of extreme directional run scores. The other eight subjects showed no mean shift but a strong excess of extreme run-score values.

As each of the 22,200 silent run scores was obtained at the same time as the button was pressed by the subject (and feedback of the feedback sample given), it seems less than parsimonious to attribute a "retro-PK-by-experimenter" hypothesis to account for apparent effects in subjects' data. The present data suggest that silent-data effects may represent real-time psi effects occurring without real-time (or any subsequent) feedback or necessary awareness of its occurrence. That the patterns of the two separate silent run-score data sets (experimenter's and other subjects') are quite different may suggest that the "agents" responsible for the effects were different (i.e., not an "experimenter effect" in the subjects' silent data). If this is so, this might suggest a realtime "psi displacement" interpretation which challenges the premises of Observational Theory.

OPERATOR-RELATED ANOMALIES IN A RANDOM MECHANICAL CASCADE EXPERIMENT

Roger D. Nelson,[†] Brenda J. Dunne, and Robert G. Jahn
(Princeton Engineering Anomalies Research, School of Engineering/Applied Science, Princeton University, Princeton, NJ 08544)

The Random Mechanical Cascade (RMC) experiment was developed to explore the possibility that human consciousness, interacting with a macroscopic mechanical system in a sensitive, carefully controlled experiment, may effect a measurable change in the behavior of that system. An earlier report detailed the design and first applications of this experiment, and this update subsumes all the technical information presented therein (Nelson, Dunne, Jahn, PEAR Technical Report 83002, Princeton Engineering Anomalies Research). The study was motivated by the results of an extensive series of similar experiments using a microelectronic random event generator (REG) wherein a number of operators achieved substantial success in attempts to generate higher or lower totals of sample counts (PK^+ and PK^-) compared to baseline behavior or theoretical expectation. In the full REG data base, the observed split between the two PK conditions could have been achieved by chance with a probability of only about one part in 10^4, and about one-fourth of the more than 30 operators achieved extra-chance results. (Nelson, Dunne, Jahn, PEAR Technical Report 84003).

These results raised the question of the vulnerability of other types of random physical systems and processes to similar effects of intention. In particular, it seemed important to ascertain whether such effects could be produced on a more macroscopic scale. A mechanical Gaussian distribution analogue device, frequently featured in large science museums, which allows a large number of balls to drop through an array of elastic pins into a set of collecting bins to demonstrate the development of a quasi-normal distribution, was adapted for the purpose. Suitably modified and instru-

---

[†]Throughout this volume, a dagger indicates the speaker(s).

mented, this statistical demonstration device has become a viable experiment for assessment of the interaction of consciousness with a macroscopic random mechanical system.

Experimental Equipment and Procedure

The Random Mechanical Cascade machine is roughly 10' x 6' in size and employs 9000 polystyrene balls 3/4" in diameter, cascading through a quincunx array of 330 3/4" nylon pins on 2¼" centers. A conveyor transports the balls from a plenum at the bottom to a funnel at the top, from which they drop into the matrix of pins. The balls bounce in complex stochastic paths through the matrix, colliding elastically with pins and other balls, accumulating finally in 19 parallel vertical collecting bins arranged across the bottom. The front of the pin chamber and of the collecting bins below it are clear Plexiglas so that both the active cascade of balls and their disposition into the developing distribution of bin populations are visible as feedback to the operator.

Each collecting bin is equipped with an optoelectronic counter at its entrance. These 19 counters are scanned on-line by a microprocessor which transmits in real-time the ordered accumulation of counts in each bin to LED displays at the bottom of the bins and to a TERAK computer where the ordered sequence of ball drops is registered on disk as a file of 9000 characters. Each file carries indexing information, including file number, instruction, operator, date, time, humidity and temperature within the pin cavity, and various experimental parameters. A logbook is maintained with the indicated index information; a photograph of each completed run distribution, including the bin totals displayed on the LEDs; the bin totals as registered by the computer; summary information including total populations right and left of the 10th bin, a right-left ratio, and the distribution mean and standard deviation; and any appropriate comments.

Each run of 9000 balls takes about 12 minutes, and most operators sit facing the machine on a couch about eight feet away. Optional experimental parameters include choice of lighted versus blank LED displays and choice of volitional versus random assignment of direction of effort. As in the REG experiment, operators freely develop their own strategies and schedule their own sessions. They are encouraged to generate large data bases, divided into series of 10 sets of runs (20 sets of runs prior to October, 1983) wherein experimental parameters are not varied and over which some informal general strategy may be maintained. All operators are uncompensated volunteers, none of whom claim special abilities.

For the formal trials reported here, data are collected in sets of three runs which include a baseline, an effort to distort the distribution to the right (PK-right or PK$^+$), and a left-directed effort (PK-left or PK$^-$), closely interspersed, with all other conditions remaining constant. This "tripolar" experimental format is important in mitigating any possible biasing effects of physical changes in the operation of the machine. Variation of humidity, for example, is found to correlate with small changes in the distribution variance and very slightly with changes in the mean.

Because the RMC is a large-scale mechanical device, the distribution of results is dependent on a number of physical features of the machine and its immediate environment that are too complex to permit theoretical calculation. In the absence of a theoretical distribution, experimental results can only be compared to some empirical standard that fairly represents the distribution in the absence of operator influences. Although there is some evidence that even those runs designated as baselines may not be totally devoid of operator effects (Jahn, Nelson, Dunne, PEAR Technical Report 85001), such runs are nevertheless treated as the best available estimate of unbiased performance. All tables and numerical statements of significance reflect this presumption; in particular, the t-scores for PK-right and PK-left and the ΔPK values all are computed using the paired data (PK$^+$ vs. BL and PK$^-$ vs. BL) derived from the tripolar sets.

Statistical Treatment

Although an approximate model of the path of one ball might be developed using sophisticated Markov chain techniques, the complex of collisions is so fine grained that the conceptually simpler quasi-binary model analogous to that employed for the REG experiment may also serve heuristically to represent the RMC. In particular, as runs accumulate the envelope of the 19 bin populations closely approaches a Gaussian curve. There is a slight kurtosis, attributable in part to the first and last bins absorbing balls which would have made more steps from the mean but were prevented by the walls of the machine from doing so, and to a few balls falling too directly into the three central bins.

Using bin units as the statistical variable, the empirical distribution mean, μ, is approximately 10.025 and the standard deviation, σ, about 3.25 bins. Using a binary model with unit probabilities $p = q = .5$, and $\sigma = \sqrt{\nu pq}$, an expected number, ν, of "binary equivalent events" can be estimated for the path of one ball: i.e., $\nu = 4\sigma^2$ or about 40 effective binary decisions. Thus, in the RMC experiment a "trial" may be considered to be the 40 "binary equivalent samples" in a single ball's path into one of the 19 bins. Since there are 9000 such "trials" in a run, the statistical power of each run is considerable, comprising approximately 360,000 binary equivalent bits. (By comparison, a typical REG session of 20 runs yields 200,000 bits.) The expected mean of repeated runs is that of the distribution, 10.025, with a standard deviation about that value of .035.

The original formal series length of 20 runs was arbitrary and yielded an informatively stable estimate of the compounded mean for each of the three conditions. However, experience indicated that a shorter series of 10 sets of runs would be more comfortable for the operator, while still sufficient to distinguish trends from stochastic variation. The stability of parameter estimates for the distribution is indicated by the small standard error, $\sigma_{\bar{x}}$, for estimates of the mean. For a series of 20 runs, the standard error is .0078, yielding a 95% confidence interval around the grand baseline mean of $10.010 < \mu < 10.040$; for 10 runs the standard error is .0111 with a commensurate confidence interval. Thus, it is clear that persistent small changes in the mean of the experimental runs can cumulate rapidly to significant deviations from expected values.

Experimental Results

The RMC experiment has been in operation using the formal protocol described for nearly 4 years, and 21 operators have accumulated a total of 70 series (see Table I). Seven of these operators have generated a total of 16 series with terminal means that are unlikely by chance at the 5% level.

Table I

SUMMARY OF 70 RMC SERIES (21 OPERATORS)

Condition	Successful Series In Direction of Effort	Series $p < .05$
PK^+	N = 40 (57%)	N = 4 (6%)
PK^-	N = 46 (66%)	N = 12 (17%)
ΔPK^*	N = 47 (67%)	N = 12 (17%)

*The probability against chance is computed by a two-sample t-test.

Although the experiment is intended primarily to assess the series-level interaction with the machine of each operator independently, concatenations across series and across operators may be useful for particular purposes. Table II presents the results of a grand concatenation across all data.

Table II

SUMMARY OF CONCATENATED RMC DATA
(70 SERIES, 21 OPERATORS)

Condition	N	Mean	S.D.	t	p (one-tailed)
Baseline	964	10.02557	.03449		
Right (PK$^+$)	964	10.02631	.03450	0.466	.321
Left (PK$^-$)	964	10.01948	.03453	-3.890	5×10^{-5}
Δt (independent estimates)				3.080	.001
Δt' (two-sample t-test)				4.347	1×10^{-5}

Despite the combination of individuals with widely different performance, the results show a highly significant departure from expectation for the left-going efforts, while the right-going efforts are not significant.

Discussion

The RMC has proved to be an effective and high-yield experiment on the interaction of consciousness with physical systems, but in several respects the results are quite complex and will require considerable further work to explicate. Most notably, it has so far presented a profound asymmetry of effect, especially for one of the prolific operators. While the overall left-going efforts compound to a large cumulative deviation, the overall right-going efforts show little difference from baseline, although a few individual operators succeed with this instruction. Explorations of a broad range of potentially relevant physical and psychological variables may help explain this outcome and lead to more general insight. For example, one operator achieves quite different results under the two modes of instruction (volitional or random assignment), and this operator has demonstrated a similar differential effect in REG experiments as well. Also of potential consequence for ultimate comprehension is the apparent vulnerability of the baseline results to operator influence, as was also found in the REG data. The baseline distribution appears quite smooth and normal (chi-square = 7.75, with chi-square$_{.95}$ = 8.67, 17 df) while both PK distributions are relatively rough (chi-square$_R$ = 21.63 and chi-square$_L$ = 35.05, with chi-square$_{.05}$ = 27.59, 17 df).

Thus, several aspects of the results in this macroscopic experiment show statistically significant alterations that correlate with operator intentions. These comprise important complements to the results of the microelectronic REG experiment, since the scale and the style of the two physical systems are so different despite the similarity of their information content. Properly interpreted, these comparative results should aid in modeling the interaction of consciousness with such random physical systems.

RANDOM EVENT GENERATOR PK IN RELATION TO TASK INSTRUCTIONS

John Palmer[†] and James R. Perlstrom (Institute for Parapsychology, Box 6847, Durham, NC 27708)

In random event generator (REG) PK games that provide real-time feedback to the subject, a potential psychological conflict arises when the feedback indicates that scoring is in the opposite direction to the subject's intent. For example, when a subject is aiming for psi-hitting and the feedback indicates psi-missing, the subject may be tempted to alter his or her intent midstream and aim for significant psi-missing as a more attainable goal. A possible way to minimize this conflict is to instruct the subject to aim for either hitting or missing, i.e., to aim for high variance.

There also is a rationale for asking a subject to aim for low variance. If there is any truth to speculations that most of us are afraid of psi, unconsciously if not consciously, psi may be less threatening if we are asked to use it to reinforce the natural order of things. One psychologically appealing (if not strictly accurate) way of presenting such a task in the context of an REG PK game is to instruct the subject to keep the feedback display line as close as possible to the chance line, i.e., to aim for low variance.

Inspired by the preceding considerations, the authors undertook an REG PK experiment systematically comparing three instructional sets: "normal" directional scoring, high variance, and low variance. We chose for the REG task the game VOLITION developed at the Psychophysical Research Laboratories (PRL). The visual feedback consists of a line moving horizontally across a computer monitor screen. As scoring (defined by a cumulative Z-score) increases in the intended direction, the line is oriented upward with respect to the horizontal baseline. A decrease in scoring is likewise represented by a downward orientation of the line. For the purposes of this experiment, other forms of auditory or visual feedback were for the most part eliminated from the software because they are only appropriate for a directional set.

The feedback represented the output of a Bierman/RIPP binary REG, modified and thoroughly tested by PRL staff prior to our having acquired it. The REG, which works on an electronic noise principle, is a circuit board that fits inside our APPLE II+ microcomputer.

For this experiment, software options were selected that caused each button press by the subject to generate a run of 100 trials at a trial rate of 6700 per second. Each game consisted of 50 runs, each run adding a segment to the feedback line. At the end of the game, a table appeared on the screen giving the cumulative Z-score and associated p-value for that game.

Paired with each of the 50 runs fed back to the subject was a "silent" run not fed back but stored in the computer. The order of the two kinds of runs alternated within the game in an FS, SF, FS ... sequence.

Following each game, the number of hits in each run was stored on an APPLE diskette. The software also computed various statistical measures for each game, as described below. At the end of the experiment, these data were restructured and manually transferred to our PDP 11/23 computer for further analysis using BMDP software.

The subject sample consisted of 30 volunteers, mostly past or present Duke University students. All had been to an orientation session at the lab on a prior occasion, and 15 had participated in previous psi experiments at the lab. Most had already completed a Participant Information Form and the Myers-Briggs Type Indicator. Two additional subjects were actually tested but their data were eliminated (prior to experimenters' knowledge of their results) due to equipment malfunction.

Subjects were randomly assigned to each of the three conditions based on a random permutation of the numbers 1-30 performed by the REG. The conditions represented the three instructional sets: directional (D), extreme (E), and middle (M). (The E-condition aimed for high variance and the M-condition for low variance.) Ten subjects were assigned to each condition. Each subject completed four successive games, all with the same set. Subjects in the D-condition completed two high-aim games and two low-aim games in either HLLH or LHHL sequence, alternated between subjects in this condition.

Each subject was greeted by the experimenter (J.R.P.) who explained the task, including all three instructional sets. On the screen were the results of a bogus game with a directionally significant positive score to aid in the exposition. After setting up the first game on the computer, the experimenter moved behind a curtain where he remained until the four games had been completed. Once the experimenter had left the subject, the subject opened an envelope indicating the assigned condition (and the order of directional aims if in the D-condition). This method was used to keep the experimenter blind to the condition assignments. After completion of the four games, the experimenter debriefed the subject and introduced a card-shuffling task (to be discussed in a separate report). The experimenter maintained a casual, friendly, respectful, and supportive demeanor throughout. Most subjects seemed to enjoy the experiment very much.

As a control, within 90 minutes of each session the experimenter generated four simulation games which employed the same software, data recording, etc., as the experimental games. However, a single button press activated all four games.

Three dependent variables were specified: (1) *run variance*, a chi-square representing the sum of the squared run-score deviations about mean chance expectation (MCE) for each game; (2) *game variance*, the squared cumulative Z-score for each game (normalized by a double square-root transform); and (3) *game deviation*, the signed Z-score for each game (applicable only to the D-condition).

The two variance measures were planned to be analyzed by 3 x 2 x 4 mixed analyses of variance (ANOVA) with instructional set, feedback mode (feedback vs. silent) and game as the factors. (For purely exploratory purposes, this analysis was also performed on the game deviation scores.) It was planned to analyze the game deviation scores in the D-condition by a 2 x 2 within-subjects ANOVA with aim (high vs. low) and feedback mode as the factors. Where possible, cell means were planned to be evaluated for significance against MCE by single-mean t-tests. The criterion for significance was preset at $p < .05$, two-tailed.

The only significant result in the three planned ANOVAs was a main effect for instructional set on the game variance scores ($F = 3.65$, 2, 27 df, $p < .05$). Examination of the cell means revealed that the effect was attributable to a relatively high mean in the E-condition (.875) and a relatively low mean in the M-condition (.729), which is in line with the instructional sets. The effect was somewhat stronger in the silent mode than in the feedback mode, but not significantly so. Because of the transform, these means could not be evaluated with respect to MCE. When a table of the untransformed game variance means was examined, the only one to reach significance was the mean for the M-condition, silent mode. This mean was .644 ($t = -2.44$, 9 df, $p < .05$). However, it should be noted that the raw-score distribution is highly skewed.

Ironically, the strongest statistical result emerged from the exploratory overall ANOVA of the signed game deviation scores. A significant main effect for instruction set ($F = 4.45$, 2, 27 df, $p < .05$) was superseded by a significant set-by-game interaction ($F = 2.78$, 6, 81 df, $p < .02$). Further examination revealed that this result is attributable to significantly positive deviation scores in the second and third games of subjects in the E-condition, collapsed over feedback mode.

The simulation data were evaluated by computing the full three-way ANOVAs for run variance, game variance, and game deviation scores, respectively. Only one of the 21 possible effects met the .05 criterion of significance (at p = .006). This result is well in keeping with the null hypothesis.

At this point, not much more can be claimed for the experimental results than for the simulation results. Given the large number of effects examined, the relatively small number that were significant (combined with the marginal levels of the p-values), and in particular the failure of the significant results to converge in a meaningful pattern, it is best to treat them for now as statistical flukes. The significant main effect of instructional set on game variance does make some sense, however, and may be worth following up. On the other hand, this finding would have been more impressive had it occurred primarily in the feedback mode rather than in the silent mode. As is usually the case in exploratory research, the ultimate interpretation of these findings will depend on how they fit with findings of other experiments in REG PK.

BEHAVIORAL RESPONSE OF MICROORGANISMS TO PSI STIMULUS, PART II: STATISTICAL ANALYSES OF DATA FROM DUNALIELLA

C.M. Pleass[†] and N.D. Dey (College of Marine Studies, Pilottown Rd., Lewes, DE 19958)

A consciousness experiment in which the Doppler shift of He/Ne laser light was used to describe changes in the velocity and vector of a marine alga, Dunaliella, was reported by Pleass and Dey in 1985 (RIP 1985, 70-73). Because the subject of the consciousness experiment is living, we expect strings of baseline velocity and vector data which are, at some level, inexplicably time variant. This complicates the statistical procedures that must be used to analyze the data.

Cells of Dunaliella are approximately 10^{-5} m in length. Using whiplike flagella in a motion similar to a breast stroke, they swim at velocities up to approximately 2×10^{-4} m/sec. The authors use differential laser Doppler to obtain real-time information on velocities and vectors of individual organisms. The measuring volume is the ellipsoid where the split laser beams cross. It has a volume of approximately 1×10^{-6} cc. Cultures of Dunaliella can easily sustain 10^6 cells per cc, with intercellular spacing of the order of 10^{-4} m. Under these conditions, bursts of scattered light from the laser

Psychokinesis Studies

crossover will normally correspond to the passage of one individual cell. On those rare occasions when the measuring volume contains more than one cell, the observed velocity will be the mean. Data rates are quite high, approximately 70/sec. The apparatus is single component: It will record velocity and direction along any one chosen axis.

Since any experiment with a living system is by definition irreproducible and the baseline data must be assumed to contain trend, rhythm, and nonrandom noise, any satisfactory statistical procedure for describing the results of consciousness experiments must be robust enough to deal with these characteristics.

Baseline Data Properties

Baseline data, i.e., a stream of velocity readings taken by the computer when neither participant nor experimenter are present in the laboratory, have been collected and subjected to numerous visual inspections (via time plots) and more quantitative analyses. Figures in the Convention proceedings illustrate:

(1) Noise--the variation of velocity readings around an average value. This variation is neither a constant nor a constant percentage of the average. Standard deviations (σ) of baseline velocity readings range from 5 to 35 x 10^{-6} m/sec with coefficients of variation 100 $\sigma/\bar{x}$ from 10 to 60 percent.

(2) Trends--where velocity is consistently increasing or decreasing for periods of several hundred to several thousand readings.

(3) Periodicity--repeating cycles of varying frequency. Periodicity includes strings of velocity readings with significant autocorrelation. Note that no replicable frequencies characteristic of the organism or its environment (other than the diurnal or circadian) have been found.

(4) Trends and Periodicity--combinations of repeating cycles with consistently increasing or decreasing average velocity readings.

(5) Mean Shift--an obvious and relatively abrupt shift in the average velocity. This characteristic may be a "discontinuity" in an apparent long-range trend and may or may not include periodicity. It is relatively uncommon.

General Observations of Baseline Data: (1) All of above exist or can exist in the data stream at any given time; (2) Existence of one or more of these phenomena can only be determined after the fact, i.e., after the data have been collected and analyzed; (3) No a priori adjustment of data to "compensate" for

Statistical Analyses

PK85

The participants were asked to try to visualize the algae in the vicinity of the laser crossover during the psi period using informal, lighthearted imagery while excluding all unrelated conscious thoughts. They initiated each psi period by touching the F1 key and terminated it with F2. The psi interval was followed immediately by a control interval of the same length. After a pause of random duration (maximum 5000 raw data points), pseudo-psi and pseudo-control intervals which have identical dimensions to the real run were automatically marked in the data file. The control-period task involved reading trivia. The statistics routinely calculated were means and standard deviations. To accumulate scores, the double differences were developed into histograms with the best fitting Gaussian overlaid. <u>In each analysis the null hypothesis was that there was no psi effect extant</u>, and the data were detrended by using the double difference

$$\Sigma(\bar{X}_{control} - \bar{X}_{psi}) - \Sigma(\bar{X}_{pseudo-control} - \bar{X}_{pseudo-psi})$$

as the score for the run.

The results of these experiments were compared to results artificially generated from data collected when no psi experiments were in process. This additional level of control will be referred to as "global control." An F-test was used to compare the experimental and the global distributions of scores: $F = \sigma_g^2 / \sigma_p^2 = 1.64$. With 204 degrees of freedom this gave a probability of a chance difference less than 2×10^{-4}, suggesting that the null hypothesis should be rejected.

WAVE

Only one key press was involved. Participants were asked to touch the F1 key on the computer keyboard when they felt their psi effort was at a strong peak and to turn away immediately to the trivial control-period task. Reading a dictionary was found to be an effective way of quickly transferring attention. In this way, we hoped to observe the release of psi pressure. The peak psi period was taken to be the 25 data records (2500 raw data points) preceding the F1 key press; thus, all WAVE runs had the same data dimensions. The control, pseudo-psi, and pseudo-control periods all had the same dimension as the psi period. We continued to use the same null hypothesis, algorithm, and format for feedback.

Graphic displays of differences in means were provided as feedback, just as in PK85.

Quite striking results were obtained from individual sets. Run scores were then compared with global controls using the procedure previously outlined for PK85. In this case the experimental results had a much larger range than the global results: $F = \sigma_p^2/\sigma_g^2 = 5.99$. The probability of obtaining the result by chance is very low, $p = 10^{-6}$, again suggesting that the null hypothesis should be rejected.

It is appropriate to ask if the two "global control" distributions are similar, within experimental error, since the sample numbers are quite high and it would be difficult to explain any difference. Applying an F-test to them we find $F = \sigma_{w.g.c.}^2/\sigma_{Kg.c.}^2 = 1.11$, $p = .2$. This gives us substantial confidence in the chosen procedures.

Discussion and Conclusions

It is appropriate to use the most cautious interpretation of the results: The physics of the method used in the research is straightforward, but it is conceivable that there are alternate explanations for the differences between experimental and global data since the global data cannot, by definition, be taken at the same time. The only method that can be used to obtain global data at exactly the same circadian phase angle is to take it from a different diurnal period. This possibility will be examined.

The nonsignificant difference between the distributions of global control data from the two experiments ($p = .2$) helps to validate the statistical procedures. However, it is reasonable to question the use of the F-test, since the histograms of scores contain several extreme values. This test is used in an exploratory mode, for want of a better method of describing the differences between the two data sets. Suggestions for alternate methods of statistical processing would be most welcome.

Two statistical analyses of psi runs carried out with the green alga Dunaliella have been reported. They examine the significance of changes in psi and control period statistics derived from strings of velocity data. Taken at face value, the results suggest the rejection of the null hypothesis that there is no psi effect. However, this is the first experiment of this type to be attempted, and the results should be treated with caution until they are substantiated by further research and various alternate statistical treatments.

INFRARED SPECTRA ALTERATION IN WATER PROXIMATE TO
THE PALMS OF THERAPEUTIC PRACTITIONERS*

Stephan A. Schwartz,[†] Randall J. De Mattei,[†] Edward G. Brame,
    Jr., and S. James P. Spottiswoode (The Mobius Society,
    4801 Wilshire Blvd., Ste. 320, Los Angeles, CA 90010)

Studies by researchers in a variety of disciplines, notably biologist Bernard Grad at McGill University (JASPR, 1965, 95-129), biochemist M. Justa Smith at Rosary Hill College and Roswell Park Cancer Hospital (Human Dimensions, Spring 1972, 15-19), physicist Elizabeth Rauscher at University of California, Berkeley (RIP 1980, 140-141), and biologist Carroll Nash of St. Joseph's University (RIP 1982, 61-64) report increased vitality in treated subpopulations of cell colonies, enzymes, and seedlings in comparison with controls. In each study, treatment consisted of some variation of an historical technique known as laying-on of hands, or a modern nursing program known as Therapeutic Touch.

The variables that can affect the health and well-being of living systems are multitudinous. An alternative avenue for research is suggested in work done by Grad using near-infrared spectrophotometry of treated water samples (JASPR, 1965, 95-129). Dean and Brame continued that line of research, and their results supported Grad's findings (Proceedings of the Second International Congress of Psychotronics, 1975, 200-202).

The infrared (IR) portion of the electromagnetic spectrum was selected for monitoring, based on the assumption that what we are observing is a change in the oxygen-hydrogen (O-H) bonding. The state of O-H bonding is best observed in the infrared where the fundamental stretching frequency occurs (Rao, "Theory of Hydrogen Bonding in Water." In Franks (ed.), Water: A Comprehensive Treatise. New York & London: Plenum, 1972, p. 108), although earlier research suggests that overtones and combinations of overtones of the phenomenon occur at higher frequencies up to the ultraviolet (UV) region (Dean, An Examination of Infra-Red and Ultra-Violet Techniques to Test for Changes in Water Following the Laying-On-of-Hands. Doctoral Dissertation, Saybrook Institute, 1983, University Microfilms International No. 8408650; pp. 111-115). Because these UV bands are overtones, they are weaker and less clearly defined.

Hypotheses

Hypothesis One. The null hypothesis predicts that there will

---

*A complete 29-page report (dated 29 October 1986) is available from The Mobius Society.

be no significant difference in the ratio, defined below, resulting from infrared spectrophotometric analysis of the water from each session, whether the sample comes from a calibration control, session control, or a treated water vial. We predict that in some or all of the treated samples a change in the infrared spectra of the samples will occur such that the ratio, defined below, will have a reduced value in comparison with the session and calibration control samples. We expect that some practitioners will be more effective in producing the decreased ratio value than others.

Hypothesis Two. The second null hypothesis predicts that there will be no differential between 5-minute exposed vials and those exposed for 10 or 15 minutes. We predict that the magnitude of the change in the ratio value will increase with exposure time to the practitioner, the change being greatest in the 15-minute samples.

Protocol

Design. This pilot study, consisting of 14 therapy sessions involving one practitioner and one recipient each per session, is designed to explore an effect evidenced in the O-H bonding of water as a result of the intent and action of one person to influence another therapeutically. During the sessions practitioners had 50 ml sealed vials of bacterially static distilled water held to the palms of their hands by a cloth tube.

Each session involved the spectrophotometric analysis of five vials--three treated and two control samples. The three treated vials were in place for 5, 10, and 15 minutes, respectively. Two spectroscopists independently measured each sample on a predetermined schedule to keep uniform intervals of time between each analysis session and within each session's five spectra run.

The independent variable is the action and intent of the practitioner. With "intent" as our independent variable, an actual therapeutic session with its possibility of effective aid to a fellow human being is presumed to hold greater motivation than acting solely on bottled water.

Definition of Dependent Variable. The dependent variable is a ratio derived from the infrared spectrum. We measured the IR absorption at two frequencies (f_1 = 3620/cm, f_2 = 3350/cm) at the peak and shoulder of the absorption band. To normalize the absorbance values, a baseline representing the maximum transmission or minimum absorption for these wave numbers was constructed beginning at 3800/cm across to 2700/cm.

At 3620/cm two points are defined for percent transmittance in order to calculate absorbance: one, T_1, at the intersection with baseline; and the second, T_2, at the intersection with the spectrum.

Similarly, at 3350/cm the baseline intersection is defined as T_3 and the spectrum intersection as T_4. The absorbance at 3620/cm, A_u is defined by: $A_u = \log(T_1/T_2)$. Similarly, at 3350/cm, A_b is defined by: $A_b = \log(T_3/T_4)$. Then, the dependent variable R is given by:

$$R = A_b/A_u = \log(T_3/T_4)/\log(T_1/T_2).$$

(For further information regarding infrared spectroscopy, see AST, American Standards for Testing for Materials, committee E-13, Quantitative Infrared Analysis Procedures.)

<u>Vial numbering and utilization</u>. Sixty-one vials were uniformly marked with an integer from 1 to 61 and randomly assigned their roles as treated vials (42), session controls (14), and daily calibration controls (5).

<u>Analysis</u>. Testing the stated hypotheses involved a comparison of the mean values of R found for the three sample populations of treated, session controls and calibration controls. A nonparametric distribution of R values required the use of the distribution-free Mann-Whitney U test. The nature of the distribution was determined by the Rankit graphical method (Kletzky <u>et al</u>., <u>American Journal of Obstetrics and Gynecology</u>, 1975, pp. 688-694).

Results

<u>Hypothesis One</u>. Confirmed.

	Z	p
All Treated vs. All Controls	-2.03	0.02
All Treated vs. Calibration Controls	-2.93	0.002
All Treated vs. Session Controls	-0.26	0.4

The p-values are one-tailed and were calculated using the temperature-adjusted ratios as described in the Environmental Effects section.

<u>Hypothesis Two</u>. Not confirmed ($p > .2$).

<u>Inter-Spectroscopist Calibration Consistency</u>. The uniformity of the mean values (3.27 and 3.27) and standard deviations (0.14 and 0.15) between the two spectroscopists suggested no significant difference between their performances. Calibration controls showed relative consistency both by and between spectroscopists, indicating correct measurement technique and consistent sampling.

Psychokinesis Studies

An examination was conducted of possible artifacts of temperature, barometric pressure, and variations of sampling order which might alter R values; the results are presented below. It should first be noted that the single largest variation of R values resulted from a change in a component of the spectrophotometer.

Internal Reflection Element Variations. During the second session the germanium Internal Reflection Element (IRE) from the Multiple Internal Reflection (MIR) Unit in the IR spectrophotometer broke; in its place we substituted one of zinc selenide. The germanium IRE, with its higher refractive index, consistently produces lower ratios and, thus, artificially skewed the combined overall analysis. The germanium ratios alone (15 of 141) constitute too small an $\underline{n}$ to achieve truly meaningful results. The ratios for all samples measured using the zinc selenide IRE yield:

	$\underline{Z}$	$\underline{p}$
Treated vs. Combined Controls	-2.56	0.005
Treated vs. Calibration Controls	-3.54	0.0004
5-Minute samples	-3.06	0.001
10-Minute samples	-2.52	0.006
15-Minute samples	-3.02	0.001
Treated vs. Session Controls	-0.464	0.30
Calibration Controls vs. Session Controls	-2.8	0.002

Removing distortion due to the IRE differences increases the significance of the p-values.

Environmental Effects

The following ranges of temperature and barometric pressure were recorded during the course of the experiment: Temperature: maximum = 28.6°C, minimum = 22.3°C (range = 6.3°C); Barometric pressure: maximum = 30.1" Hg, minimum = 29.8" Hg (range = 0.3" Hg).

Ratio Values vs. Temperature. When plotted, the ratios showed a slight negative temperature coefficient across the aggregate samples. This same slight negative slope was observed in both germanium (-0.08) and zinc selenide populations (-0.055), and within all vial populations. Three studies have shown that R, as defined, has a temperature coefficient on the order of -0.025°/C (G.M. Hale, M.R. Query, and D. Williams, J. of the Optical Society of America, 1972; W.P. Pinkley, P.P. Sethna, and D. Williams,

J. of the Optical Society of America, 1977; J.W. Schultz and D.F. Hornig, J. of Physical Chemistry, 1961).

To mimic the mean effect observed in this study, a two-degree difference of room temperature would be required between sampling the treated and calibration controls. This magnitude of temperature shift was not observed; the mean shift was 0.44°C. To encompass the full range of the effect would require a change of +11°C.

To investigate whether ambient temperature or sample handling induced temperature shifts we conducted post hoc studies. The thermal time constant of the water within the vials was such that the temperature differential between sample and ambient halved every 29 minutes. Spectra from a given session were taken from 15 to 73 minutes after the time a vial left the hand of the practitioner. Second spectroscopic measurements typically occurred an hour and a half after that. A worst-case scenario showed that a vial would be 7°C above ambient at the time its first spectrum was taken.

This led to temperature factors involving the sample cell/IRE unit itself. During the course of a typical five-vial measurement session, we found that the sample-cell temperature varied above ambient by no more than 0.5°C. This rise dissipated during the approximately three-minute period it took to prepare for the next spectrum taking. These experiments also revealed that samples 7°C above ambient, which were injected into the IRE for analysis, equilibrated very rapidly and closely to the temperature of the sample cell. This is not surprising since the 1.5 ml of water in the sample-cell cavity is spread out in a shallow film within a steel casing.

These post hoc studies make it clear that since the metal has a much greater thermal capacity than the water, the sample-cell temperature is the significant factor in determining the sample temperature at the time of spectroscopic measurement. Temperature increase within the vials, caused by handling, is not a significant factor. Similarly, handling the metal sample cell is not a significant concern because of the waiting time it took to prepare the spectrophotometer for the next session.

Having established that spectra were taken at a temperature approximating ambient, we corrected for the slope observed in the regression line, producing an adjusted ratio, R_a, by $R_a = R + 0.041(T - 25)$, where R_a is the temperature-adjusted ratio, R is the uncorrected ratio, and T is temperature.

The Mann-Whitney U tests were again run using the corrected ratios from both the germanium and zinc selenide populations. The results of these calculations provided data upon which the Hypothesis One analysis was based. In fact, the Z-score difference between the two data sets was quite small; in the most pronounced category, treated vs. calibration, it changed from -2.97 to -2.93.

Barometric Pressure. The barometric pressure was logged at the time each spectrum was produced and over the course of trials covered a range of only 0.3" Hg. These were optimal experimental conditions, and because this range was so small, we can say nothing about the pressure-to-ratio relationship.

Sampling and Order Variations. There is a second possible pressure effect to consider. Air was pushed into the vials to offset the vacuum created by hypodermically withdrawing the water samples. The calibration controls were sampled four to six times each and would show the greatest influence of any such effect. The first-of-the-day calibration control sample ratios were plotted against the second-of-the-day, and so on, up to the sixth. This revealed no pattern in the relationship between mean R value and sequence of measurement.

The general experimental effect does not appear to be the product of increased pressure due to air injected into the vials nor slight variations in pH due to CO_2 absorption.

Practitioner Subpopulations. The total population of practitioners was considered as being made up of two subpopulations: practicing and nonpracticing. We compared the treated vs. calibration control results for the two practitioner subpopulations (zinc selenide IRE only). This resulted in a Z of -3.08 (p = .001) for practicing practitioners (n = 7) and a Z of -1.75 (p = .04) for nonpracticing practitioners (n = 5). Those who trained in some kind of therapeutic technique and characteristically involved themselves in such activities produced more significant results than those who had not undergone such training or who did not characteristically involve themselves in such activities.

Conclusion

This pilot study supports earlier research suggesting the existence in water of an objectively measurable infrared signature which is independent of measurements on living systems. The central difficulty in interpreting these results lies in the session controls, some of which also had altered spectra. The cause of this is undetermined. Environmental influences do not provide a compelling explanation for either the overall effect or for the changes in the session controls. Further research is encouraged.

HYPNOTIC SUGGESTION AND RSPK*

Jeannie Lagle Stewart[†] (Psychical Research Foundation and Parapsychological Services Institute, 1502 Maple St., Carrollton, GA 30117), William G. Roll[†] (West Georgia College and Psychical Research Foundation), and Steve Baumann (Spring Creek Institute)

Last year (RIP 1985, 59-62) we reported apparent PK effects on neurons of a sea snail and on piezoelectric crystals. One of the subjects was T.D.** around whom RSPK incidents had been reported in her home in Columbus, Ohio, and at locations in the Durham-Chapel Hill (North Carolina) area, March-April, 1984. T.D. was 14 years old.

T.D. returned to Durham from October 18 to 22, 1984, to take part in the tests with the neurons and crystals. She turned 15 during this visit. Other than an unintentional bending of a spoon and subsequent intentional bendings of three spoons and a fork the week before, no activity was reported since her return from Durham. In preparation for the PK tests, we decided to attempt to reactivate her PK abilities by hypnosis.

Hypnosis as a Means to Reactivate RSPK

J.L.S. described the hypnosis procedure to T.D. and invited her to participate. She accepted. J.L.S. asked her to select eight items from her purse as RSPK targets since they might have an emotional charge. T.D. chose the four utensils she had bent, her deodorant stick, toothbrush, hairbrush, and lipstick.

On October 19, T.D. and J.L.S. met at W.G.R.'s home, at noon; T.D. had brought the objects. They sat facing each other at a table on the patio by the swimming pool. T.D. said, "something's going to happen!" and reported that she felt the way she did when things had moved before. After relaxation induction, J.L.S. suggested that T.D. recall an RSPK episode and asked her to pay attention to her body and describe any area where she felt anything. T.D. grimaced, her right hand moved to her stomach, and she said, "It hurts." J.L.S. induced relaxation to decrease the pain and suggested this sensation could also be the sensation of warmth. She asked her to concentrate on her stomach and said that she would notice a slight feeling of warmth. T.D. reported sensing the warmth and J.L.S. asked her to increase it.

---

*This study was supported by a grant from Psychological Research Foundation, Aloha, Oregon.
**Pseudonym.

J.L.S. then asked T.D. to select mentally one of the objects on the table and name them all. Then she asked her to visualize the movement of an object while feeling the warmth in her stomach. J.L.S. detected an expression of fear, and they talked about how frightening the past events had been and imagined how things might move in a way that was harmless and exciting, such as moving only small, unbreakable items. Then they left to get a drink. As they walked toward the door they heard a noise and found one of the spoons on the ground (Event #1). T.D.'s hands were not in view of J.L.S. and it is possible she had picked up the spoon and thrown it.

After having checked that all objects were on the table, J.L.S. had T.D. walk in front of her to the door so she could see her hands. As she approached the doorway, a sound was again heard, and the deodorant stick was found 6' from the table (#2). J.L.S., who was watching T.D., did not see any unusual movements. Next a spoon moved 3', when T.D. was in the house under observation by J.L.S., with a wall intervening between T.D.'s location and the table (#3). Finally, when T.D. again was on the patio and as she approached the doorway, J.L.S., who was observing her from the hallway, saw something hit her head and found the fork on the ground (#4). T.D. cried "Stop hurting me" and flung the fork into the pool. They left for the laboratory.

The hypnotic procedure was used each day before the experimental sessions. J.L.S. also assisted T.D. in concentrating on the two systems, at times offering suggestions for imaging effects on each system.

Previous Instances of Fraudulent Simulation

Prior to W.G.R.'s investigation in Columbus, a TV news crew had recorded T.D. pulling over a lamp. She had been told that she could return to a friend she had been visiting as soon as there was an occurrence. When some hours had passed uneventfully, she said she pushed the lamp over so that she could leave. There were also incidents during W.G.R.'s stay in Columbus when T.D. was alone in her room at night which he believed to be simulated.

When T.D. was in North Carolina, two types of spurious incidents were noted. She would at times entertain dinner company with "table levitation" using her legs. On an occasion when she was unobserved she admitted to having hurled a glass bottle against a wall in a fit of rage (with such force that the metal top lodged in the wall).

On the other hand, W.G.R. had been with her both in Columbus and Durham during incidents that apparently could not have been produced normally by anyone. He attempted to video record the events but without success. T.D. seemed to become self-conscious when she knew she was being filmed. W.G.R. decided to use concealed video equipment at the first opportunity.

W.G.R. discussed the study with the magician, James Randi. Randi thought the most likely fraudulent procedure would be simple throwing rather than more elaborate magic. We were attentive to both possibilities in the present study.

Apparent RSPK Incidents Under Controlled Conditions of Observation

The four occurrences at W.G.R.'s home suggested that T.D. had some control over the incidents and that they might recur in the laboratory. We prepared ourselves by keeping her under close observation. In particular, we were alert to the possibility that she might pick up objects and then later throw them. We were also aware of the possibility of simple magic, e.g., effected by tying strings to objects. The possibility of more elaborate devices was presumably precluded because she had no access to the laboratory except when she was with the investigators. Our procedure was to interfere as little as possible with her movements and then to tighten conditions if the events resumed. J.L.S. carried a tape recorder to record the circumstances surrounding the incidents. W.G.R. was usually working on other matters in the laboratory since he felt that his presence might be distracting T.D. and since he had no need to observe further RSPK incidents. Aside from S.B., two other members of the laboratory staff, E.K. and W.J., and a technician, R.T.H., were sometimes present.

T.D. had been working on the two systems and was taking a break at 3:10 p.m. when a screwdriver behind her and J.L.S. moved 5' to the floor from a desk (#5). (All distances are approximate.) She picked it up, placing it defiantly in the middle of the desk. They turned to leave, T.D. in front under close observation by J.L.S. Upon passing through the doorway, J.L.S. again heard the screwdriver land on the carpet (#6). J.L.S. saw no movement of T.D.'s hands as she exited the room either time. She would have had to pick up the screwdriver and throw it over her and J.L.S.'s heads for it to have landed where it did. The second time J.L.S. was highly attentive to T.D.'s movements and had assured herself that the screwdriver was on the desk when she and T.D. left. (We now only describe incidents in the laboratory that she could apparently not have caused normally.) At 3:12, as T.D. was placing the screwdriver in a desk drawer, she and J.L.S. heard the sound of something landing on the carpet in an empty office across the hall. Five coins that had been on a desk had moved 11' (#7). J.L.S. was sitting between T.D. and the door and had T.D. under close observation. The coins' original location was 18' and behind a wall from T.D.'s position.

During a break outside, at 3:20 while J.L.S. observed T.D. (who was sitting next to her on some steps, holding a cigarette in her left hand and resting her right hand on her knee), the hairbrush from T.D.'s bag was heard to land on the walkway above and behind (#8). At 3:30, J.L.S. saw a pen hit a wall at the same time as T.D. was in view (#10). The pen, which belonged to R.H.T. with whom they were talking, came from his office, a distance of 18'. Five minutes later, when J.L.S. and T.D. were in the restroom, a deodorizer broke on the floor when T.D. was in the stall next to J.L.S., with J.L.S.'s foot touching hers (#11). T.D. was under observation by J.L.S. before entering the stall, so the event apparently could not have been staged.

Following the second experimental session, there were three incidents in 5 minutes: beginning at 4:31 a battery moved 12' (#12), a crescent wrench moved 7' (#13), and an anesthesia machine was disturbed (#14). T.D. was under observation by J.L.S. in all cases and was several feet from the origin of the movements.

Movements of RSPK Target Objects

Because T.D. seemed to have a degree of control over the occurrences (only "permissible" objects moved rather than valuable equipment), on the next day of testing, October 21, 1984, we set up a table with RSPK target objects, such as tools and pieces of equipment. T.D. had no access to the target table at any time. W.G.R. concealed a video camera in an unused testing console and focused it on the target area. Since S.B. felt it was unethical to film without informing T.D., she was told that a camera was installed. She reverted to the self-conscious stance characteristic of her when she knows she is being filmed. After some hours with no activity, we dismantled the equipment.

After a hypnosis session, at 5:10 when T.D. was in the hallway facing J.L.S. and in full view of her, a target hose clamp was heard to fall to the floor in an adjacent, empty office (#37). Since this had no direct access to the target room, the clamp presumably moved 35' and in a curved path from the target table. At 5:24 a (nontarget) roll of wire moved 8' in an empty office when T.D. was in the adjacent hallway, facing J.L.S. and S.B., and with both hands on the door frame to another office (#38). Then at 5:35 a 12" target socket wrench moved into an adjacent, empty office while J.L.S. and S.B. were facing her at the end of the target table, with their backs to this and standing between it and her (#39). The loud sound and an indentation on the door indicated that the wrench had hit this before coming to rest in the office. It apparently moved 18' and in a curved path to have hit the door where it did.

On October 22, at 1:31 there was a noise from the computer console behind J.L.S. and T.D. T.D. sat on the other side of

J.L.S. who observed her with both hands in her bag, looking for her airline ticket. When J.L.S. turned, she saw the computer paper move and found a 2½" target level on the console, a distance 40' and along a curved path from its position (#46).

At 2:01 a pocketknife on a desk 2' behind J.L.S. and T.D. moved 10' while J.L.S. was on the phone and when T.D. was holding J.L.S.'s free hand with both of hers (#49). At 2:02 when they were in the same positions, a metal bracket from an empty office across the hall was heard to land in the hall, 11' from its location (#50). At 2:16 when T.D. and J.L.S. were sitting on the desk in the same room, J.L.S. saw a wallet hit the left side of T.D.'s head (#52). S.B. had earlier left it with his pocketknife on the desk.

There were three more events with target objects, each moving 10 feet: At 2:25 J.L.S. brought T.D. into the target room for guided relaxation to slow down the rate of the events. As W.G.R. observed T.D. sitting down in front of the window he heard a target battery hit this (#54). W.G.R. and J.L.S. were seated between T.D. and the target table, and she had had no opportunity to interfere with the objects there. One minute later they heard a target "L" bracket hit the window under similar circumstances (#55). Then at 2:30 a target drill bit hit the window when T.D. was standing in the doorway of the room observed by W.G.R. (#56). Her back was to the room, both hands resting on the sides of the door frame.

From July 25 to 31, 1985, W.G.R. and J.L.S. attempted to replicate the effects in the temporary quarters of the Psychical Research Foundation near Durham, NC, using a video camera concealed above the target table. T.D. discovered this after the first day. When no effects were recorded on the second day, we ceased operating it. On the third day of testing, July 29, two target objects moved to their target locations during a period when T.D. was with J.L.S. However, the effects were not associated with any sounds that allowed us to pinpoint the times of the incidents and thereby T.D.'s position in relation to them. Since the camera, which would have provided both items of information, was not in operation, too much uncertainty surrounds these effects to consider them evidential. On July 30 there were two events when T.D. was not supervised.

Discussion

We have reported 21 incidents when T.D. was under observation and when she apparently could not have caused them either by simple throwing or skilled magic. Eight involved target objects placed in areas to which T.D. had no access.

The use of hypnosis to reactivate PK provided a tool in studying this phenomenon under controlled conditions, and the therapeutic setting offered an atmosphere of acceptance for T.D. to be herself, including her spontaneous, psychic self.

The lack of evidence for PK in the second period could stem from three differences between the two periods. First, all who came into contact with T.D. reported a difference in her behavior during the second period, generally describing her as "more mature." Her lack of physical coordination and jerkiness were also reduced. Possibly these changes resulted in a weakening of PK. Secondly, T.D.'s motivation to perform seemed lower. She often expressed the need for objects to move quietly, if at all. In talking about her current concerns, she spoke entirely of her social life and clothes, a typical 15-year-old's interests. Her concern for her psychical expressions was minimal, quite different from the first period when these dominated her conversation. Thirdly, the setting, the persons involved, and the tasks were different in the two periods.

FREE-RESPONSE ESP STUDIES

GANZFELD TARGET RETRIEVAL WITH AN AUTOMATED TESTING SYSTEM: A MODEL FOR INITIAL GANZFELD SUCCESS

Charles Honorton[†] and Ephraim I. Schechter (Psychophysical Research Laboratories, 301 College Rd. East, Princeton, NJ 08540)

A total of 187 psi Ganzfeld sessions have been completed in five experimental series at the Psychophysical Research Laboratories (PRL) using an automated testing system which controls target selection and presentation, the judging procedure, and data recording and storage.

PRL participant demographics have been reported elsewhere (Psychophysical Research Laboratories 1984 Annual Report, 113-138). Participants (receivers) have the option of bringing a friend to serve as their sender. If they choose not to do so, a laboratory staff member serves as sender.

At the beginning of each session, sender and receiver are stationed in nonadjacent, sound-isolated, and electrically shielded rooms. The receiver's room is an Industrial Acoustics Corp. 1205A Sound-Isolation Room, consisting of two 4" steel walls separated by a 4" airspace. The walls, door, and ceiling of the sender's room are treated with 4" Sonex acoustical material, similar to that found in commercial broadcast studios. Both rooms are copper screened and are 15 ft. apart on opposite sides of the experimenter's monitoring room, which provides the only access.

A computer video interface controls a random access videocassette recorder (VCR), allowing film clips and other "lifelike" material (dynamic targets) to be used in addition to still pictures (static targets). There are 160 targets, made up in 40 pools of 4 dynamic or static targets each and stored on 4 VHS-format videocassettes.

Target selection is performed by a PRL staff member who has no contact with either experimenter or receiver until after the judging procedure has been completed. The target is selected via

computer through a hardware random number generator (RNG),
yielding a value between 1 and 160. The pool and videocassette
numbers are calculated and the computer informs the target selector which of the four videocassettes to feed into the VCR. No
further information concerning the target is displayed. Once the
appropriate videocassette has been inserted, the screen is blanked
and the target selector leaves the monitoring room with the remaining three videocassettes.

Two physically separate and electrically isolated audio recorders are used by the system, one to present audio stimuli (prerecorded relaxation exercises, session instructions, and white noise)
and the other to provide a permanent record of the receiver's
Ganzfeld mentation, judging period associations, and judging period
interactions with the experimenter. Both sender and receiver undergo the 15-minute relaxation exercise prior to the beginning of
the sending/mentation phase of the session. Receiver instructions
are given at the end of the relaxation tape and are followed by 30
minutes of white noise.

A vertical-interval switcher selectively controls the computer
and VCR display modes of three color TV monitors (one each for
experimenter, sender, and receiver). During the sending/mentation
phase of the session, the sender's TV monitor is switched to VCR
mode for the duration of each of six sending periods, and the target is displayed for 73 seconds each time.

During the judging period, the experimenter's and receiver's
TV monitors switch into VCR mode, allowing them to view the four
target possibilities. The sender's TV remains blank during this
period. Target and decoys are presented in random order. When
the receiver is ready, a rating form appears at the bottom of the
monitor, and the receiver uses a computer input device to rate the
perceived similarity between Ganzfeld mentation and each of the four
possible targets. The computer converts the ratings into ranks.
The sender leaves his or her room only after the judging task has
been completed, then enters the receiver's room along with the experimenter. The actual target is shown to provide feedback. The
data for each session are saved in a floppy disk file.

The cumulative hit rate (32%) is statistically significant
(Stouffer $Z = 1.92$, $p = .027$, one-tailed). This outcome is consistent with a meta-analysis of 28 published direct-hits Ganzfeld studies (JP, 1985, Table A1, p. 84). A Mann-Whitney U test comparing
the effect size of the current data set with the meta-analytic sample
indicates that they do not differ significantly ($Z = 1.08$, $p = .279$,
two-tailed).

Sessions with dynamic targets (video segments) are independently significant ($n = 87$, 39% hits, Stouffer $Z = 2.47$, $p = .0068$, one-tailed), while those with static targets are at chance. While suggestive, the difference in success rate for the two target types is not significant (chi-square = 3.08, 1 df, p = .079, two-tailed).

Our primary objective has been to identify individual differences associated with initial psi Ganzfeld success. While studies using experienced participants have generally been more successful than those with novices only, new investigators planning replication studies will generally not have access to experienced participants. Thus, specification of participant characteristics associated with initial success is especially important.

100 "first-timers" have each contributed a single psi Ganzfeld session. Two questionnaires have been used to explore individual differences: the Participant Information Form (PIF), a 55-item demographic survey developed at PRL, and Form F of the Myers-Briggs Type Indicator (MBTI). PIF data are available for 91 of the first-timers, and MBTI profiles are available for 74. In addition to the PIF and MBTI, we have examined the effects of prior psi-testing experience and participants' session options (choice of sender, light, and noise intensity) on initial psi Ganzfeld performance. In all, we have examined the effects of 27 variables on initial Ganzfeld performance, and the findings summarized below should be treated as exploratory until they are confirmed.

Only 18 of the first-timers had previously participated in psi experiments. They achieved a significant hit rate (55%; exact binomial p = .005, one-tailed) and were more successful than those without prior psi-testing experience (chi-square = 5.42, 1 df, p = .02, two-tailed).

Participants involved in mental disciplines such as meditation obtained significant hitting (n = 71, 35% hits; exact p = .036) while those not involved in such practices obtained chance results. Reported personal psi experiences correlated significantly with psi performance among both first-timers (r = .256, t = 2.50, 89 df, p = .014, two-tailed) and experienced participants (r = .734, t = 3.24, 9 df, p = .005, one-tailed).

First-time Ganzfeld performance correlated significantly with Feeling and Perceptive (FP) dimensions of the Myers-Briggs Type Indicator. Characteristics associated with the FP dimensions include analysis of subjective activity, interpersonal sensitivity, flexibility and adaptability, and motivation for new experiences. FP types achieved significant hitting (n = 33, 55% hits, exact p = .00027) and were more successful than non-FPs (Fisher's exact p = .0011, two-tailed).

Extraverted FPs were more successful with friends than with lab senders while the reverse was true for the introverted FPs (Fisher's exact p = .013, two-tailed). This finding reflects a general tendency for extraverts to bring friends and for introverts to rely on lab senders (Fisher's exact p = .037, two-tailed).

These findings suggest a model for first-time Ganzfeld success: (PRIOR TESTING + MENTAL DISCIPLINES + PSI EXPERIENCES + FP). Due to the small number of participants with prior psi-testing experiences, only six participants met all four criteria (100% hits; Z = 3.5). The 28 participants meeting the remaining three criteria obtained a 64% hit rate (Z = 4.2). Only 16% of those not meeting all three criteria (n = 45) obtained hits (16% hits; Z = -1.32).

The 95% confidence interval for the success rate of the three-factor model suggests that the population success rate is between 43%-89%. Power analysis, using the lower bound of 43%, with alpha and beta set to .05 and .20 respectively, indicates that a sample size of 36 cases will be needed to confirm the three-factor model. Since 38% of the first-timers in our present sample conform to the optimal model, we anticipate that an additional 100 first-timers will be required to achieve the desired sample size. Our next several first-timers series will serve this purpose.

REPLICATION OF AN "INCLINE" EFFECT IN BLIND JUDGING SCORES*

Michaeleen Maher (Dept. of Psychology, New School for Social Research, 66 W. 12th St., New York, NY 10011)

In a prior experiment (Maher, RIP 1983, 18-21) an incline effect was observed in the scores of two experienced blind judges who, under different judging conditions, had made three attempts to match the same series of ESP mentation protocols to videotape targets. Both holistic and analytical strategies had been provided as part of the judges' instructional sets, and scores had tended to improve with repeated judgings of the material. In fact, the judge who spent the most time evaluating the protocols achieved the highest score (i.e., made the greatest number of correct target/protocol matches).

The present confirmation experiment tested the hypothesis that blind judging scores would show significant improvement over the threefold judging process when the same mentation protocols were newly evaluated by a group of 20 inexperienced judges. A repeated measures Analysis of Variance (ANOVA) gave evidence for significant differences in scores for the three judging conditions: F = 12.40, 2, 38 df, p < .0001. Tukey a posteriori analysis showed that judges' final scores were significantly higher than

---

*This work was supported by a grant from the Parapsychology Foundation, Inc.

their initial scores: q = 6.78, 38 df, p < .0005, one-tailed; and that their intermediate scores were also significantly higher than their initial scores: q = 5.04, 38 df, p < .005, one-tailed.

However, while judges' scores improved with repeated attempts at matching the mentation protocols to the videotape targets, judges' rated confidence in the matches bore no relationship to success. When mean confidence ratings for final correct target/protocol assignments were contrasted with mean confidence ratings for the incorrect assignments, the result (t = -.016, 19 df) was thoroughly nonsignificant. So, although judges improved their scoring with the implicit and explicit strategies provided for the second and third runs of judging, they were apparently not conscious of the benefits of these strategies. That is, they were unable to articulate these benefits in terms of assigning a higher level of confidence to successful matches than they had assigned to unsuccessful ones.

The hypothesis of psi was tested and confirmed by comparing the distribution of judges' successful final matches to the theoretical distribution expected by chance. The result (t = 3.63, 19 df, p < .005, one-tailed) permitted the inference (which is conventionally made when free-response GESP data preclude a chance interpretation) that the subjects who had provided the mentation protocols had responded to the ESP targets with psi (in this case, clairvoyance).

An alternative but no less plausible interpretation of significant blind judging results is that it is judges' psi that is exhibited in judges' fortuitous target/protocol assignments. While particularly striking target/protocol correspondences make credible the supposition that judges are identifying targets by deducing salient target features from the descriptions given in subjects' free-response protocols, Child and Levi (JASPR, 1980, 171-181) among others have cited examples of seemingly remarkable target/protocol correspondences that occurred when protocols were mismatched with the wrong targets.

The issue of subjects' versus judges' psi is explored with respect to the present findings, and it is argued that the results offer some modest support for the conventional interpretation of blind judging results (that is, that blind judges are using cognitive abilities other than psi, as indeed they are being asked to do). It is suggested that the observed "incline" in judges' scores is opposite to the "decline" that might have been expected if judges had been using psi to make forced-choice target/protocol assignments. Also, although Tart (RIP 1975, 80-82) has maintained that gifted subjects will show learning (or a success "incline") if they are given feedback on their forced-choice ESP calls, judges in the present experiment received no feedback, because they were to be asked to evaluate the same material three times. Therefore, the "incline" in judging success cannot be attributed to a forced-choice psi-star learning curve.

Another line of inference supports the speculation that judges were not using psi. When judges were given an opportunity to discern and hold constant some of the subjects' misleading personality characteristics (such as style of expression and favored cognitive themes), judging improved dramatically. This unique opportunity was afforded because the subjects in the experiment had each provided two mentation protocols, one for each of two psi-impression periods. There were two videotape targets, and both were used for every subject, one during each of the psi-impression periods. For the initial judging, blind judges attempted to match each of the randomized mentation protocols against the two videotape targets without knowing that two protocols were provided by each subject. This often led to both of a subject's protocols being assigned to the same videotape target. Judges' introspective comments suggested that they may have been misled in these assignments by irrelevant subject personality characteristics which reminded them more of one videotape target than the other. When they later attempted to match the two mentation protocols of a given subject to the two different videotape targets, they were obliged to hold these personality variables constant while they probed for other factors which could help them to distinguish which of the two target videotapes had been playing during each of the psi-impression periods. Apparently they were able to make these finer discriminations, because judging improved. This effect suggests that clues to the target are embedded in subjects' mentations, but that they must be distinguished from irrelevant and potentially misleading facets of subjects' personalities which otherwise might be mistaken for clues.

It is suggested that blind judging results may be improved if an attempt is made to address this potentially relevant factor in the design of the experiment. Blind judges conceivably could be drawn from among subjects' close friends or relatives, or perhaps unknown judges could be provided with a subject's introspective nonpsi passages to be used as a control for the same subject's psi passages.

An analytical procedure which comprised the third and final stage of judging further improved some judges' scores, but not enough so that total group scores for the third judging represent a significant improvement over scores for the second judging. Several attempts have been made to develop analytical techniques for quantifying psi content in free-response mentation protocols (e.g., Honorton, JASPR, 1975, 353-359; Jahn, Dunne, and Jahn, JP, 1980, 207-231). The underlying assumption here appears to be that psi can effectively be assessed and quantified as bits of target-relevant information embedded in the mentation protocols (the more target-relevant bits, the more psi). However, psi may prove to be more difficult to quantify than the underlying assumption presupposes. While these techniques for "objective determination of information rate" have had their successes, they employ a clerical strategy which may often be ignored by a human judge, who is free to base his or her target assignment on a single compelling (or not so compelling) correspondence. A direct hit has the advantage of being a hit whether it was arrived at through complex or manifold correspondences or through a mere nuance of similarity between the protocol and its target.

It is suggested that new attention needs to be given to the problem of developing effective judging strategies. Both quantitative and qualitative approaches need further scrutiny. An intriguing possibility is that both will lead to equivalent assessments of psi content, but that the different approaches are suitable for different individual judges. If improved judging techniques can be developed, they may tell us more about the nature of psi and its manner of cognitive expression during clairvoyance or GESP.

In the meantime, the improvement in judging obtained with repeated blind judgings of free-response psi protocols may give pause to skeptics and dispirited experimenters alike.

EXPLORING HYPNOTIZABILITY, CREATIVITY, AND PSI:
CONSCIOUS AND UNCONSCIOUS COMPONENTS TO PSI
SUCCESS IN THE GANZFELD*

Nancy Sondow (789 West End Ave., #5D, New York, NY 10025)

Psi functioning in the Ganzfeld, hypnotizability, and creativity appear to share common aspects suggesting openness to unconscious processing. This study was designed to cast a wide exploratory net in the hope of elucidating their interrelations. Speculations were stated as 18 hypotheses to be formally tested. In this report, results of 12 hypotheses relating to psi success are presented.

An underlying assumption was that psi information first enters at an unconscious level; thus, openness to the unconscious should aid in the psi task, while personalities that habitually censor, repress, or inhibit unmodified unconscious material might also habitually repress intrusions of psi information into consciousness. Openness to unconscious material implies tolerance for "primary-process thinking." There is a fairly consistent pattern to indicate that a change of consciousness to a state dominated by primary-process thinking in response to the Ganzfeld experience relates to psi success. The intent of this study was to examine individual differences in cognitive habits relating to openness to unconscious material as possible predictor variables in selecting subjects more likely to demonstrate psi success on demand.

---
*This research was partially supported by a grant from the Parapsychology Foundation, Inc.

Hypnotizability and creativity seemed to be promising candidate predictors because each has been speculatively and empirically linked to psi success, each depends on openness to unconscious processing, and they have been found to correlate positively with each other. A construct of "effortless experiencing" over creative and hypnotic tasks (which seemed to indicate free access to unconscious material) has been shown to explain the significant positive relationship between creativity and hypnotizability (P. Bowers, Intl. J. of Clinical and Experimental Hypnosis, 1978, 184-201). A modified effortlessness scale to measure the degree of effortlessness in the Ganzfeld was created. Effortlessness was expected to relate positively to psi.

In short, it was thought that hypnosis, creativity, and psi success might be related in a personality syndrome involving effortless experiencing of unconsciously processed information, the ability to shift flexibly from one "state of consciousness" or way of processing to another, and lack of repression as a defensive style. A question posed was whether the Ganzfeld technique produces psi success in unselected subjects, or whether a psi-conducive personality syndrome might be selected in future Ganzfeld studies to increase repeatability.

Each of 60 adult volunteers (30 of each sex) completed two sessions. In the first, small groups of 2 to 8 subjects took a trait test of hypnotizability--a 12-item group version of the Stanford Hypnotic Susceptibility Scale, Form C, administered on tape; four measures of creativity (self-report, Barron-Welsh Art Scale [Palo Alto, CA: Consulting Psychologists Press, 1963], an eight-item Independence of Judgment Scale [Barron, 1963], and a Tolerance for Ambiguity Scale taken from Budner, J. of Personality, 1962, 29-50); dream recall frequency; dream quality (how "dreamlike" one's typical recalled dreams are--from "logical, realistic, ordinary, as if awake" to "chaotic, bizarre, disconnected"--which is a measure of tolerance for uncensored primary process material and lack of defensiveness); absorption; and Gestalt Completion. Trait tests were not scored until both sessions were completed. Thus the experimenter was blind to trait scores during the psi task to avoid the possible confound of unconscious differential handling. Since the experimenter was not blind to ESP results after the Ganzfeld, an experienced outside judge who was blind to psi scores scored some hypnotizability items.

Subjects were scheduled individually for the second (Ganzfeld) session. Each either brought a friend to act as "sender" or were provided with a sender. Forty color photographs from National Geographic were arranged in ten packs such that each picture was as different as possible from the other three in color, form, content, and theme. Each pack of pictures had a duplicate pack of slides for "sending" to control for handling cues. The pack for the session was chosen in a quasirandom way by generating an integer from 1 to 10 using the random function of a Casio scientific calculator, contingent on (1) using each of the ten packs six times, (2) avoiding three or more repetitions of the same pack in a row, and (3) not using the same pack more than once for sender/receiver pairs. While the subject was reclining in Ganzfeld isolation in a sound-attenuated room listening to the 10 minutes of taped muscular and autonomic relaxation instructions which preceded the 35 minutes of white noise, the experimenter gave the session pack to an assistant with written instructions for randomizing the target and the time of the five-minute sending period. The experimenter then entered the lab and remained isolated from the sender and assistant. The randomizer constructed a private binary code by first writing down the four possible combinations of heads and tails that could occur in two coin tosses, in any preferred order, numbering the four ordered parts, tossing a coin twice and writing down each outcome, finding that ordered pair in the written list, and writing down the corresponding number, translated to the appropriate letter.

The assistant performed the target randomization, recorded and sealed it in an envelope, removed the appropriate slide from its pack by looking at its letter label, and either took the target slide to the sender at the beginning of the sending period, retrieving it at the end, or acted as both randomizer and sender. Neither experimenter nor subject had contact with the assistant or sender from the time the target was randomized until the judging was completed.

Free-response mentation was transcribed by the experimenter through a one-way intercom and also taped. At the end of the Ganzfeld, the subject filled out a postsession questionnaire measuring aspects of state of consciousness in the Ganzfeld: mentation quality, how altered the state, percent time in altered state, time estimate, and a five-item effortlessness scale. Subject (and experimenter) each ranked and rated the four pictures in order of target likelihood. Direct hits and sum-of-ranks from subjects' judgments tested psi success and subjects' Z-scores from ratings tested correlations. All trait, state, and effort variables were predicted to correlate positively with psi (with the direction of time estimate and effort flipped).

Psi scoring was not significant overall. Subjects has 12 direct hits. A sum-of-ranks analysis also was nonsignificant. There was support for only one of 12 formal hypotheses concerning psi. Dream quality correlated significantly positively with psi success as predicted (Pearson $r = +.25$, 58 df, $p < .05$, two-tailed). Effortlessness correlated negatively with psi, contrary to prediction. In short, formal findings were null after correction for selection.

Because the effortlessness scale correlated with psi in the direction opposite to expectation, the scale was broken into its five component questions: effortlessness of imagery, details of images immediate or added later, ease of interpretation of images, amount of control of next image, and to what extent the Ganzfeld experience "just happened" or the subjects "made it happen." The latter three all correlated negatively with psi (where difficult interpretation, control of the flow of imagery sometimes consciously directed, and imagery "made to happen" corresponded to psi success). "Happen" and interpretation were independent factors. Since "happen" correlated most strongly with psi, it was examined further. Partialing out "happen" from the correlation between effortlessness and psi ($r = -.235$, 58 df, $p < .07$, two-tailed) destroyed the relationship ($r_{ES,H} = +.02$). Thus, the "happen" component can explain the negative correlation between effortlessness and psi success.

Subdivisions of subjects by natural cuts (e.g., high/low hypnotizables, sex, previous Ganzfeld experience or naive) yielded interesting post-hoc findings. "Happen" correlated negatively with psi for all cuts of the data. When the sample was cut simultaneously by sex and by high/low hypnotizability, the significant negative relationship between psi score and "happen" appeared for three of four independent groups ($r = -.49, -.54, -.28, -.75$). Although post hoc, the strength and consistency of the results through many cuts of the sample suggests the effect, which is opposite to what was predicted, is not spurious.

"Happen" scores ranged only from "just happened" to the midpoint, a three-point range. Further exploratory analysis showed that if "happen" is treated as a binary variable by dichotomizing it with scores on or off the "just happened" endpoint, the pattern of results did not markedly change.

This study began with the premise that psi was an unconscious process and therefore that open access to the unconscious should aid in detecting it. An implicit assumption was that unconscious psi interactions can be blocked by inhibitions of unconscious material. Thus, those persons least blocked should demonstrate the most psi ability. A forgotten question was how the subject's conscious orientation to the psi task might focus on the information desired, rather than allowing him or her to be flooded by irrelevant information. If it is possible to acquire information psychically, how does one get information about the target and avoid getting just as much information about other pictures in the pack? The most strikingly consistent post-hoc finding of the present study suggests a serendipitous answer to this unasked question. The "happen" component of the effortlessness scale may be a measure of a conscious component steering or orienting the stream of consciousness toward relevant information.

Of the measures planned to reflect lack of repression, the best seems to have been the dream quality score. High scores indicate home recall of bizarre and unrealistic dreams (i.e., little repression). A positive relationship hypothesized between psi success and such lack of repression is weakly supported by the entire sample, where the correlation is marginally significant. It is more strongly supported by uniformly positive correlations through all cuts. Dream quality correlates most strongly with psi in subgroups with below-chance psi scores (less than 25%) in both subjects' and experimenter's judgings (those with previous Ganzfeld experience [$r = +.42$], high-hypnotizable males [$r = +.46$], and low-hypnotizable females [$r = +.36$]). Thus, dream quality appears to relate positively to psi success most strongly in subgroups where there is no positive deviation from mean chance expectation. This variable may be separating psi-missing from psi-hitting only if there is enough missing.

Although psi appears to have aspects that indicate an unconscious process, the unexpected negative correlations between "happen" and psi suggest that there may be an important conscious component to psi success in the Ganzfeld, perhaps equivalent to the "demand" component of the "old method" described by White (JASPR, 1964, 21-56) in her analysis of introspective reports, e.g., a conscious orientation to the task and a motivation to succeed that remains in awareness.

This idea is consistent with the introspection of a successful subject with previous Ganzfeld experience who marked a two rather than a one on the "happen" scale. He described his recognition of the personal symbolic meaning of the images that were drifting into his mind during the Ganzfeld, which he would dismiss as his own unconscious preoccupations, and he would make a conscious effort to clear his mind of them and see something totally different, something about the target. He had only a few such images, but they were highly specific to the target.

It may be that this extra conscious effort (which is different from conscious striving in that it does not block the manifestation of unconscious material, but sorts through it and continually re-orients one to the psi task) is an integral component to psi success. Some with potential "high ability" may become "open to contents of their unconscious," letting associations and ideas "just happen" and not orienting clearly to the task of obtaining information about the target (and not about the control pictures or other irrelevant information). This may actually result in just as much psychically acquired information, but if it is not focused on the target picture the psi effect will not be detectable with this judging procedure.

In retrospect, one might postulate three components to success in the psi task, namely (1) openness to the emergence of unconscious material in consciousness (which this experiment attempted to tap with the trait measures employed, most successfully with dream quality); (2) an orientation to focus on the particular information required (which might be tapped by the "happen" scale); and (3) the ability to recognize the connections between the mentation and the target (judging ability), which may involve both ease with primary-process associations and absence of emotional resistance. The first component without the second may lead to staying in personal preoccupations or to undirected psi which may alight on compelling control pictures or go further afield. The first and second without the third may lead to low psi detection with subject judging, but higher psi detection with independent, trained judging.

In a correlational study, a design with a more stable psi measure (e.g., multiple sessions) might better preclude confounding by psi-missing due to uncontrolled factors such as an aversive emotional reaction to the content of a specific target picture in a single trial. A longer, more detailed effortlessness scale, collected over more domains of consciousness, might further illuminate variables of interest in psi success and to what extent a variable such as "happen" is either a cognitive habit tied to more stable personality traits or a strategy that can be suggested or trained.

This experiment attempted to explore psi in relation to subject selection for variables related to openness to unconscious material in an attempt to increase the reliability of psi on demand. Predicted results were null after selection. However, the pattern of results and post-hoc findings suggests that conscious control may be a stronger factor in psi success than unconscious structure. Future research examining and perhaps suggesting cognitive strategies employed while attempting to gain psi impressions may further delineate components of a successful strategy.

FORCED-CHOICE ESP AND TIMING STUDIES

SUCCESSFUL PERFORMANCE OF A COMPLEX PSI-MEDIATED TIMING TASK BY UNSELECTED SUBJECTS

William Braud[†] and Donna Shafer (Mind Science Foundation, 8301 Broadway, Ste. 100, San Antonio, TX 78209)

A motoric timing task was developed as one of a number of computer-based psi tests designed especially for children. This particular task was one that demanded minimal cognitive processing on the part of the subject. The participant simply pressed a computer key whenever he or she felt the time was right. Which particular key was pressed was irrelevant; the important element of the task was the timing of the response. Key presses occurring at correct times produced rewarding feedback in the form of pleasant bell-like sounds; incorrectly timed key presses resulted in miss (buzzer) sounds. Subjects were instructed not to think about the task but simply to respond at what they felt were the right moments and "let their fingers do the guessing." We hoped that such a task would yield better psi results than typical verbal and imaginal tasks which would seem to require a greater degree of conscious, cognitive processing and hence be more susceptible to error-producing distortions.

Between the fall of 1982 and the winter of 1983, we conducted many tests with this psi task, not with children as originally planned but with adult participants. It was used as an ongoing, routine experiment from which we deliberately excluded any special instructions, induction techniques, or additional motivational procedures. We did this in order to learn whether a simple, casual experiment such as this would be capable of supporting significant psi performance over a relatively long time period with minimal experimenter involvement.

Radin and Bosworth (JASPR, 1985, 453-583) have reported the results of experiments similar to ours, prompting us to describe our study at this time as a conceptual replication of their work.

Method

Subjects

Fifty-one individuals participated in the study. Forty-six of the participants were unselected volunteers from the community; the remaining five participants were the two authors, two visiting parapsychologists, and the Foundation's librarian.

Procedure

It was decided in advance to test volunteers on a continuing basis until data from 100 runs had been collected. Subjects could participate in one or more runs, according to their inclinations. The experimenter (D.S.) explained the procedure and demonstrated it for six trials. The volunteer participant then practiced the task for 12 trials. Finally, one or more formal tests, each of 36 trials, were completed.

The task was described to the participant as one of clairvoyance in which the aim was to identify correctly a target that had already been selected by the computer. The technical aspects of the procedure were as follows. After preliminary information for a run (volunteer's name, date, time, number of trials, condition, experimenter) had been entered into the computer, the final carriage return for these inputs selected a clock value which served as the first seed for the computer's own random function algorithm. The computer was a Commodore 64 microcomputer, programmed in interpreted BASIC. The resulting random number (in the range 0 through 1) was converted to an integer in the range 1 through 6. The volunteer's next press of any key selected the current clock value as a new seed for the algorithm and generated a new integer in the 1 to 6 range. If the two integers matched, a hit was scored and a low-volume bell-like feedback sound was provided. The response-generated integer for that trial became the target integer for the next trial, and so on until 36 trials had been completed. A hard-copy paper printout was then produced which listed the number of times each integer had been selected as target and as response along with the number of hits and misses.

The chance probability of a hit is 1/6 or 0.17. Since the clock stepping rate (one step every 1/60th of a second or every 17 msec) exceeded the volunteer's possible reaction speed, since the initial clock value seed occurred at a quasirandom time and was unknown to the volunteer or to the experimenter, and since hitting required an exact match between two numbers which were produced by a complex pseudorandom algorithm which was unknown to the volunteer and the experimenter, no conventional sensorimotor response strategy should be able to bias the outcome in favor of an excess of hits. A statistically significant excess of hits, therefore, could be taken as evidence for a successful psi interaction with the computer system. Extrachance hitting would indicate the presence of psi-mediated instrumental timing responses.

Randomness tests

The first author conducted three types of empirical tests of the randomness of operation of the computer system in the absence of interactive psi attempts. The first randomness test consisted of four blocks of control trials, with block lengths of 600, 600, 1800, and 600 trials, respectively. A second randomness test consisted of a single block of 3600 trials. A third randomness test consisted of 100 blocks of 36 trials each. For these randomness control tests, computer-generated time delays ranging from 0 to 15 seconds were substituted for key presses.

Predicted outcome

This was an extremely straightforward study in which statistical analyses were deliberately kept at a minimum in order to obviate any ambiguities of interpretation. The following two a priori predictions were made:

(1) The hit scores for the randomness control runs would not depart significantly from chance expectation.

(2) The hit scores for the 100 experimental runs would significantly exceed chance expectation.

Prediction 2 was tested by a single-mean t-test comparing the 100 scores with the number of hits expected for each run of 36 trials (i.e., 6). It will be recalled that three sets of empirical randomness tests were done. The third set provided 100 scores and was amenable to an identical t-test analysis. The first and second sets yielded only total block scores and were therefore assessed by means of a Z-score analysis. The criterion for statistical significance was set at $p < .05$, one-tailed.

Results

As predicted, the number of "hits" for the various randomness tests did not depart significantly from chance expectation, indicating no inherent bias in the computer system. Also as predicted, there did occur a significant excess of hits during the experimental runs ($t = 2.04$, 99 df, $p = .02$, one-tailed). The use of the t-test guaranteed that the effect was fairly uniformly distributed among the various runs and was not contributed by only one or a small number of runs.

Discussion

The present results provide a successful conceptual replication of Radin and Bosworth's (1985) findings. Unselected participants were able to regulate the timing of their key-press responses to achieve an extrachance hitting rate. This accomplishment necessitated unconsciously selecting a rapidly changing clock value that would appropriately seed a pseudorandom algorithm to yield an integer that matched a similarly randomly generated target integer. The participants were unaware of the precise method whereby hits were produced, and the successful completion of the task was beyond their conventional sensorimotor and cognitive capabilities. Their success demonstrates what Stanford (JASPR, 1974, 34-57) has called a psi-mediated instrumental response (PMIR), with timing behavior appropriately and unconsciously modified to yield rewarding outcomes, and is consistent with a "goal-oriented" interpretation of the psi process.

The experiment succeeded in accomplishing its major purpose. It was able to support significant psi hitting over an extended period of time and for a large number of unselected subjects, with minimal experimenter involvement. For this reason, the procedure is recommended as a useful, effortless psi task.

CHILDREN'S ESP SCORES IN RELATION TO AGE

Susan Shargal (P.O. Box 184, Auburn, NH 03032)

A study was done in 1979 to investigate under controlled conditions the validity of an apparently common belief that younger children have a greater likelihood of having ESP abilities than do older children. Common belief coincided with some personal experiences of the author with young children who appeared to "know things" in a way that older children and adults generally did not. Also as part of this dissertation research, the relationship of ESP with a relevant personality measure (body boundary) was investigated. In 1982, a second study was done in order to attempt a longitudinal follow-up to see if the significant results of the first study would replicate and to try to refine the procedure to eliminate problem areas in the first study.

Review of the literature at the time the dissertation was designed indicated the absence of a study using a population of normal children in which all controllable aspects were held constant except for the ages of the children. The procedure of the first study attempted to control everything that could be controlled and to rate or record everything that could not. Thus, as well as examining the relationship between hits on the ESP test and age and the body boundary scores, numerous other factors were explored. These included such data as time of day, experimenter mood and rating of rapport with the child, the color marker the child selected, and delayed versus immediate feedback.

The results of the first study indicated that not only did the first graders score better than the older children (2 x 2 ANOVA with grade and body boundary score as factors; grade was significant at p = .031, but body boundary score was not), they also had a mean number of hits that was significantly above chance (p = .025). It is noteworthy that although there was some expectation on my part that the hypothesis of a decline in ESP performance with age was generally true, significant results with this experimental design seemed unlikely. Even more surprising was the significant above-chance scoring, which had not been part of the original hypotheses.

The literature indicated that success would be most likely between people in a relationship and/or with emotionally arousing material. For ethical and practical reasons, the children were strangers to me and the material was chosen to be emotionally neutral. The task, however, of "guess the number" (using a variant based on the Fisk-West clock cards) is one that children are usually familiar with and enjoy. No special rewards were deemed necessary, as it has been my experience that children generally find positive adult attention to be sufficiently rewarding. Normal children are generally motivated to do well, and efforts were made to help them view the task as a game. The children generally seemed to enjoy the experience and so reported to their teachers (this information was obtained as part of my attempt to "record everything"). Also, I made the decision to score only for direct hits rather than using variance scoring. The decision was made according to what would be more convincing to my dissertation committee. It is only in hindsight that I realized that exact-hit scoring also made sense because young children do not know how to estimate. (It is a learned skill.)

The second study (in 1982) was an attempt at a longitudinal measure. This goal was not possible to achieve since the children remaining in the school from the original first-grade group were not representative of the original population. The majority of high scorers had left the school, apparently between third and fourth grade. Since I was returning to the school (I did not realize the above until I analyzed the data), it was suggested that I also test the new group of first graders. In addition, I decided to administer a second set of targets using a clairvoyance rather than GESP procedure in answer to some criticism of the first study. Since I had some reservations about the likelihood of success with a clairvoyance procedure, I used an adaptation of Schmeidler's "well-wishing" method: Without informing the children that anything had changed, I went behind the desk during the second set and concentrated on a blank target corresponding to the target the child was working on, thinking, "Get it right."

There was no significant difference between the condition means, so the scores were combined (just as had been done with the feedback conditions in the original study). To my surprise, since so few studies of psi replicate successfully, the first graders again scored significantly above chance ($p < .025$).

Subjects for the first study were first, third, and fifth grade students at a public elementary school. The final sample consisted of all the children who fulfilled the following criteria: in a regular class and within the normal age range for the grade (i.e., had not repeated or skipped); fluent in English; of at least average intelligence (as determined by the teacher, guidance counselor, and school records); without major physical, emotional, behavioral, or learning problems; with parental permission; and not denying the possibility they could "guess the right number" for the hidden target (i.e., "sheep"). Although four children were not included because they did not fulfill the belief criterion, their responses indicated that the issue more likely was that they thought they couldn't do it rather than that they thought it couldn't be done. Only one child (during a pilot study) replied "Because there are twelve numbers and you only get one guess." The final sample consisted of 115 children, approximately equally distributed by grade and by sex. Each child was given a 15-target answer sheet. There were 15 first graders in the second study, each given two 15-target answer sheets.

Precautions were taken so that the children could not see the targets or were unlikely to receive any sensory cues from me, and so that I could not see their answers until after the number was circled. Details of the procedure and sample target sheets (blanks) are available upon request.

EFFECTS OF ELECTRICAL SHIELDING ON GESP PERFORMANCE

Charles T. Tart (Dept. of Psychology, University of California, Davis, CA 95616)

Some little-known experiments by Andrija Puharich in the 1950s suggested that general extrasensory perception (GESP) performance in percipients (who had been preselected to show regular, statistically significant hitting on the test used) could be enhanced by having such percipients work inside a solid-wall, electrically shielded enclosure. Such an enclosure is known as a Faraday cage. This apparent amplification of GESP ability occurred only if the

Faraday cage was electrically connected to the earth (grounded) and/or if it was maintained at a steady, high-voltage DC potential with respect to ground. An ungrounded, electrically floating cage apparently inhibited GESP performance by dropping the normally significant GESP test scores under ordinary room conditions to chance levels. The present study tested these effects in a double-blind design.

Psychically talented percipients were not available, thus lowering the likelihood of finding Puharich's effect if it is indeed valid. Thirteen undergraduate students in one of the author's experimental psychology classes were used because they were available. They alternated roles as percipients and experimenter/agents. The experimenter/agents were kept blind to exactly how many electrical conditions were to be tested and what the electrical condition of the Faraday cage was during any given session. Only the grounded and ungrounded conditions were used, and they were varied at random.

A test called the Circular Matching Abacus Test (CMAT), which involves matching ten cards without replacement, was used for testing GESP performance. The CMAT is evaluated on the null hypothesis that the scores form a Poisson distribution with a mean and variance of one. The CMAT is similar to the test originally used by Puharich.

In spite of not being able to use percipients who were known to be psychically talented, there was significant hitting in the grounded Faraday cage condition (mean score of 1.22 hits per run, with an exact Poisson probability of .032, one-tailed), as predicted. Scoring was not significantly different from chance expectation (mean of .905 hits per run) in the floating condition, as predicted. The difference between conditions was significant ($p = .03$, one-tailed) by a Mann-Whitney U test.

The possible mechanism of this effect is unknown and probably requires further research in nonparapsychological areas dealing with the effects of electrical fields on the human nervous system. It is unlikely that electromagnetic signals per se are the actual carrier mechanism for GESP. Perhaps the electrically quieter environment of the Faraday cage affects physiological factors which in turn affect GESP performance. Regardless of our lack of theoretical understanding, the possibility of electrically amplifying or inhibiting GESP performance can be of practical value and deserves further investigation.

COMMENT: ELECTROMAGNETIC MEASUREMENTS OF THE SHIELDED ROOM AT U.C. DAVIS

G. Scott Hubbard[†] and W.R. Vincent (SRI International, Room G-203, 333 Ravenswood Ave., Menlo Park, CA 94025)

   Dr. Charles Tart of the University of California at Davis has presented data displaying a statistically significant difference in psi performance between trials collected in a shielded room which was electrically grounded and trials collected in an ungrounded condition (see pp. 53-54). If it can be demonstrated that some electromagnetic phenomena directly enchanced or interfered with psi functioning, the implications for the field of parapsychology would be extremely important. As a result, arrangements were made for staff from SRI International to visit U.C. Davis on 17 July 1986. At that time, we conducted a series of measurements designed to characterize the electromagnetic properties of the shielded room.

   All measurements were made using commercially available spectrum analyzers; however, the low-noise, wideband preamplifiers and the low-frequency electric- and magnetic-field sensors were custom designed by W.R. Vincent. The frequency range of the measurements was 10 Hz to 110 MHz. Electric and magnetic fields were measured separately over the range of 10 Hz to 100 kHz; above 100 kHz, the two fields converge so that a single measurement using a 2/3 m rod antenna was sufficient. Measurements were made of the electromagnetic ambient within a meter of the shielded room. In addition, we measured the fields inside the shielded room for both the grounded and ungrounded conditions. All data were recorded by photographing the analyzer display.

   We found that: (1) The facility is not effective in shielding against low-frequency magnetic fields. This is not a surprising result because such fields penetrate most shielded rooms with ease. (2) Reasonable shielding was achieved against low-frequency electric fields; an attenuation of > 60 dB (1000:1) was observed. (A dB is a logarithmic unit that compares a measured value to a reference value; e.g., 60 dB is a factor of 1000 in voltage, thus a 1 V/m field incident on the room would be reduced to 1 mV/m inside.) (3) Against high-frequency fields, however, the measured attenuation was only > 35 dB (60:1). By comparison, a commercial shielded room should provide > 100 dB (100,000:1) attenuation in the same frequency range.

   With regard to the main hypothesis of Tart's work, <u>no change was evident over the entire measured electromagnetic frequency range between the grounded and ungrounded conditions</u>. This finding is consistent with the theory and practical applications of shielded rooms. Grounding of a shielded room is primarily for safety, not for enchancing shielding effectiveness. In our opinion, the significant difference between conditions found by Tart is a very good example of the experimenter effect.

EVENT-RELATED BRAIN POTENTIALS AS CLAIRVOYANT INDICATORS IN A SINGLE-SUBJECT DESIGN, FORCED-CHOICE TASK

Charles A. Warren[†] and Norman S. Don[†] (Kairos Foundation and School of Public Health, University of Illinois at Chicago, Box 6998, Chicago, IL 60680)

The use of event-related potential (ERP) techniques in the investigation of clairvoyance has been extremely limited. The term ERP is here defined broadly as that transient brain electrical activity which occurs time-locked to specific events--either external events, endogenous events, or overt motor behavior. This study used pattern-recognition procedures to determine whether time-varying voltage changes and brain-wave frequency changes could be used to distinguish correct from incorrect psi trials.

In an illustrative study using ERPs in a cognitive task, W.G. Walter (J. of Psychosomatic Research, 1965, 51-61) measured the time-related changes in voltage occurring prior to a subject's judgment of whether he had been shown the correct missing piece of a geometric puzzle. The subject was first shown the main body of the puzzle (starting at time S1) with a candidate for the missing piece being flashed one second later (time S2). This procedure was repeated numerous times as a variety of candidate missing pieces were flashed one at a time. An average of those cases where a difficult puzzle had been presented revealed a greater transient negative voltage shift (termed the contingent negative variation, or CNV) over the one-second S1-S2 interval as compared to the average of the easy puzzle cases. This result suggested that the S1-S2 negativity reflected the greater mental effort required for the difficult puzzle.

In a CNV study of psi Hartwell (EJP, 1979, 358-364) tested whether CNV patterns occurring in a cognitive-motor task would also occur when the task was transformed into a psi task. The results did not support this hypothesis.

Our paradigm is similar to that of Walter except for (1) the use of stimuli concealed from the subject (S); (2) use of a much longer time period between trial onset and time of judgment (10 sec or more); (3) requirement that S make an overt forced-choice response on each trial; and (4) use of a self-paced response.

Based on Walter's study our working hypothesis was that if greater cognitive activity were required to achieve a hit, then negative-going changes prior to the overt response should discriminate correct from incorrect trials. From our discussion with the subject it was clear that special mental preparation was required to achieve the desired mental state. Additionally, fast Fourier transforms (FFTs) were calculated for four time intervals leading up to the response to reveal broad-based, sequential spectral changes associated with hits and misses.

Method

Subjects

All measurements were made on one right-handed subject with a reputation for achieving high scores on ESP-card tasks.

Procedure

Target preparation. The targets were five ESP cards--one of each symbol, each sealed within three opaque, Kraft paper envelopes by an assistant. Another assistant wrote a single digit (1,2, 3,4, or 5) on the back of each of the outermost envelopes. Neither person was connected with the experiment nor known to the subject or experimenters. At no time was the subject in possession of the stimuli.

A list of 100 random digits (1-5) from a random number table (Hodgman, C.R.C. Standard Mathematical Tables, Chemical Rubber Publishing Co., 1959) was used to select the envelopes during the experiment. S had no access to the list.

Testing protocol. Electrodes were applied to the subject. Throughout the experiment S remained in the chamber adjacent to the control room, seated in a high-back recliner chair equipped with a lap table, which effectively prevented him from rising from his chair or turning around. During the session S was required to fixate on a small white dot on a black background. His left hand rested, palm down, on a styrofoam support while his right hand rested at the base of the manipulandum, a numeric calculator key pad mounted on a base. The S's fingers and thumb rested on the five keys identifying the five response choices; movement of the hand was unnecessary.

The experimenter initiated the trial by placing the target envelope indicated by the random number list face up on top of S's immobile left hand for 10 seconds. The random number list and the numeral on back of the envelope were not visible to the subject. The experimenter removed the envelope and S waited from 12 to 18 seconds (self-paced) before pressing the button to indicate his response. He then waited two seconds (self-paced) and was allowed to blink and move his eyes. No trial-by-trial or outcome feedback was ever given to him. The experimenter waited more than two seconds before presenting the next target. (The mean time between onset of consecutive button presses was 28.2 sec [s.d. = 4.45 sec].) One hundred trials were run in approximately 45 minutes.

EEG Recording. Non-polarizing, silver/silver-chloride electrodes were applied to the scalp with Beckman paste at Fz, C3, Pz, C4, and O1 referred to linked ears. EOGs, used to detect eye-movement artifacts, were recorded as the difference between electrodes placed above and to the right side of the right eye. A forehead ground was used. Electrode impedances were well below 10k ohms; Grass model 7P122 amplifiers with 8-second time constants were used in a Grass Model 78 polygraph. One-half amplitude high frequency cut-off was set at 35 Hz; a 60 Hz notch filter was used. One hundred microvolt pulses were recorded before and after the experiment to calibrate each channel. Data were recorded along with an event channel on a Vetter FM tape recorder for off-line analysis.

Data Analysis

Ten seconds of EEG data plus the EOG and event channel were digitized at 10 msec per point, yielding 1000 data points 9.5 seconds of which were prior to the button press. A total of 100 trials were collected and computer edited to exclude trials contaminated by artifacts due to eye blinks and movements and excessive electrode drift. Twenty-two percent of the trials were excluded. All 100 trials were included in the tally of hits and misses.

Two types of single-trial data derived from the 1000 data-point trials were utilized: FFTs of the data points of each EEG channel and the waveforms, the latter being defined as the time-varying voltages as represented by 500 points. This reduced data set, developed for computer computational reasons, was obtained through adjacent point averaging (effectively passing the waveform data through a low-pass filter). Four 256-point FFTs were calculated for each data channel; the frequency range was 0 to 50 Hz with resolution of 0.391 Hz. Both the waveforms and FFTs were analyzed by Stepwise Discriminant Function Analysis (SDFA) (Dixon, BMDP Statistical Software, U. of California Press, 1985; Foley and Sammon, IEEE Transactions on Computers, 1975, 281-289). The SDFA developed a pair of linear equations which utilized the brain data of a given channel to maximally predict right (RTE) and wrong (WRO) responses. The equation yielding the highest score determined the classification. The accuracy of these equation pairs in correctly classifying responses will be referred to as the performance or hit rate of the SDFA.

Results

The subject scored 49 correct trials out of 100 ($Z = 7.125$, $p < 10^{-11}$); expected performance was 20%. Of the 78 trials with artifact-free EEG data the subject scored 39 correct.

For each channel the first 10 WRO and the first 10 RTE trials were used as a "training set" to develop 5 pairs of equations (for Fz, C3, Pz, C4, and O1) discriminating RTE from WRO trials. These equations were then applied to three "test sets" of RTE and WRO trials, constituting the remaining trials. Each test set contained 10 RTE and 10 WRO trials, except for the third set which contained 9 RTE and 9 WRO. Hit rates, defined as the number of hit trials divided by the sum of hits plus misses, were calculated for each test set. The average hit rate was calculated as the weighted mean of the hit rates of each test set. To be significantly above chance ($p < .05$, one-tailed, normal approximation to binomial), a hit rate of 60.80% had to be attained. Chance performance of an equation is 50% (equal chance of correctly predicting a WRO or a RTE trial). The number of test sample values significantly above chance was 8 out of 15 for both the FFT and the waveform data.

Performance of the equation pairs on the training samples was generally very high, undoubtedly due to overfitting of the data, but dropped as they were applied to independent samples. This testing of the equations on independent sets of trials, then, provides evidence of the usefulness of the predictive model.

The average hit rates of the equation pairs across the three test sets of trials using the FFT data were Fz: 36.6%; C3: 67.3%; Pz: 58.7%; C4: 61.7%; O1: 72.7% Thus, the average hit rates for the FFT data were significantly above chance for C3, C4, and especially for O1 ($Z = 3.963$, $p < 10^{-4}$). The average hit rates of the equation pairs using the waveform data were Fz: 26.7%; C3: 62.0%; Pz: 67.0%; C4: 67.0%, while O1 showed no predictivity. Thus, the average hit rates for the waveform data were significantly above chance for C3, Pz, and C4.

Among the frequencies selected by the SDFA of the FFTs from all channels and epochs was a preponderance of high frequencies, despite the 35 Hz, low-pass, half-amplitude filter. Thirty-five frequency values were found in the beta region from 15 to 50 Hz. Only six values were found below 15 Hz. Among the low frequencies two values were selected in the delta range (0-3.9 Hz), three in the theta (4-7.9 Hz), and one in the alpha range (8-12.9 Hz).

Waveform data averages of the 39 RTE and 39 WRO trials were computed. For channels Fz, C3, Pz and C4 the RTE curves are negative with respect to WROs for a significant portion of the first 5 seconds and then become positive.

Discussion

The ESP hit rates reported here are consistent with results from precognition and clairvoyance experiments in our laboratory with this subject. The findings of all our studies lead us to conclude that this subject is capable of repeatably generating exceptional scores, and we feel the precautions we took to prevent cheating were effective.

The SDFA classification model based on the FFT data proved to have highest cross-validity from leads C3, C4 and O1, while waveform data models showed greatest cross-validity at leads C3, Pz and C4. Thus, the most successful FFT models seemed to have a more diffuse locus than the waveform models, which were central-parietal only.

It is likely that the reason O1, so successful in the frequency domain, dropped out as a discriminator in the time domain is due to the latter's low-pass filtering. Such filtering effectively blocked frequencies above 25 Hz, which played a strong role in the success of the FFT models.

The FFT results are consistent with the predominance of high-frequency brain waves found in the "deeper" stages of meditation and among subjects more highly practiced in meditation (J.P. Banquet, Electroencephalography and Clinical Neurophysiology, 1973, 143-151; N.N. Das and H. Gastaut, Electroencephalography and Clinical Neurophysiology, 1957, Supplement 6, 211-219).

In contrast to a variety of studies (e.g., Kelly, Parapsychology Review, 1977 (No. 4), 1-9; Morris et al., JASPR, 1972, 253-268; Stanford and Stevenson, JASPR, 1972, 357-368; Honorton et al., JASPR, 1971, 308-323), we found the alpha band only slightly related to psi hitting. This finding may be specific to our subject, who tends to show much greater power in the high-frequency region than in the alpha band.

The ERPs which permit discrimination of psi hits from misses may reflect the operation of either psi processing or cognitive processing after psi processing has occurred. The resolution of the question of which aspects of brain electrical activity most closely track psi processing will certainly depend on further experiments with subjects displaying high psi scoring abilities.

The marked average waveform negativity of hits with respect to misses found during the first five seconds in channels Fz, C3, Pz and C4 seems consistent with studies of ordinary cognition. Averaged brain-wave data occurring prior to complex visual stimuli display greater negativity when those stimuli were correctly rather than incorrectly perceived (D.W. McAdam and E.H. Rubin, Electroencephalography and Clinical Neurophysiology, 1971, 511-517; S.A.

Hillyard, et al., *Science*, 1971, 172, 1357-1360; Hillyard, *Physiology and Behavior*, 1969, 351-357). Warren (*The Contingent Variation and Late Evoked Potentials as a Function of Task Difficulty and Short Term Memory Load*, Unpublished Doctoral Dissertation, U. of Illinois at Urbana-Champaign, 1974) found that one prerequisite for the emergence of transient negativity, related to a variable-difficulty visual discrimination task, was frequent changing of mental set.

The prime contribution of this study is that we have developed classification models based on ERP data capable of accurately discriminating hits from misses (up to 72.7%) in a psi task. We hope that future studies using such ERP monitoring will yield indicators of psi states of even greater accuracy and will also establish linkages to subjects' phenomenological descriptions while in these states.

DISPLACEMENT EFFECTS IN ESP AND PK

EFFECTS OF COGNITIVE STYLE AND TYPE OF TARGET ON DISPLACEMENTS

James E. Crandall (Dept. of Psychology, University of Idaho, Moscow, ID 83843)

The present research is a continuation of a series of studies of displacements (Crandall, JASPR, 1985, 27-38; Crandall, JASPR, 1987, pp. 11-21; Crandall and Covey, JASPR, 1986, pp. 393-408; Crandall and Hite, JASPR, 1983, 209-228). The evidence has been fairly consistent that psi-missers score significantly above chance on displacements to adjacent targets whereas psi-hitters score below chance on displacements, under conditions favorable to psi. We conceive of displacement effects as involving two opposite but complementary components: the tendency of missers to score above chance on displacements due to their improper focus, and the tendency of hitters to score below chance on displacements due to their suppression of signals from background stimuli. Along with Tart, we now view the latter as a process that will have an overall benefit for hitting the intended targets.

Study 1

The purpose of Study 1 was to examine the effects of cognitive style (visual or verbal) and different types of targets (high or low imagery) upon displacements of hitters and missers. As discussed in earlier reports, we believe that significant displacement effects may be easier to obtain than significant hitting on intended targets. If so, this approach might be more revealing than more traditional lines of investigation.

Previous research in this area does not provide a strong empirical base for specific hypotheses. According to what could be called the "right hemisphere" point of view (for example, Broughton, RIP 1975, 98-102) we might expect stronger displacement effects among visualizers, especially with high-imagery targets. Verbalizers would not be expected to show much of an ESP effect (displacements) with either type of target. However, another point of view (for example, Maher and Schmeidler, JASPR, 1977, 261-271) might predict an interaction between cognitive style and type of target. In this case we would expect stronger displacement effects with visualizers than verbalizers on high-imagery targets, but with low-imagery targets we would expect stronger effects with verbal subjects. There are precedents for both of these sets of hypotheses, so we made no choice between them.

Method

Visual and Verbal Cognitive Styles. Paivio's Individual Differences Questionnaire (IDQ), revised by Hiscock (J. Consulting and Clinical Psychology, 1978, 223-230), was used as a measure of preferred cognitive style. This yields separate scores for visual imagery and for verbal processing.

Targets. Using normative data provided by Paivio, Yuille, and Madigan (J. Experimental Psychology Monographs Supplement, 1968) we selected five high-imagery and five low-imagery words. It was not possible to vary simultaneously the meaningfulness of targets since there are virtually no words of high imagery value that are low on meaningfulness. Consequently, both sets of words were selected to be approximately equal on meaningfulness and familiarity and to be identical in word length. High-imagery words were "avenue," "barrel," "elbow," "maiden," and "tripod"; low-imagery words were "answer," "belief," "event," "method," and "theory."

Response sheets showed two columns of 25 blank lines, with one set of target words typed above each column. (The order was counterbalanced.) Target sheets were folded inside another paper, sealed in an envelope, and the envelope stapled to the back of the response sheet. The target sheets were similar to the response sheets, but with the words randomly types on the lines. The RAND Corporation random number tables were used to set the order of the words.

Subjects. One hundred students from an introductory psychology course participated. Five were discarded either for making responses that did not correspond to the targets or for repeating the same pattern of responses over and over throughout the entire experiment.

Results and Discussion

Scoring and checking were done by myself and students from a parapsychology seminar. (Special thanks are due to Michelle Dutton, Karen Maier, and Chris Morris for their help with both studies.)

Since the visual and verbal subscale scores from the IDQ were positively correlated (r = .40, 93 df, p < .001, two-tailed), we used difference scores to identify 32 visualizers and 32 verbalizers (the upper and lower thirds of the distribution). Scoring on intended targets was not significantly different from chance, nor were there any significant differences in comparisons of the two types of subjects and targets.

Displacements were analyzed by a three-way ANOVA (Visualizers/Verbalizers x Hitters/Missers x High/Low Imagery Targets). The three-way interaction was significant (F = 4.568, 1, 35 df, p = .037). Tests of simple main effects revealed that among visual subjects, missers scored higher than hitters on high-imagery targets (F = 3.398, 1, 70 df, p = .069) whereas among verbal subjects the missers scored higher than hitters on low-imagery targets (F = 9.776, 1, 70 df, p < .005). Other pairwise comparisons were not significant. The results appear to conform to the second set of hypotheses discussed above, that is, ESP (displacement effects in this case) is influenced by the interaction (congruence) of cognitive style with type of target.

Study 2

This study was designed as a replication of the first, but with one modification. We attempted to influence missers' call frequencies by providing background stimuli corresponding to the targets.

Method

Targets and background stimuli. The same words and format for the target sheets as in Study 1 were used. However, each of the 25 high-imagery words was bracketed by the word "maiden," typed in red about 10 mm to the left and right of each target word. The word "belief" bracketed the low-imagery targets. These two bracketing words were selected because they were called equally frequently by visual and verbal subjects in the first study, and in both cases the calls of these words were very close to chance (5). To prevent chance differences in target frequencies from influencing calls, each target was used five times.

Subjects. Introductory psychology students again participated. Of the 120 subjects, two were discarded for making irrelevant responses.

Procedure. The procedure was essentially the same as that used in Study 1.

Results

There were 39 visualizers and 38 verbalizers. Again, scores

on intended targets were not significantly different from chance. The bracketing words had no significant effect on subjects' calls. With regard to displacements, the three-way interaction was not significant in this case. However, missers again scored higher on displacements than hitters, $F = 10.399$, 1, 48 df, $p < .002$. Tests of simple main effects revealed that missers scored significantly ($p = .013$ to $p = .043$) higher than hitters in all conditions except the one involving visual subjects with low-imagery targets. Here, missers scored below chance and nonsignificantly lower on displacements than did hitters. This was also true in the first study, indicating that visual subjects have trouble processing psi information from low-imagery targets. The only inconsistency between studies was that there was a displacement effect for verbalizers with high-imagery targets in the second study, but not in the first. However, these targets were relatively high in meaningfulness, and this would be congruent with a verbal style. An important next step is to develop materials that are genuinely incongruent with a verbal style of processing.

Discussion of Possible Artifacts*

The random-without-replacement procedure for selecting targets in the second study resulted in a below-chance number of target repeats. This will tend to give missers an advantage over hitters with regard to displacements. If chance fluctuations in target repeats did influence the pattern of results, the visual, low-imagery condition, where no displacement effect occurred, should be different in some way(s) from the other conditions. A three-way ANOVA was conducted using the number of target repeats as the dependent variable. There was no significant main effect for score (missers/hitters) nor were there significant interactions of this variable with cognitive style and/or type of target. In fact, all F-values were less than 1.00. The same was true for comparisons of subjects' call repeats.

As a further means of evaluating the importance of artifacts, the calls of subjects in the three conditions where displacement effects were found were scored against the original targets listed in reverse order. Any artifact(s) should again produce displacement effects. However, missers did not score higher on displacements than either chance or hitters in this case. In fact, their mean was nonsignificantly lower than that of hitters. Consequently, artifacts appear not to have been responsible for the present results.

Postscript

Since the time that this paper was submitted to the Program

---

*Editors' Note: See Postscript.

Committee, several persons involved in trying to understand possible artifacts in these displacement analyses have continued to explore one possible source which may not have been adequately tested in this line of research. This artifact has to do with non-randomness in subjects' calls: subjects tend to make fewer call repeats, or doubles, than would be expected by chance. This lack of call doubles can interact with the subject's scoring tendencies on direct targets (i.e., whether the subject is hitting or missing) to produce artifactual displacement scores in the direction opposite of direct-target scores. The tests for this artifact reported here (scoring calls against targets listed in reverse order and an ANOVA comparing the number of call doubles among various conditions) may not have been sensitive enough.

To determine the exact nature of such an artifact and to develop a correction factor, a team of researchers at the Institute for Parapsychology, under the direction of their statistical consultant, Dr. Donald Burdick, are presently carrying out the necessary simulations and calculations. When these are completed, the data from the present and following two studies will be reanalyzed using the correction and will be reported elsewhere. In the meanwhile, the results reported here and in the Crandall-Kanthamani and Kanthamani-Khilji papers should be considered tentative.

FURTHER EVIDENCE OF THE RELATION OF DISPLACEMENT EFFECTS TO FAVORABILITY OF ESP TESTING CONDITIONS, WITH A DISCUSSION OF POSSIBLE ARTIFACTS

James E. Crandall[†] (Dept. of Psychology, University of Idaho, Moscow, ID 83843) and H. Kanthamani (Institute for Parapsychology)

The purpose of this investigation was to seek independent confirmation of certain displacement effects that have been rather consistently found at the University of Idaho (Crandall, JASPR, 1985, 27-38; Crandall, JASPR, 1987, 11-21; Crandall and Covey, JASPR, 1986, 393-408; Crandall and Hite, JASPR, 1983, 209-228). Under favorable testing conditions we have found three kinds of effects: (1) missers on direct targets score above chance on +1/-1 displacements; (2) missers score above hitters on the displacements; and (3) hitters score below chance on displacements. These effects have also been found by Schmeidler (see Crandall, JASPR, 1985, 27-38). With unfavorable conditions, the effects have not been significant.

In an effort to investigate further the generality of these displacement effects, J.C. contacted John Palmer and H. Kanthamani to see if they had data they would be willing to share. Both provided brief descriptions of recent studies. We agreed to examine one study described by H.K. since it seemed especially promising. This study was designed to induce two different sets in subjects, an "active" set and a "passive" one. A number of other studies have found that a relaxed but motivated orientation is more favorable to the occurrence of psi than a more active, effortful, striving one with regard to both ESP and PK. Consequently, J.C. hypothesized (without seeing the data or knowing the previous results) that displacement effects should be larger in the passive condition. (H.K. had not analyzed the data for displacements at this time.)

Method

Procedure

The subjects in the passive-attention (PA) condition were given instructions to relax, recall a pleasant experience, and try to visualize it. Subjects in the active-attention (AA) condition were encouraged to be active and try hard and were given a number of mathematical problems to work on. Both orientations took about 10 minutes.

The ESP test involved 5 runs of 25 trials each, using standard ESP symbols (star, cross, square, circle, and wavy lines). Individual target sheets were sandwiched between two sheets of construction paper and enclosed in a manilla envelope which was stapled to the back of the response sheet.

Subjects

Three groups of high school students participated. Each group was divided into two subgroups, with each subgroup being randomly assigned to one of the two conditions. In all, there were 45 subjects in the PA condition and 51 in the AA condition.

Analyses and Results

Results with direct hits have been reported elsewhere (Kanthamani, RIP 1984, 82-85.) With regard to displacements, most of our earlier research has involved but one or two runs. When multiple runs were used (Crandall and Covey, JASPR, 1986, 393-408), we found the following method of sorting the data to be most effective. First, hitters and missers were identified by their direct-target scores over the entire series of runs. Second, we retained for analysis of displacements only those runs where missers were missing and hitters were hitting. Displacements were then averaged over however many runs were retained for a given subject. This method produced stronger displacement effects than other ways of sorting the data. Consequently, the same procedure was used here. There were 16 missers and 23 hitters in the PA condition, with 25 missers and 20 hitters in the AA condition. The 10 subjects who scored at chance were eliminated. Data for two other subjects were incomplete and were not forwarded to J.C.

Initial scoring for displacements and checking were done by J.C. and his students. A computer program scored hits, displacements, target and call repeats, and frequencies of calls for each of the five targets. A copy of the printout was sent to H.K. who independently scored all the data. Discrepancies were verified and corrected by J.C. The analyses were redone and a copy mailed to H.K.

The expected number of forward and backward displacements for a run of 25 trials is 9.6: $.4(N - 1)$. Since the number of runs retained for analysis varied (from two to five) among subjects, we calculated each subject's mean number of displacements per run. In the PA condition the means were 10.88 for missers and 8.82 for hitters. In the AA condition the means were 9.86 and 9.00, respectively. A two-way Analysis of Variance (ANOVA) yielded a nonsignificant interaction, $F = 2.824$, 1, 80 df, $p = .093$, and a nonsignificant main effect for experimental condition: $F = 1.408$, 1, 80 df, $p = .237$. The difference between missers and hitters was highly significant: $F = 16.991$, 1, 80 df, $p < .0001$. Consistent with J.C.'s hypothesis, the difference between missers and hitters was over twice as large in the PA as in the AA condition. Tests of simple main effects showed a highly significant difference in the PA condition, $F = 15.563$, 1, 80 df, $p < .0002$, but a nonsignificant difference in the AA condition: $F = 3.245$, 1, 80 df, $p = .075$.

Missers in the PA condition scored above chance (9.6) on displacements, $t = 3.127$, 15 df, $p = .007$, and hitters scored below chance: $t = 2.689$, 22 df, $p = .013$. In the AA condition displacements of hitters and missers were not significantly different from chance.

The results were very much in line with those of earlier studies showing that displacement effects are more likely to occur under favorable conditions. Although the difference between missers and hitters was not completely eliminated in the AA condition, it should be noted that this condition was not completely inimical to the occurrence of psi. There were some favorable aspects even here, such as the way the subjects were treated and the nature of the instructions which indicated to the subjects that the procedures used would help ESP. Although an active set appears to be less favorable to ESP than a more passive orientation, the general atmosphere of the AA condition was clearly much more favorable than that of an earlier study (Crandall, JASPR, 1985, 27-38) in which a rude, unsympathetic experimenter resulted in missers showing significant negative displacement.

Discussion of Possible Artifacts*

One possible confounding variable in any study of displacements concerns the number of target repeats. If there are fewer of these than would be expected by chance, missers would be expected to show more displacements than hitters. The same would be true for number of call or response repeats. If either of these variables was responsible for the displacement effects found here, we would expect to find a difference in target or call repeats between the PA and the AA conditions. Two, two-way ANOVAS (Missers/Hitters x PA/AA Condition) were conducted, one for target repeats and the other for call repeats. In both cases, none of the main effects nor interactions was significant. In fact, in each case the F-values for the main effect of score (missers/hitters) and the interaction of this variable with experimental condition (PA/AA) were less than 1.0. Consequently, there is no indication here that variations in either target or call repeats were responsible for the larger and significant displacement effects found in the PA condition.

Conclusions

There are two implications of the above that might well be kept in mind when looking for displacement effects: the latter seem to be most likely to occur under conditions favorable to psi, and data should be analyzed separately (and compared) for missers and hitters on the direct targets. Given the contrary tendencies of these two groups, their respective positive and negative displacement scores are apt to cancel each other out in any simple experimentwide averaging of displacement scores. There probably are many existing sets of data, collected for various purposes, that could easily be analyzed for displacements. Such analyses could provide valuable information concerning the specific factors and conditions that either facilitate or inhibit the occurrence of these effects. In this way we could learn more about the processes controlling this aspect of psi.

DISPLACEMENT EFFECT REVISITED

H. Kanthamani[†] and Anjum Khilji (Institute for Parapsychology, Box 6847, Durham, NC 27708)

Interest in ESP displacement scores seems to have been revived, mainly from the work of James Crandall, in recent years.

---

*Editors' Note: See Postscript, pp. 65-66.

In a series of studies, Crandall has shown how +1 and -1 displaced hits form an alternative way of looking for psi than the traditional direct-target scoring method. In another paper, Crandall and Kanthamani provided further confirmation of a type of displacement effect found in a set of data previously collected at the Institute for Parapsychology (see pp. 66-69). Further examination of the same data undertaken independently by us led to the present paper.

Before we proceed, let us recapitulate the central aspect of Crandall's hypothesis, which tests an interesting interaction of two types of psi scores: hitting and missing on direct targets and the displacement scores being above or below chance. In other words, Crandall predicts that hitters on direct targets would show missing on the adjacent +1 and -1 targets, while the missers would do the opposite, i.e., obtain displacement scores greater than chance. The old idea of "improper focusing" as a cause of psi-missing tends to get some support here in that such improper focusing may yield greater +1 and -1 hits. Similarly, the concept of "trans-temporal inhibition" among hitters might gain importance by the fact that hitters are expected to miss on the displaced targets. Crandall tests these predictions by selecting only those runs which are above chance among hitters and those which are below among the missers.

All this raised our curiosity to explore what happens in the rest of the data. Do they go against his predictions, go the same way, or just not contain any evidence of psi? If we consider seriously the model of "improper focusing leading to psi-missing," then we should expect accelerated +1 and -1 hits in such runs irrespective of whether they are taken from a hitting session or missing session. Similarly, it can be expected that a hitting run should have the same internal characteristics whether it is part of an overall high-scoring group of runs or a low-scoring group. It would seem too simplistic to expect this kind of a relationship between the directional psi process and the displaced process, and makes us wonder if it might be artifactual (see Postscript, pp. 65-66).

We have adopted two methods to test such a relationship. (1) Crandall's method, in which hitting runs were selected from above-chance scorers and missing runs from below-chance subjects. These selected runs were then subjected to +1 and -1 displacement analyses. All sessions with an overall chance score were deleted from this analysis. (2) In the second type of analysis no such selection was made. Each subject's hitting runs were compared with his or her missing runs for the displacement scores. Chance-score runs were not included. It may be mentioned that there is a certain amount of overlap between these two methods of analysis, even though they address slightly different issues. In both cases it was expected that there would be a significant difference between the two groups of data. It was further expected that the missing runs would have higher average displacement scores compared to chance and that the hitting runs would have average displacement scores less than chance. The difference between the two means was to be analyzed by a t-test, using the independent-sample method for the first, and the dependent method for the second analysis. All p-values were one-tailed.

Method

Data for the present study came from previous work not originally concerned with displacement. Three sets of data were chosen which were readily available in our files, and each set formed a different series.

Series 1. The first set is essentially the same as that of the Crandall-Kanthamani paper (see pp. 66-69), and some of the results are identical to what was presented there. This study involved subjects doing ESP tests under either a "passive-attention" condition or "active-attention" condition. Details of this procedure are available in RIP 1984, 82-85. Three groups (N = 26, N = 37, N = 33) of high-school students participated in this study. Approximately half of each group was tested in the passive condition and the other half in the active condition, for a total of 45 and 51 in the two groups, respectively. The ESP test was a standard clairvoyance test for groups, in which each subject completed 5 runs of 25 trials each. The overall results had shown significant differences between the two conditions in each group, although the consistency of the scoring rate varied from group to group. Thus, it was hard to establish if one condition was more psi conducive than the other. It was thought worthwhile to see if a displacement analysis would answer this question any better. A total of 94 subjects' data was available for this purpose. This set was collapsed across the three subgroups and reanalyzed for displacement scores separately under the two attention conditions.

Series 2. This was an extension of Series 1 using the same methodology and with a student experimenter testing the subjects. The ESP test was one of precognition, and each subject completed five runs either in the passive-attention set or active-attention set. The subjects were tested in small groups, and a total of 25 participated in the passive condition and 41 in the active condition. Overall results failed to show evidence of psi in either of the conditions or in the difference between the two. This data set was chosen to see if overall chance scores on direct targets would yield similarly nonsignificant displacement scores or whether displacement scores would be any better. This was done by analyzing the +1 and -1 displacement scores for each condition separately and contrasting them.

Series 3. This was a single-subject study in which the second author (A.K.) had completed 100 runs of a clairvoyance test over 20 sessions. These data were collected during a religious fast which A.K. observed strictly during 1984. In each session she completed five runs of an envelope clairvoyance task, once in the morning and once again in the afternoon. The overall results showed moderate evidence of psi (CR = 1.9), which was independently significant in the morning runs (CR = 2.2). This data set was chosen for its uniqueness and also to see if the displacement scores would give better evidence of psi than the direct-target scores did. Since this was a small amount of data, it was decided to combine both the morning and afternoon sessions for the displacement analysis.

Results

Series 1. The Method I analysis, in which the hitting runs of the hitters and the missing runs of the missers were compared for their displacement scores, showed a strong effect in the passive-attention condition and a weak effect in the active-attention condition. There were 10 subjects whose overall scores were at chance and who therefore did not enter into this analysis. In the passive group, the mean displacement scores of the hitters (N = 23) in their hitting runs was 8.83, while it was 10.88 among the missers (N = 16) in their missing runs. The difference between these two scores is highly significant (t = 4.237, 37 df, p << .001). In the active condition, the hitters (N = 20) averaged 9.00 and the missers (N = 25) 9.86 in their hitting and missing runs, respectively. The difference between the two means is marginally significant (t = 1.739, 43 df, p < .05).

The Method II analysis gave similar results. Here each subject's displacement scores on hitting runs were compared with those of missing runs. Among the 40 subjects who had both types of runs in the passive condition, mean displacement scores of 8.84 on the hitting runs and 10.72 on the missing runs were obtained. The difference between these two means gives a t of 4.495 (39 df, p << .001). An equal number of subjects in the active condition averaged 9.33 displacement hits in the hitting runs and 9.61 in the missing runs. The difference here, however, was nonsignificant.

Series 2. In the passive condition, according to the Method I analysis, mean displacement scores of the hitters (N = 10) on hitting runs and missers (N = 13) on missing runs were 9.20 and 9.87, respectively. The difference between them was nonsignificant. Similarly, in the active condition also there was no significant difference between the two groups, although the mean displacement of the missers (N = 19, M = 9.57) was slightly higher than that of the hitters (N = 20, M = 9.03). These averages improved slightly by the Method II analysis. In the passive condition, the two scores were 9.22 and 9.95 for hitting and missing runs contributed by 23 subjects. The difference between these two gives a t of 1.488

(22 df, p = n.s.). Similarly, in the active condition (N = 40), the average score of the missing runs was larger (9.23) than that of the hitting runs (8.64); however, the difference was not significant: t = 1.489, 39 df, p = n.s.

Series 3. Since this series included only one subject, we considered the session as the unit of analysis. Accordingly, out of the 20 sessions 18 were above chance in their total scores, 6 below, and 2 exactly at chance. In the Method I analysis the hitting runs showed an average of 7.94 hits on displacements and the missing runs an average of 9.57 hits. The difference between these two was marginally significant, with a t of 1.716, 16 df, p < .053. The same trend was seen for Method II with greater significance. The hitting runs averaged 8.27 hits on displacements and the missing runs 9.85 hits; their difference gives a t of 2.413 (16 df, p = .014).

Discussion

The results of the first series gave strong evidence for displacement effects and pointed out the superiority of one condition over the other. Such a generalization could not be made from the direct-target measure. Whether the displacements are a genuine effect or not has to await reanalysis using the correction referred to elsewhere (see p. 66). Nevertheless, the robustness of the effect is evident from both methods of analysis.

Results of Series 2 provided only weak evidence for the displacement effect, whereas those of Series 3 are somewhat stronger. Comparing the two methods of analyzing the displacement effect, Method II appears to be more powerful than Method I. Also, Method II appears to be more meaningful, as there is less selection to be made within the data. Nevertheless, it should be remembered that, as noted earlier, the two methods are not independent.

MISSING AND DISPLACEMENT IN TWO RNG COMPUTER GAMES

Ephraim I. Schechter (Psychophysical Research Laboratories,
    301 College Rd. East, Princeton, NJ 08540)

ESP displacement data reported by Crandall (JASPR, 1983, 209-228; 1985, 27-38; RIP 1985, pp. 40-43; this volume, pp. 62-66; Crandall and Covey, JASPR, 1986, 393-408; Crandall and Kanthamani, this volume, pp. 66-69) suggested retrodictive analyses of pilot series with Psychophysical Research Laboratories (PRL) random number generator (RNG) computer games, VOLITION and Psi Invaders. In the forced-choice ESP studies reported by Crandall, participants with below-chance direct-hits scores ("psi-missers") showed significant or strong displacement hitting, while participants with above-chance direct-hits scores ("psi-hitters") showed less displacement. He calls the missers' tendency towards displacement hitting the "psi-missing displacement effect" (PMDE).

Crandall's reports have already extended the PMDE to more than one type of displacement and to studies by more than one researcher. He has found the PMDE in studies of displacement to targets immediately preceding and following the one for the current trial and in a study of displacement to "background" stimuli that accompany the current trial's target. The effect has been seen in data from studies by Schmeidler (Crandall, JASPR, 1985, 27-38) and by Kanthamani (Crandall and Kanthamani, see pp. 66-69; Kanthamani and Khilji, see pp. 69-73) as well as in Crandall's own studies.

Data from PRL's RNG games VOLITION and Psi Invaders provide an opportunity to examine the displacement characteristics of missers and hitters in still another context. The ostensible task in these games is PK rather than ESP. In addition, the tasks involve a possibility for displacement different from the target-sequence and background-stimuli contexts reported by Crandall. Both games gather two sets of RNG samples (nearly) simultaneously. The results of one sample are fed back to the player by way of the game's computerized display (the "feedback" [FBK] condition); the results of the other are "silent" and are never fed back to the player (the SIL condition).

With displacement defined broadly as the tendency to systematically call (or affect) aspects of the situation other than the one defined as the target, the SIL RNG can be viewed as a displacement target in VOLITION and Psi Invaders. That is, the FBK RNG is the intended target towards which the participant's focused effort is likely to be directed because of its effect on the game display and play. The SIL RNG does not affect the game at all and, in most cases, the participant is not even (consciously) aware of its existence. Since the two RNG samples on any trial are independent, there is no reason to expect any relationship between FBK-RNG hitting and SIL-RNG hitting. Systematic hitting on the SIL RNG rather than the FBK RNG, then, fits the broad definition of "displacement" offered above.

From this perspective, the data reported by Crandall lead to the predictions (retrodictions) that (1) participants who obtain below-chance scores on the FBK RNG (missers) should have above-chance scores on the SIL RNG, and (2) missers' SIL-RNG scores should be more positive than hitters' SIL-RNG scores.

The data used to test these retrodictions are those of the VOLITION Pilot Screening Series 1 and the Psi Invaders Screening

Displacement Effects

1 series. (Other data from these series were reported by Berger, Schechter and Honorton, RIP 1985, pp. 1-3.) Early versions of the VOLITION and Psi Invaders programs were used in these series; PRL's PsiLab// package contains more recent versions.

VOLITION is an RNG game in which cumulative performance on the FBK RNG is plotted, as the game progresses, against theoretical trend lines. This provides the participant with a clear picture of performance relative to the goal. In the series reported here, VOLITION made use of an RNG board that contained two independent noise-diode RNGs. The program sampled each RNG 100 times on every run to provide the FBK- and SIL-RNG data. Which RNG was used for the FBK sample and which for the SIL sample, and which sample was taken first, were determined pseudorandomly for each run.

VOLITION Pilot Screening Series 1 involved 20 participants each playing 10 100-run games, with 10,000 FBK-RNG binary trials and 10,000 SIL-RNG binary trials per game.

Psi Invaders is a modified version of the popular video game "Space Invaders." The player must "shoot" invaders who are attempting to "bomb" the player. The player uses a game controller to move a "laser cannon" and avoid being bombed, and presses a button on the controller to "fire" the laser and shoot the invaders. Output from a 100-trial FBK-RNG run determines whether or not the laser fires when the button is pressed. The series reported here used an early version of the PRL PsiLab// RNG, based on the RIPP RNG designed by Dick Bierman. Two consecutive 100-trial RNG runs were taken with each button press to provide the FBK- and SIL-RNG data. Whether the FBK or the SIL sample was taken first was pseudorandomly determined for each button press.

Data from 16 of the 17 participants in the Psi Invaders Screening 1 series are reported here. (The number of games per participant varied, as did the number of trials per game. The seventeenth participant played only 2 games, while the other 16 participants averaged 9.6 games apiece [s.d. = 1.5]. Since the number of RNG trials per game was not fixed, this early version of Psi Invaders was susceptible to optional stopping. The program has since been modified and the version supplied with PRL's PsiLab// has a fixed number of trials per game. The data being analyzed here, however, are based on SIL-RNG performance, which was not shown to the participant during game play and would not have been a factor in optional stopping. In addition, the analysis is retrodicted and the details of the "hitter/misser" relationship could not have been predicted at the time the data were gathered.)

The overall FBK-RNG and SIL-RNG Z-score for all of a participant's games were used in the analyses. The SIL Z-score was the dependent variable; the FBK Z-score was used to determine whether the participant was classified as a "hitter" or a "misser." Two participants with FBK Z-scores of 0.00 were dropped from the analysis of the VOLITION data.

For each study, the mean SIL Z-score for hitters and the mean SIL Z-score for missers were compared to the expected Z of 0.00 with single-mean t-tests. The tests of the misser means were one-tailed, since the existing PMDE data retrodict that the misser SIL mean should be above 0.00. The tests of the hitter means were two-tailed, since the PMDE data available at the time the analyses were done were not specific as to the direction of the difference for hitters.

The hitter and misser SIL-condition mean Z-scores were compared to each other with independent-groups t-tests. Since the PMDE data retrodict that the misser SIL means should be above the hitter SIL means, one-tailed tests were used.

In both games, as retrodicted, the SIL-RNG data resembled Crandall's displacement data. Participants who scored below chance on the FBK RNG ("psi missers") scored significantly above chance on the SIL RNG (VOLITION: mean Z = .819, t = 1.947, 9 df, p = .041, one-tailed; Psi Invaders: mean = .711, t = 3.377, 6 df, p = .008, one-tailed). Those who scored above chance on the FBK RNG ("psi hitters") scored nonsignificantly below chance on the SIL RNG (VOLITION: mean = -.356, t = -.962, 7 df, p = .635, two-tailed; Psi Invaders: mean = -.392, t = -1.229, 8 df, p = .254, two-tailed). The difference between hitters' and missers' SIL-RNG scores was statistically significant in both games (VOLITION: t = 2.04, 16 df, p = .029, one-tailed; Psi Invaders: t = 2.702, 14 df, p = .009, one-tailed).

Seven participants played both games; they are among the eight "multiexperiment participants" described by Berger, Schechter, and Honorton (RIP 1985, 1-3). To insure that the similarity between the VOLITION and Psi Invaders displacement data is not due to these players alone, the analyses were redone without these participants' data. The results indicate that the overall patterns do not depend on the common participants. Missers scored above chance on the SIL RNG (VOLITION: mean Z = 1.02, t = 1.566, 3 df, p = .11, one-tailed; Psi Invaders: mean = .793, t = 1.702, 2 df, p = .116, one-tailed), and hitters scored below chance on the SIL RNG (VOLITION: mean = -.352, t = -.823, 6 df, p = .554, two-tailed; Psi Invaders: mean = -.746, t = -1.898, 5 df, p = .115, two-tailed). The difference between hitters' and missers' SIL-RNG scores was statistically significant in both games (VOLITION: t = 1.838, 9 df, p = .049, one-tailed; Psi Invaders: t = 2.364, 7 df, p = .025, one-tailed).

In addition, 300 Psi Invaders simulation games were run. The simulations use the same computer program as the real games, except

that they do not produce a display on the video monitor and the
time between runs is pseudorandomly varied rather than being determined
by a player's button presses. The simulations are run
with no participant or observer present.

Since the simulation games were not divided into sets matched
to the numbers of games and trials per game of the real participants,
they were analyzed with the game, rather than the "participant,"
as the unit of measure. The product-moment correlation between
FBK and SIL Z-scores across games was not statistically significant
($r = -.09$, 298 df, $p = .22$, two-tailed). When the 153 experimental
games were analyzed the same way, the correlation was
statistically significant ($r = -.158$, 151 df, $p = .048$, two-tailed).
This indicates that the relationship between hitters' and missers'
SIL Z-scores is not likely to be due to an equipment artifact.

If the retrodicted patterns reported here can be confirmed as
predictions for new data, we will be able to widen the definition of
"displacement" in "psi-missing displacement effect" and extend the
PMDE logic to ostensible PK tasks.

PSI AND GEOMAGNETIC FACTORS

PERSISTENT TEMPORAL RELATIONSHIP OF GANZFELD RESULTS TO GEOMAGNETIC ACTIVITY, APPROPRIATENESS OF USING STANDARD GEOMAGNETIC INDICES

Marsha H. Adams (Time Research Institute, Box 620198, Woodside, CA 94062)

Two studies show persistent temporal relationships between observations of successful versus unsuccessful psi performance and a geomagnetically quiet period preceding them. These reports show different time intervals preceding the enhanced psi functioning. Analysis of a third data set shows a hard temporal relationship to geomagnetic activity, but in yet another time interval.

Replication across each of the psi data sets suggests that the temporal relationship to the geomagnetic field (GMF) is valid. However, the variability of the quiet-time interval preceding successful psi functioning indicates that the causal influence that may affect psi function may not be adequately described by the geomagnetic indices alone. It has been proposed that influence on psi performance is determined by some other factor closely related to geomagnetic activity which co-varies with the geomagnetic indices.

Physical characteristics of the geomagnetic field that might influence psi function are explored, in particular, the occurrence of extremely low frequency (ELF) and ultra low frequency (ULF) micropulsations. The relationship of these influences to GMF activity is discussed, and the possibility that these characteristics are incompletely represented by the geomagnetic indices is explored. A possible seasonal effect is also investigated.

ASPECTS OF THE MEASUREMENT AND APPLICATION OF GEOMAGNETIC INDICES AND EXTREMELY LOW FREQUENCY ELECTROMAGNETIC RADIATION FOR USE IN PARAPSYCHOLOGY

G. Scott Hubbard[†] and Edwin C. May (SRI International, Room G-203, 333 Ravenswood Ave., Menlo Park, CA 94025)

A great deal of interest has been generated in the parapsychological literature by recent publications claiming correlations between psi performance and geomagnetic-field (GMF) indices. An established correlation between geomagnetism and psi performance would represent the first environmental factor that might explain the variability of results in parapsychological research and would provide a powerful predictive tool for establishing "psi-conducive" experiment times. Because the implications of such a correlation for the field of parapsychology are extremely important, we decided to investigate these claims in some detail. Included in our review were (1) research on the biological effects of electromagnetic radiation (EMR), (2) other claimed correlations with geomagnetic indices, (3) derivation and use of geomagnetic indices, (4) measurement of low-frequency electromagnetic radiation, and (5) statistical methods used to examine the data.

The often-cited justification for examining low-frequency EMR correlates to psi is laboratory research on behavioral effects of extremely low frequency (ELF) electromagnetic radiation (3 to 300 Hz). However, a recent review by W.R. Adey (Physiological Reviews, 1981, 435-514) criticizes the data on behavioral effects in general as: "... lacking necessary rigor in experimental design, often defective in control procedures, ... and plagued by experimental data so noisy that even statistical evaluation does little to establish credibility for claimed interactions." He also points out that "most reported effects have not been independently confirmed."

Although plausibility arguments for examining psi correlates to EMR are drawn from ELF research, the most widely used EMR measurements in the parapsychological literature are the geomagnetic indices. These indices reflect global or hemispherical variations in the horizontal component of the geomagnetic field in the ultra low frequency (ULF) region extending from DC to about 3 to 10 Hz.

The parapsychological publications we studied often cited as evidence the work of H. Friedman et al. (Nature, 1963, 200, 626-628) which examined possible correlations between geophysical parameters, admissions to psychiatric hospitals, and behavioral trends in the hospital wards. On inspection, however, the papers presented by this group appear to us to provide essentially no justification for the present use of geomagnetic indices. In the 1963 reference, the authors conclude (p. 627): "The total range of geomagnetic activity, as reflected in planetary (ap) and more local (ak) natural magnetic field intensity parameters, does not reveal any significant relationship with psychiatric hospital admissions" (our emphasis).

As noted earlier, the method that researchers have chosen to examine the question of EMR effects on psi functioning is to look for correlations between existing psi data and the geomagnetic field indices. It is our contention that the GMF indices are not a useful tool to test these hypotheses.

The GMF indices were first developed in the late nineteenth century as a method of collecting qualitative information about planetary magnetic phenomena. During the era preceding satellite communications and extensive transoceanic cables, short-wave radio was an important form of worldwide communications. At that time, the indices served as valuable "weather stations" because short-wave radio was extremely sensitive to intense GMF activity. Stated simply, the indices are an excellent detector of global magnetic storms but were never intended to provide highly quantitative measurements of local geomagnetic activity.

Because these indices are averages reflecting global GMF, there may be little correlation between local geomagnetic activity and the index. Research by Bubenik (Final Report, SRI Project 3731, SRI International, Menlo Park, California, June 1983) recently demonstrated that the coherence between geomagnetic measuring stations falls off dramatically at distances greater than 600 miles. The lack of coherence may be further exacerbated by special local conditions. For example, San Francisco Bay Area measurements by Fraser-Smith of Stanford University in 1979 showed that ULF magnetic fields generated by the Bay Area Rapid Transit electric railway are one to two orders of magnitude greater than average natural background values. Since the published index is determined from a weighted average of data reported from 13 worldwide measurement stations, the GMF activity may be relatively quiet in one area while the index is reflecting a magnetic disturbance detected at several other sites. Geomagnetic indices are therefore poor indicators of the local magnetic conditions that may possibly influence psi performance.

In the parapsychological literature, a number of different indices have been utilized to find correlations with psi performance. Most often cited are the ap, aa, Ap, and Kp indices. All of these indices are derived from the same type of data; they do not represent different measurements. The principal difference is that the "a" and "A" indices are linear whereas the "K" indices are quasi-logarithmic. The use of these indices for correlational studies is complicated by a number of factors. In particular, it has been demonstrated that the values in the commonly used indices are neither normally distributed nor continuous. As Bubenik states

(Journal of Geophysical Research, 1977, 2875-2878): "... the indices in their present form are probably less representative of the natural fluctuations in geomagnetic activity than is generally believed. The artificial components directly affect the most common studies undertaken with these indices. Correlations, in particular will be influenced by the artificial components in the indices" (our emphasis).

To conduct meaningful correlational studies, we suggest that local measurements of the geomagnetic field using standard instrumentation should be employed. For practical measurements, a single-axis magnetometer having room temperature shielding would be sufficient.

In addition to local GMF measurements, appropriate statistical techniques must be used. One example of a widely used technique is signal averaging. To apply this technique to the psi/GMF arena, let us assume that we have made local measurements of the horizontal component of the magnetic field, H, averaged over one-hour intervals. Further assume that we have a number of events consisting of good psi performances and that we are interested in H up to five hours before and after the psi task.

We average the magnetic field across all sessions for each time interval to produce column means. Using a method such as Analysis of Variance (ANOVA), we must now determine if all the column means were drawn from the same population. If they were, then the analysis ends with the conclusion that there was no significant correlation between the GMF and the good psi trials.

Under the condition that the ANOVA shows significant differences in the column means, a second analysis is imperative because geomagnetic field measurements are not necessarily statistically independent and cannot be considered random variables in the usual sense. Forbush et al. (Reviews of Geophysics and Space Physics, 1982, 971-976; Solar Physics, 1983, 113-122) have demonstrated that by ignoring possible persistent components in the geomagnetic field, a gross underestimate of the residual variance may occur, leading to a highly inflated F-ratio. In their test example, when they included a correction for the persistency effects, the F-ratio was reduced from 4.96 to 1.16. This corresponds to a p-value increase from 10^{-15} to 0.3!!

In geomagnetic data, one source of the persistency is well known and arises because of the 27-day rotation period of the sun. There is also a two- to three-day persistence corresponding to the mean lifetime of geomagnetic storms. Even if the time period of the magnetic-field measurements is small compared with a given period of persistence, Forbush suggests that a variance correction be made.

To determine if there is a significant difference between a set of GMF data for good psi performance and a set for poor performance, the ANOVA (corrected for persistency and linear trends) must show a significant Good x Poor interaction term. In the absence of an a priori hypothesis, this interaction term must be significant before pairwise t-tests can be applied to determine which time intervals are important.

While there is considerable controversy over the possible effects of ELF and ULF electromagnetic radiation on behavior, the question of EMR interference with performance on psi tasks is a valid area of investigation. Again, we believe that the GMF indices are inappropriate to examine this question. We urge that local ELF and/or ULF measurements be conducted simultaneously with the psi task under investigation. Once these data are collected, a statistical procedure that properly addresses the possible nonrandomness in the signals must be applied.

ATTEMPTED CORRELATION OF ENGINEERING ANOMALIES WITH GLOBAL GEOMAGNETIC ACTIVITY

Roger D. Nelson[†] and Brenda J. Dunne (Princeton Engineering Anomalies Research, School of Engineering/Applied Science, Princeton University, Princeton, NJ 08544)

Two investigators have independently reported patterns of higher psychic performance in spontaneous cases (Persinger, RIP 1985, p. 32) and in remote-viewing trials (Adams, RIP 1985, p. 25) on days of lower geomagnetic activity or on the first or second day following a minimum. Such correlations of physical parameters with any of the various categories of anomalies may be an important step toward basic understanding of the phenomena. Three large data bases generated over the past several years in the Princeton Engineering Anomalies Research (PEAR) program are suitable for similar exploration of such correlations (Nelson, Dunne, Jahn, PEAR Technical Reports 83003, 84003, and 85004).

Various measures of geomagnetic activity are available, but public records generally are averages over a global or hemispheric dimension. The several indices are highly correlated or in some cases are simply transforms of each other. A magnetic tape providing several geophysical data bases was obtained from the National Oceanic and Atmospheric Administration (NOAA),* and the average antipodal (aa) index of geomagnetic activity for the

---

*NOAA, National Geophysical Data Center, 325 Broadway, Code E/GC4, Boulder, CO 80303.

Northern Hemisphere over the time period of the PEAR data base was extracted.

Remote Perception

A subset of the aa index was created corresponding to all formal Precognitive Remote Perception (PRP) trials. These are the data most similar to those used in previous investigations and were treated in a similar manner and with other analytic approaches. Table I shows Pearson product-moment correlations of the 334 PRP trial scores with the aa index for several days surrounding the trial.

Table I

CORRELATIONS OF PRP SCORES WITH THE aa INDEX

Relative Day	Correlation, r	t_r (333 df)
-4	-.0165	-.301
-3	-.0233	-.425
-2	-.0234	-.427
-1	.0252	.459
0	-.0079	-.115
1	-.0482	-.880
2	.0243	.443
3	.0275	.501
4	-.0396	-.722

There appears to be no correlation of the PRP scores with aa index values in this data set, either on the day of the trial or anywhere in the week surrounding the trial. To provide context, correlations of date with score ($r = -.0247$, $t = -.450$) and date with the aa index itself ($r = .2573$, $t = 4.581$) were computed. The lack of correlation of date with score is expected in a data set that is uniform across time. The highly significant correlation of the aa index and date indicates a seasonal variation or autocorrelation within the index. It is also evident that the distribution of index values is highly skewed, so that the use of any statistics that assume normality may give spurious indications in tests of correspondence or difference among subsets.

In contrast to the straight correlational method described above, some investigators have selected the best and worst scores from their data sets and have sought correspondence of these with the geomagnetic measures. The PRP data were also examined in this mode. A set of high scores and low scores were selected and the corresponding aa indices compared for the day of the perception and the week surrounding it. Table II shows the average aa index for high and low scores.

Table II

AVERAGE aa INDEX FOR HIGH AND LOW PRP TRIALS

Relative Day	aa High (N = 47)	aa Low (N = 44)
-4	30.851	31.246
-3	32.617	30.864
-2	34.617	28.909
-1	31.681	30.864
0	27.915	29.364
1	32.404	30.000
2	29.979	34.068
3	28.681	34.841
4	28.298	27.886

To evaluate grossly the importance of apparent differences, a two-sample t-score was computed for two of the largest differences, remembering the caveats concerning nonnormality. For day -2, the difference is opposite that predicted and has a t of -1.58 (on log transformed data, t = 1.30), while day +3 has a positive difference: t = 1.65 (log transformed data, t = 1.19). The day of the trial for high scores does have a low average aa value, but the variation of these data is so great (the standard deviation ranges from 14 to 20) that the appearance of patterns may be deceptive. There is no clear indication of a meaningful relationship of data from the PRP experiment to geomagnetic activity. While the aa index for high scores shows a minimum coinciding with the day of the trial, three other perspectives suggest caution in interpretation: this minimum is not significantly different from its neighbors; the differences between values for high and low scoring are nonsignificant; and the regressions of scoring on aa index values for the days surrounding the trial show small and nonsignificant slope.

Psychokinesis Experiments

A similar but less extensive examination was made of data from psychokinesis experiments in the PEAR data base. Samples of highly successful PK data from the Random Event Generator (REG) and Random Mechanical Cascade (RMC) experiments were selected, and correlations with the aa index were computed for days corresponding to the experimental sessions. For the REG, a sample of 1046 PK⁻ runs showed a slight, nonsignificant correlation opposite the predicted direction ($r = -.028$, $t = -.917$, 1045 df), and for the RMC, in a sample of 262 PK-left runs the correlation was also nonsignificant (r = -.061, t = -.977, with 261 df). Thus, in these data also there is little to indicate a correspondence of anomalous performance with the global geomagnetic index.

Discussion

The possibility that a correlation might be found between a measure of geomagnetic activity and the results of anomalies experiments is not borne out in the PEAR data base, even though the subsets selected were large and contained strong evidence for effects. However, some aspects of this study may have more general application in the search for correlates to anomalous effects. Perhaps of first importance is to characterize the measures that are being compared to determine what statistical models may be appropriate. In the aa data, there are two important deviations from the well-understood normal distribution: skew and strong autocorrelation; in addition, the variance is large and also autocorrelated. In contrast, the experimental data are statistically very well behaved. This is a situation in which sequential patterns need to be supported by other indicators of relationship between the variables. Simple correlation procedures are a powerful and easily interpreted approach which is very useful in a complete examination of relationships of this nature. It also seems important in pursuing further the question of geomagnetic influence to obtain relatively local measures, preferably in the context of a controlled experimental design, since local variations are not only large but likely to be relevant.

EXPERIMENTAL DREAM TELEPATHY-CLAIRVOYANCE AND GEOMAGNETIC ACTIVITY

Michael Persinger (Behavioral Neuroscience Laboratory, Laurentian
   University, Ramsey Lake Rd., Sudbury, Ont., Canada,
   P3E 2C6) and Stanley Krippner (Saybrook Institute)*

Data from the first night each subject spent at the Maimonides Dream Laboratory (see Ullman and Krippner, in M. Ebon, Signet Handbook of Parapsychology, New York: New American Library, 1978) were utilized to determine whether a particular pattern of geomagnetic (GM) activity was evident. Only subjects being tested for dream telepathy or clairvoyance (T-C) were selected, because previous research did not suggest a link between GM activity and

---

*Presented jointly by Stanley Krippner (Saybrook Institute) and George B. Schaut (Laurentian University).

precognition (e.g., Schaut and Persinger, Perceptual and Motor Skills, 1985, 412-414).

The only form in which data are available for all the Maimonides sessions is as a count of judges' hits and misses, based on ranked correspondences between dream protocols and potential targets (art prints) in a target pool (I.L. Child, American Psychologist, 1985, 1219-1230). If the actual target had been ranked for similarity to the dreams and postsleep interview in the upper half of the target pool (e.g., #1, #2, #3 in a pool of six), the outcome was considered a hit. If the actual target was ranked in the lower half of the pool (e.g., #4, #5, #6 in a pool of six), the outcome was considered a miss. The median score of the three judges was used to determine hits and misses.

The ranks were divided into four categories. A "high hit" (HH) is a rank in the top quartile (e.g., #1 or #2 in a pool of eight; #1 in a pool of six), a "low hit" (LH) is a rank in the second quartile (e.g., #3 or #4 in a pool of eight; #2 or #3 in a pool of six). A "high miss" (HM) is a rank in the third quartile (e.g., #5 or #6 in a pool of eight; #4 or #5 in a pool of six); a "low miss" (LM) is a rank in the fourth quartile (#7 or #8 in a pool of eight; #6 in a pool of six). This procedure yielded 62 experimental T-C nights available for analysis: 18 HH, 29 LH, 7 HM, and 8 LM.

Method

It was decided to use GM activity as measured by the Aa index. Aa values for the Northern Hemisphere were determined from Mayaud (IAGA Bulletin, 1973, No. 33) and consequent monthly updates. Subjects were coded according to gender and to the closeness of their dream's correspondence to the target (i.e., HH, LH, HM, and LM groups).

The major design involved multivariate analyses of variance (MANOVA). The repeated measure was the Aa value for the three days before, the day of, and the three days after the day the experiment was initiated (a total of seven days). The range of the key day plus and minus three days was selected because GM activity tends to be correlated within this period, being particularly correlated between a given day and plus and minus one or two days. Except for specific periodicities, the intercorrelations between GM activity on a day and more than three days before or afterwards are not statistically significant. The two major main factors (non-repeated) in the MANOVA were gender and group. Because the numbers of subjects within the HM and LM groups were small, these two groups were combined for the analysis.

The major analyses involved $\log_{10}$ transformations of the daily Aa values. This was done to reduce the contributions from single days and to increase the homogeneity of variance among groups and between repeated measures. All analyses were also completed using the original Aa values as square-root transformations because the latter were not as extreme as the log modifications. A posteriori contrasts were completed using correlated t-tests for each group and independent t-tests (between groups on a given day) to determine the source of any factor-by-repeated-measure interactions.

Correlated t-tests, with alpha levels set at .01 (to reduce the effect of multiple analysis), were completed for each group for the Aa values of each of the seven days during the experiment and the Aa average for the month in which the experience occurred. The latter analyses were completed to determine the absolute activity of the days of the experience compared to the typical monthly values rather than restricting the analyses to the relative differences between the key day and the days before and afterwards.

Results

MANOVA for all 62 subjects according to the three major groups (HH, LH, LM plus HM), gender, and the seven repeated measures (Aa values of key days plus and minus three days) demonstrated no significant groups or gender interactions. However, there was a significant ($F = 2.53$, 12, 336 df, $p = .003$) interaction between groups and GM activity over days for the log-transformed Aa values. There was also a nearly significant daily difference ($F = 2.54$, 6, 336 df, $p = .03$). There were neither gender-by-day nor gender-by-group-by-day interactions. The group-by-day interaction was significant ($p = .01$) for the absolute and square root Aa values as well.

A posteriori tests showed that the only near-significant difference among days for the four groups occurred three days before the key day (Day -3). On this day, GM activity was higher ($F = 3.40$, 58 df, $p = .02$) for the HM group than the LH group. This finding was confirmed by Duncan's analysis ($p = .05$). Correlated t-tests for within-group comparisons (alpha set at $p = .01$) demonstrated that the nights of the experiments for Group I (HH) were quieter than both Day -3 ($t = 2.99$, 17 df) and Day -2 ($t = 3.04$, 17 df). The night of the experience (plus 1) was significantly quieter than the average of the month ($t = 4.55$, 17 df, $p = .001$).

For the second group (LH), correlated t-tests indicated that only Day -3 ($t = 2.80$) was significantly quieter than the monthly averages. There were no significant differences between the key days and the days before or afterwards. Combining Groups 3 and 4 (14 df), no statistically significant differences in GM activity were found on any of the days.

Discussion

The HH group, the one that showed the greatest psi, demonstrated a pattern where there was no pre-experience elevation in GM activity compared to monthly values. Instead, there was a sudden <u>decrease</u> in GM activity; this activity was significantly lower than for the month or for the days before or afterwards. This latter pattern and not the pattern displayed by the HM group is typical of profiles that have been found in the cases of spontaneous T-C (e.g., Schaut and Persinger, <u>Perceptual and Motor Skills</u>, 1985, 412-414).

The use of Aa values must be viewed with some caution. In its attempt to determine the extent of geomagnetic perturbations, these values are derived from a quasilogarithmic process that omits temporal patterns in the data to derive numerical values. The best index for the study of anomalous behavior of laboratory subjects would be one based on readings from devices in or adjacent to the laboratory itself. Optimally, these readings should be considered in relationship to solar and lunar effects, competing field effects (e.g., radiation), and biological cycles of the subjects being studied.

GEOMAGNETIC FACTORS IN SPONTANEOUS TELEPATHIC, PRECOGNITIVE, AND POSTMORTEM EXPERIENCES

Michael A. Persinger and George B. Schaut[†] (Behavioral Neuroscience Laboratory, Laurentian University, Ramsey Lake Rd., Sudbury, Ontario, Canada P3E 2C6)

Several studies (Persinger, <u>Perceptual and Motor Skills</u>, 1985, 320-322; <u>JASPR</u>, in press; Schaut and Persinger, <u>Perceptual and Motor Skills</u>, 1985, 412-414) have shown that spontaneous telepathic experiences concerning the death or crisis to significant others tend to occur on days when the geomagnetic activity is quieter than the days before or after the experiences. The pattern has been consistent for experiences that have occurred both in this century and the latter part of the previous century.

The geomagnetic activity measure that was used is called the aa (average antipodal) index. Values are available for global geomagnetic activity from the year 1867 to present (Mayaud, <u>IAGA Bulletin</u>, 1973). Although there may be station differences with respect to amplitude of change, the general activity as indicated by aa is strongly representative of the <u>global</u> geomagnetic condition. For example, its correlation with other more pervasive global indices exceeds 0.90.

We decided to see if the geomagnetic V-shape effect (which refers to the graphic display of days with higher geomagnetic activity surrounding the key day of lower activity) was replicable in another collection of spontaneous telepathy cases. In addition, to determine if the effect was specific to telepathy experiences and not a general aspect of spontaneous psi, instances of precognitive and postmortem experiences were used as case controls. The numbers of cases in the first and second data sets (numbers in parentheses) for each phenomenon were: telepathy-clairvoyance, or T-C (58,75), precognition (56,49), and postmortem experiences (75,65). All of the cases were collected from the "My Proof of Survival" and "True Mystical Experiences" sections of FATE magazine. Every case that involved these three phenomena and contained the day, month, and year of occurrence was used in the analysis.

The basic design of analyses involved two procedures. The first was MANOVA (multivariate analysis of variance) which allows for repeated and nonrepeated measures simultaneously. The repeated measures were the daily geomagnetic values (aa indices) for the three days before, the day of, and the three days after the experience. The nonrepeated levels were: (1) phenomena: telepathy, precognition, or postmortem experiences, and (2) replication. A second analysis simply compared the aa values on the days of the experiences with the monthly average and yearly average aa values. In the latter case, nonparametric analyses were also used when problems of heterogeneity of variance were encountered. However, log transformation attenuated this risk.

MANOVA showed no significant difference between replications ($F = 0.56$, 1, 372 df, $p > .01$) but a highly significant difference ($F = 11.20$, 2, 372 df, $p < .001$) between classes of experiences. A posteriori analysis (Scheffe's) indicated that geomagnetic activity for the entire week was lower for the T-C cases than for the other two classifications. However, by far the strongest and most striking effect was the class-by-days interaction ($F = 4.42$, 12, 2232 df, $p < .001$). This was due exclusively to the quieter geomagnetic conditions on the days of the T-C experiences (X ± S.E.M. = 13.9 ± 1.0) compared to the days on which the precognitive (26.0 ± 2.2) and postmortem (27.5 ± 1.9) experiences occurred.

MANOVAs were also conducted between the aa values on the days of the experiences and the averages for the months and years in which the experiences occurred. A posteriori correlated t-tests indicated that the aa values for the days of the T-C experiences (13.9 ± 1.0) were significantly lower than those for the months (20.9 ± 0.5) and years (21.3 ± 0.4) in which they occurred; however, the monthly and yearly values did not differ significantly from each other. On the other hand, the aa values for days on which the precognition (26.0 ± 2.2) and postmortem cases (27.5 ±

1.9) occurred were not significantly less than those for the months (22.9 ± 0.8; 21.9 ± 0.6, respectively) or years (22.6 ± 0.5; 22.4 ± 0.4, respectively) in which they occurred. There was a marginally significant tendency for postmortem experiences to occur on days when the geomagnetic activity was higher than the monthly average.

Finally, we compared the results of the T-C cases with the geomagnetic daily patterns for two other sets of data: the Stevenson and the Gurney, Podmore, and Myers collections. All three analyses showed the V-shaped relationship, with the geomagnetic activity being significantly lower on the day of the experiences compared to the days before or afterwards or relative to the monthly or yearly averages. These results suggest that the geomagnetic effect, whatever mechanism it might entail, has been systematically associated with the occurrence or report of T-C cases.

As an internal check for consistency, only the apparitional modes of experiences were used for the T-C (n = 37), precognitive (n = 27), and postmortem (n = 117) cases. These T-C cases occurred when the geomagnetic activity was quieter before and during the days of the experiences compared to days after the experiences. However, the precognition and particularly the postmortem experiences tended to occur on days when there was a rapid relative increase in geomagnetic activity. Only the postmortem experiences demonstrated a statistically significant, though weak, effect.

The mechanism for the effect is not clear. A variety of metaphors have been suggested, such as the occurrence of extremely low frequency (ELF) electromagnetic fields. It is known that certain ELF bandwidths are facilitated during periods of transient <u>relative</u> decreases in geomagnetic activity. How such conditions facilitate the occurrence of T-C given the occurrence of preconditions --death or crisis to a significant other--remains to be determined. It is clear that the phenomenon is quite robust and can still emerge despite the relatively crude measures of global geomagnetic activity.

GEOMAGNETIC EFFECTS IN A GESP TEST ARE ALTERED BY ELECTRICAL SHIELDING

Charles T. Tart (Dept. of Psychology, University of California, Davis, CA 95616)

Marsha Adams (<u>RIP 1985</u>, p. 25) reported finding lower values of geomagnetic-field (GMF) activity on several days preceding more successful laboratory GESP performance. She used a data base of several hundred remote-viewing trials carried out at SRI International. This difference was statistically significant for one day before more successful remote-viewing trials. Michael Persinger (RIP 1985, p. 32) studied GMF activity and the occurrence of spontaneous ostensible GESP experiences. Though his measure of GMF activity was different from Adams's, various GMF activity measures are highly correlated. Persinger found significantly lower GMF activity on days of spontaneous ostensible GESP experiences (compared to preceding and following days) in three separate studies of different case collections. If the findings of Adams and Persinger are valid, it might be possible to increase the yield of GESP in experiments by canceling experiments that are scheduled on days when GMF activity is high. This would be an important advance in parapsychology, where a major problem is the very poor signal-to-noise ratio in GESP studies.

An already-completed study of the effects of electromagnetic shielding on GESP performance (see pp. 53-54) was reanalyzed for possible correlations of GESP scoring with GMF activity. Methodological details of that study are presented in that abstract.

The Adams study involved remote viewers preselected for very good GESP performance, so the contrast between their good performance (at least "good correspondence with unambiguous unique matchable elements, but some correct information") and poor performance ("some correct elements, but not sufficient to suggest results beyond chance expectation" or worse) involved large differences in GESP functioning. Similarly, Persinger's analyses of spontaneous cases also involved very high levels of ostensible GESP functioning--otherwise it would have been unlikely for the case to have been published and therefore be accessible to Persinger. When looking for correlations, a high degree of variability in at least one of the variables being correlated increases the chance of discovering such a correlation, if it exists in nature.

The data analyzed here suffer from the distinct handicap of having been collected from unselected percipients who showed only small, even if statistically significant, amounts of GESP. Thus, the likelihood of finding a significant correlation between GESP performance and GMF activity was reduced, even if it exists. The fact that some electrical shielding was involved led me to analyze the data anyway. "Good" GESP runs were defined as those with a score of three or more hits ($p < .08$, one-tailed) while a run with a score of zero hits was defined as a "bad" GESP run. The planetary A index, a measure of GMF for 24-hour periods, was used for analysis. This measure correlated highly (.90 and higher) with the Sigma Kp measure used by Adams for the time period of my study.

In the present study Adams's finding of significantly lower GMF activity on the day immediately preceding more successful remote-viewing trials was directionally confirmed, but not significantly so. Persinger's findings of significantly lower GMF activity on days of spontaneous GESP events in three studies were paralleled for deliberate laboratory GESP. Ignoring the electrical condition (grounded or ungrounded) of the Faraday cage, good GESP performance was associated with quieter GMF activity (p = .056, one-tailed, using a Mann-Whitney U test because of the nonnormality of the distributions).

When the data were more closely analyzed, the GMF/GESP relationship was found to occur when the shielding structure, a solid-wall Faraday cage, was in an electrically floating condition with respect to ground (p = .063, one-tailed), but not when it was electrically grounded.

These are weak confirmations in terms of size and marginal statistical significance, but given that they were found under the unfavorable conditions of low GESP performance, compared with the much more robust GESP functioning in the Adams and Persinger studies, they are supportive of a possible link between GESP functioning and GMF activity.

The U.C. Davis Faraday cage is constructed of .005 inch thick copper. At the ultra low frequencies of basic GMF activity, this shielding would be expected to have virtually no effect at all on transmission of magnetic fields and electromagnetic radiation through the cage. Speculating on possible mechanisms for the difference between the grounded and floating Faraday cage conditions is somewhat premature before further confirmation, but perhaps some high-frequency harmonic component of the GMF that affects GESP performance may be shielded by the Faraday cage. The original study found, however, that a grounded Faraday cage produced significantly higher GESP performance from the percipients, so an alternative explanation may be that the apparent amplification of GESP performance found in the grounded Faraday cage condition may have washed out the GMF effect.

If other researchers confirm the suggestions of a link between higher GESP performance and quieter GMF activity, this might be coupled with the suggestion of enchanced GESP performance in a grounded Faraday cage to increase the yield of GESP in experiments: Carry out experiments in grounded Faraday cages when GMF activity is low. Further research is needed to investigate these possibilities.

METHODOLOGY

MONTE CARLO METHODS IN PARAPSYCHOLOGY

George P. Hansen (Psychophysical Research Laboratories, 301 College Rd. East, Princeton, NJ 08540)

The term "Monte Carlo" is applied to any problem-solving computation utilizing random numbers. These procedures are being used more and more frequently in the statistical evaluation of parapsychological research. M.R. Barrington (JSPR, 1973, 222-245) used such a method in evaluating a sheep-goat experiment. H.G. Boerenkamp and G. Camfferman (EJP, 1983, 435-454) used the approach in evaluating a novel method of testing for psi in daily experience. R. Hyman (JP, 1985, 3-49) used the method in estimating effects of multiple analysis on the Type I error rate.

There are a number of advantages in using Monte Carlo procedures, but there are some pitfalls. This paper discusses some of the critical aspects that must be considered when undertaking such a computation. In addition, an example problem was analyzed to illustrate the method. This involved simulating a free-response ESP experiment in which two statistical measures, sum of ranks and direct hits, were used. True probability values were estimated for cases in which both indices were applied. Tables were generated (not included here).

Sources of Random Numbers

There are two methods commonly used to provide random numbers for simulations. Pseudorandom number generators are the most frequently used. These are essentially mathematical algorithms which can produce long strings of apparently random numbers. In actuality, these are deterministic. If one knows the formula and starting point, the same string can be recreated. (For an overview see Radin, JP, 1985, 303-328.) The other method uses a physical process (e.g., radioactive decay) along with appropriate circuitry to produce "truly random" numbers.

Computer languages typically contain pseudorandom number

generators that are called by commands such as the RND function in BASIC. Many are very poor in performance. Further, usually little or no documentation is available for the general user. One of the biggest problems is that the numbers often repeat at short intervals. An investigator is not limited to the generators provided by the language or system. Pseudorandom generators can be implemented in software; however, special coding may be required.

The alternative to pseudorandom algorithms is a hardware random number generator (RNG). This has a number of advantages. It can provide a virtually unlimited quantity of random numbers. No special programming is required to implement it. Standardized devices along with protocols for testing have been developed (most notably the PRL PsiLab// [Psychophysical Research Laboratories, 1985]).

Programming Considerations

To achieve an adequate degree of accuracy, a large number of Monte Carlo trials may be required. Because this approach is probabilistic, the theoretical answer is only approximated. The error is a function of the square root of the number of trials. Thus, each additional decimal digit of accuracy requires 100 times as much calculation as the preceding one. Accuracy requires time, and this may turn out to be the most important consideration when conducting a simulation. Indeed, some simulations can take weeks or months to run. However, there are methods of speeding the calculations.

Variance Reduction

To improve the speed and/or accuracy of a simulation, a number of computational techniques can be employed. These are known as variance reduction methods (Monte Carlo Methods, Methuen, 1967). In certain types of computations, these procedures provide enormous gains in efficiency; however, many of these require some mathematical sophistication.

Machine Factors

Although variance reduction methods have made solution of some problems feasible, another practical consideration in Monte Carlo simulation is the machine and language available. On some systems, a simulation might not be feasible while on others it may be.

Usually the most effective method of increasing speed is to write the program (or some part of it) in assembly language. In one of my simulations on the Apple, I found an increase in speed of over 300 times that of BASIC. A drawback is that assembly-language programming and debugging are more difficult than they are in BASIC. A caution that must be observed when using assembly language is that a hardware RNG should not be sampled too rapidly or nonrandom results will be obtained.

A second method, when using high-level languages, is to compile the program, if possible. A number of compilers are commercially available. A third method is to use a device, such as the Accelerator card of Titan Technologies, to speed processing. This and similar cards for the Apple typically increase speed 3 to 3 1/2 times. These cost in the range of $200 to $250 (mail order). Such cards speed assembly-language programs as well as those written in higher level languages. Some of the IBM and work-a-like microcomputers accommodate coprocessors which can speed calculation.

Debugging

After one has decided to conduct a simulation, a program must be written and debugged. For many applications in parapsychology, the problems are conceptually simple and the programs easy to write. The work is often in the debugging. At times this can be difficult because the correct output may be unknown. However, there are several strategies that can be used in checking the results.

Perhaps the first and most obvious check is to examine the results and see if they "make sense." Boundary conditions should be examined. Approximate hand calculations might be attempted here. One might also employ structured (nonrandom) input (e.g., 1,2,3,1,2,3,1,2,...). If the sequence is well chosen, it may allow independent calculation of the result for the specific input. Another method of checking is to write several versions of the code and compare the results. Still another approach in verifying the program is to conduct the simulation on a very small version of the problem (ideally one in which the correct results can be easily computed by hand).

Multiple Analysis: An Example

In order to illustrate the Monte Carlo method, a simulation was conducted. This simulation addressed a problem found in certain statistical analyses of psi experiments in which two indices are used in testing for significance.

There are a number of reasons an investigator might wish to use several indices to check for statistical significance. For instance, in a free-response ESP experiment psi-hitting might manifest in several ways. There might be generally positive scoring with few negative trials or there might be a number of strong hits but also strong misses. The former case could be detected by a sum-of-ranks statistic while the latter might be best detected by a direct-hits measure. A researcher might wish to allow for both possibilities. Another reason one may desire to use multiple indices is that the use of discrete distributions can impose a more severe requirement than is intended.

When similar cases arose previously, the Bonferroni method could have been used to correct for multiple analysis. This procedure is quite conservative because it assumes statistical independence of the measures. For many cases, this is unrealistic and can be grossly overconservative.

Probabilities of Sums of Ranks or Direct Hits

The specific problem undertaken was to simulate mathematically the results of a free-response ESP experiment. The conditions included a specified number of independent trials, with each trial having a probability of a hit of .25 (one target and three decoys in the judging pool). The procedure involved ranking the target and decoys during judging (ranks 1 to 4, with a rank of 1 being best match). Given such a procedure, direct hits or sum of ranks could both be used for statistical evaluation.

The simulation of this procedure is quite straightforward. Random digits (1,2,3,4) were generated; these simulated the judge's ranking of targets. For one cycle of the simulation, $\underline{n}$ random digits were produced (where $\underline{n}$ is the number of trials in the experiment being simulated. These digits were summed (to determine the sum of ranks), and the number of 1s was tallied (to determine the number of direct hits). This procedure continued for at least 20,000 cycles, and the distributions of the sums of ranks and direct hits were found.

A short BASIC program was written to perform the simulation. The randomness was supplied by a PsiLab// RNG. Simulations were done for experiments with 10, 20, 30 and 40 trials, and tables were generated.

One needs to be a bit cautious when interpreting results of simulations. Confidence limits should be calculated to establish accuracy (Simulation and the Monte Carlo Method, Wiley, 1981).

It was found that in a twenty-trial experiment the probability of obtaining 10 or more direct hits or a sum of ranks of 41 or less is approximately .046 (the upper confidence limit for $\sigma = .01$ is .050). If one were to assume that these measure were independent and use the Bonferroni method, the calculated probability would be approximately .059. The conservative analysis would fail to reject the null hypothesis, but the more accurate analysis indicates that the null hypothesis should be rejected. Using data from the Monte Carlo simulation gives greater statistical power.

Conclusions and Recommendations

Because these methods are nonstandard, authors who report results of simulations should give some details about the method used. The number of trials should be listed, and the source of randomness should be described. The statistical accuracy of the result should also be included. If the computer program is short, a complete listing might be included in an appendix.

REPRESENTATION AND PERFORMANCE EVALUATION APPROACHES IN PSI FREE-RESPONSE TASKS

A. Jean Maren (Psychophysical Research Laboratories, 301 College Rd. East, Princeton, NJ 08540)

Qualitative examples cited in free-response studies often show a very strong correspondence between transcript and target. (See, e.g., Terry and Honorton, JASPR, 1976, 207-217.) The current methods for free-response trial evaluation are effective for statistically measuring possible extrachance correspondence. However, these methods are not primarily oriented towards providing a formal or systematic characterization of the nature of the transcript-to-target correspondences.

As an example of this problem, a percipient in one of the recent Ganzfeld trials at the Psychophysical Research Laboratories (PRL) gave half an hour of mentation for a static-image target showing two fire-eaters giving a public performance. In the image, one fire-eater had flames coming from his mouth, a second was about to or had just finished performing, and a ring of spectators surrounded the two performers. The percipient's mentation included 35 references to flames and/or fire, as well as a number of episodes which had unusual correspondence to the organization of components in the target image.

In this case, the percipient correctly selected the target from a pool of four images. This led to our recording the trial as a "hit." Although this is a pleasing result, the formalism for evaluating the results of the trial reduces a large amount of very interesting data to a single number with $P = 0.25$.

In order to develop a method for formally and systematically characterizing possible transcript-to-target correspondence, it is necessary to first develop a means for formally representing the information content of both transcript and target and then to develop a methodology for transcript-to-target matching. Approaches that draw on concepts and techniques from artificial intelligence (AI) may be very useful in this context, as fundamental and ongoing work in AI deals with symbolic representation and pattern matching.

Representing an overall characterization of a target may be done using approaches based on bit-descriptor lists (JP, 1980, 207-231). Individual target components may also each be described using lists of the component descriptors. The relationships among components are not only significant in themselves but form a basis for creating a description of the structural organization of the target (M. Vernon, A Further Study of Visual Perception. Cambridge: Cambridge U. Press, 1952). Target processes include motion and explicit or implicit dynamics in the target.

The significant components of the "Two Fire-Eaters" include the two fire-eaters, the flames shooting from the mouth of one of the fire-eaters, and the spectators. The entire scene is set in an outdoor courtyard environment.

The structure that symbolically represents the organization of the components in the "Two Fire-Eaters" groups the component "Flames" with the proximal and similarly oriented component "Fire-Eater 1." The next perceptual grouping combines the newly made node (Flames, Fire-Eater 1) with "Fire-Eater 2" based on the similarity and proximity of the two fire-eaters. This produces a new, more complex node. Finally, the spectators, the complex node representing the fire-eaters and the flames, and the environment are grouped into a single node which represents the entire target. This can be symbolically diagrammed using a formalism based on LISP list representation of complex lists (P.H. Winston and B.K.P. Horn, LISP (2nd Ed.). Reading, MA: Addison-Wesley, 1984):

> Two Fire-Eaters =
> (Environment, Spectators, (Fire-Eater 2, (Flames, Fire-Eater 1))).

Although the "Two Fire-Eaters" target is a single image, two processes are strongly implicated: the eruption of the flames from the mouth of the first fire-eater and the transformation of fuel and air into combustive residue.

Transcripts from Ganzfeld experiments often contain many episodes or distinct impressions which can be characterized by a unique representation. In a recent Ganzfeld session for which "Two Fire-Eaters" was the target, there were 67 distinct episodes.

The basic approach to matching will be to generate structures or representations for each transcript episode and to match each episode representation against the target representation. If a match (even a partial match) is found, then a "goodness of fit" measure can be calculated based on the degree of correspondence of components, component features, relationships, and processes, as well as

the overall structural match of the target and the episode. If the
episode structure does not exactly match the target structure, then
the structures can be further broken down into their component sub-
structures and each of these can be tested for possible match.

One of the episodes in a transcript for which "Two Fire-
Eaters" was the target illustrates this approach to episode-to-target
matching. The episode, which was an internal visual image of a
funeral pyre, is structurally diagrammed below:

> Funeral Pyre Concept =
> (Environment, Spectators, (Flames, (Person, Logs))).

Matching this episode against the target results in a positive
match between the "Environment" and "Spectators" nodes of both
the episode and target. The complex nodes (Flames, (Person,
Logs)) and (Fire-Eater 2, (Flames, Fire-Eater 1)) do not match
structurally on the first match attempt. This is because the component "Flames" in (Flames, (Person, Logs)) is on the first level
of this structure, while the component "Flames" in (Fire-Eater 2,
(Flames, Fire-Eater 1)) is on the second level (i.e., embedded in
another set of parentheses).

When the complex node (Flames, (Person, Logs)) is matched
against the substructure (Flames, Fire-Eater 1), a partial match
does result; the "Flames" nodes correspond to each other. The
match of (Person, Logs) to "Fire-Eater 1" is again only partially
successful: the component "Person" matches to "Fire-Eater 1," but
the component "Logs" is unmatched. The relationships between the
components of the episode and the target are similar, and there
are also similarities between the processes invoked by the flames.

This example illustrates in a simple manner the matching of an
episode against a target representation. The structure components,
relationships, and processes in episodes can each be compared to
the target. This allows detailed exploration of how psi may potentially affect a percipient's Ganzfeld mentation.

It is too early to evaluate how effective the approaches described will be in facilitating an understanding of how psi can influence percipient mentation. Nevertheless, the two-stage approach
of target and transcript representation and episode-to-target pattern matching offers a potentially useful means of examining the potential influence of psi. Over the next five years, it should be
possible to develop AI systems for target/transcript representation
and performance evaluation. The use of AI systems for performance evaluation would facilitate the training of psi capabilities, because precise and detailed feedback could be given to the percipient.

JUDGING STRATEGIES TO IMPROVE SCORING IN THE GANZFELD

Julie Milton (Department of Psychology, University of Edinburgh,
    7 George Square, Edinburgh, Scotland, U.K.)

Despite the popularity of free-response methods in ESP tasks, there is as yet no research-based consensus on how best to judge the correspondence between free-response mentation and the (usually) pictorial targets. For example, should the target be chosen on the basis of spectacular correspondences alone, ignoring the weaker ones? Should more weight be given to images that are vivid or bizarre? Is a semantic correspondence worth more than a correspondence of form? The exploratory study described here was an attempt to investigate various ways of optimizing scoring by identifying mentation most likely to be target related. The present author independently judged the correspondence between mentation reports and picture target sets from a Ganzfeld GESP experiment run by Dr. Deborah Delanoy in which 20 percipients (10 male, 10 female, aged 19-48) took part in two 35-minute trials each.

Procedure

Having transcribed the percipient's taped verbal mentation report, the author noted whether or not she was confident that the trial would be successful according to the degree of spontaneity and bizarreness of the percipient's mentation. She then divided the transcript into individual mentation items and noted into which, if any, of a number of mentation categories (such as "bizarre," "vivid," "fleeting," etc.) each mentation item fell.

Next, the author opened the target set pack for the trial provided by Delanoy, and assigned rating points between 0 (no correspondence) and 5 (perfect correspondence) for the correspondence between each of the four pictures in the target set and each mentation item. She also noted which kind of correspondence occurred: the mentation could relate to a picture literally, formally, conceptually, or associatively, or several of these at once, in which case a picture could receive, for example, several "associative" points and several "formal" points for a single mentation item.

When the whole transcript had been judged, the number of rating points was summed for each picture and used as a guide to place the pictures in rank order of correspondence to the mentation. These point sums were also used to calculate ESP Z-scores. The author noted whether or not she was confident that the trial had been successful on the basis of the occurrence of outstanding matches between individual mentation items and a single picture in the set and also noted whether two or more pictures in the set correspond unusually well to the mentation report. When the judging of all the trials had been completed, Delanoy provided the author with the identities of the targets.

Results

All analyses were planned in advance of feedback at the end of the experiment. Data from 37 of a total of 40 trials were independently judged; two of the missing trials were those in which the author was the percipient, and the third was a trial whose outcome was known to the author before the independent judging of the experiment began.

Overall scoring was nonsignificantly above chance (p = 0.11, two-tailed), according to the sum-of-ranks analysis of Solfvin et al. (JASPR, 1978, 93-110). A sum of target ranks of 81 was obtained (mean chance expectation [MCE] = 92.5). The distribution of target ranks is shown below.

Target Rank

	1	2	3	4
Frequency	13	10	8	6

A number of areas of inquiry were of interest; each will be dealt with in turn.

(1) Mentation Categories. For each trial, Wilcoxon T tests compared the proportions of item-by-item rating points assigned to the target on the basis of each mentation category to the proportion assigned on the remaining mentation that did not fall into that category. Out of the 18 mentation categories for which mentation occurred in a sufficiently large number of trials (N > 5) for the Wilcoxon test to be applied, none showed scoring significantly greater than that on the remaining imagery.

(2) Correspondence Types. Using the same analysis as in (1) above, it was found that (a) scoring on the target on the basis of no one correspondence type (literal, formal, conceptual, or associative) was significantly better than that on the basis of remaining correspondences, (b) 30.7% of formal-correspondence points related to the target as compared to 28.3% of literal points (MCE for both being 25.0%), but the difference between the two was not significant, and (c) imagery that percipients could describe in terms of formal qualities but that did not form recognizable scenes or objects was only slightly and not significantly more accurate on correspondences of form than remaining imagery; on formal correspondences alone, 31.0% of such unrecognizable imagery related to the target as compared to 30.5% of all remaining imagery.

(3) Scoring on Strong versus Weak Correspondences. No significant difference in scoring was found when all the trials were reranked on the basis of strong correspondence point sums (using item-by-item point allocations of 3 or more to calculate the sum) and on the basis of weak correspondence point sums (using points of 2 or less), according to a sum-of-ranks analysis. Sums of ranks of 84.0 and 80.0 were obtained for "strong" and "weak" ranks respectively.

(4) Confidence Calls. Three different kinds of confidence call could be made on each trial. The first was made if the percipient's mentation was unusually spontaneous and bizarre; the second if individual mentation items matched unusually well to one of the pictures in the set; and the third if the ESP Z-score for the trial calculated for the first-ranked picture was one of the nine highest in the whole experiment (this criterion having been planned before the beginning of the experiment). For the transcript-based confidence calls, the mean target rank was 2.33, which is closer to chance (MCE = 2.50) than the mean target rank on the remaining trials of 2.00. However, both the high Z-score confidence calls and confidence calls based on spectacular matches improved upon the remaining trials, with mean target ranks of 1.67 and 1.50, respectively, although neither differed significantly from the mean ranks on the remaining trials (mean rank = 2.25, 35 df, t = 0.59, and mean rank = 2.26, 35 df, t = 0.87). There was no significant difference according to a t-test comparing the mean rank assigned to the target on trials receiving confidence calls based on high Z-scores and those receiving confidence calls based on good individual matches.

(5) Identification of Displacement. In her previous Ganzfeld experimentation, the author noticed that on trials in which two or more pictures in the target set corresponded unusually well to the mentation report, the picture that turned out to be the target often received very little correspondence. Although such an observation may be spurious for a number of reasons (such as selective memory), it was decided to examine empirically whether the occurrence of unusually good matches to two or more pictures in the target set was an indication that displacement was occurring in the trial. Because of time restrictions, it was not possible to test directly for displacement using the procedure described by Child and Levi (JASPR, 1980, 171-181); instead, a one-tailed t-test was performed to test the prediction that the mean target rank on such "displacement-called" trials would be significantly lower than that of the remaining trials. The mean target rank of 2.58 was slightly below chance, although not significantly different from the mean target rank of 2.00 on the remaining trials (t = 1.53, 35 df).

Discussion

Overall, scoring was nonsignificantly above chance, which may

have indicated a weak or nonexistent level of ESP in the study.
This being the case, the null results obtained in the analyses
designed to isolate particularly psi-related mentation may have
been due to a general lack of ESP in the studies, and the hypotheses which they represent may not have received a fair test. The
author plans to continue this line of research with data in which
overall scoring was significant.

AN ETHNOGRAPHIC APPROACH TO THE STUDY OF PSI:
METHODOLOGY AND PRELIMINARY DATA

Marilyn Schlitz (Mind Science Foundation, 8301 Broadway,
 Ste. 100, San Antonio, TX 78209)

Employing a method for collecting and analyzing qualitative
data drawn from ethnographic research (Spradley, The Ethnographic Interview, New York: Holt, Rinehart, Winston, 1979),
this paper reports preliminary data obtained from interviews
with three selected PK researchers: William Braud, Julian Isaacs,
and Helmut Schmidt. Various patterns suggesting shared cultural
practices and beliefs have been identified, providing important
insights into the nature of PK experimentation.

Methodology

The ethnographic method includes descriptive, structural,
and contrast questions introduced during formal and informal interviews. To illustrate these steps, I turn to excerpts from interviews with one of the three informants. I began by asking him to
describe his procedure for carrying out a PK experiment when he
himself acted as the PK subject (descriptive question). He utilized
the term "psyched up" to describe his personal preparation. I
then sought further clarification on the meaning of "psyched up."
Rather than asking what the term means, however, I asked him how
he goes about getting "psyched up" (a structural question). To
this he responded:

> In preparing to carry out an experiment, I bury all the
> papers that I am writing. I go for long walks, get into a
> meditative state, and take things very seriously. In taking long walks I imagine myself and the task. I walk in
> the dark, imagining myself as the task. In the experiment I don't want the display to go to the right or left,
> so during the walk I proceed in a very straight line....

Based on this brief excerpt it is possible to note several
features of the ethnographic interviews. First, this information is

something that has not been included in any formal experimental report even though it is seen by the informant as a vital component of experimental preparation. Second, we have obtained folk terms (e.g., "psyched up") which provide insights into the informant's conceptualization of the phenomena we are probing. Third, based on these passing comments we now have a framework for asking further questions about the role of academic work in PK performance and the value of exercise, visualization strategies, and meditation. Such comments become the roots of an analysis that follows further descriptive and structural questions from this informant and others.

Contrast questions are introduced to further our attempts to discover meanings behind the vast wealth of cultural beliefs and practices involved in PK experimentation. Again turning to the statement by the previous informant, we find a certain contradiction between "getting psyched up" and getting "into a meditative state." By presenting these two expressions as a contrast we will find a greater degree of detail and clarification. Once the contrast was pointed out, my informant provided the following description:

> That is a funny thing about PK. On the one hand you need to relax, and on the other hand you need this hard push. It is similar to the practice of athletes. You read about these guys who calm themselves before running a hundred-yard dash.... When you are learning to meditate they tell you not to work too hard. You should have a relatively easy lifestyle, not like the driving executive. At least for me that is how it should be--otherwise it is too distracting. If I write a paper I have too much to think about. It always comes in, even when I am trying to clear my mind. You need to cut out this type of interference.

The three types of questions--descriptive, structural, and contrast--were employed in the interviews with each of the three informants. Analysis of interviews with one informant led to questions with the following informants, and vice versa. In this sense, the questions provided cultural corroboration. Following the ethnographic interviews, the data were analyzed using domain, taxonomic, and componential analyses.

Domain analysis involves the identification of symbolic categories which include other categories (domains). Domains, which represent units of cultural knowledge, are often implicit rather than explicit in the minds of the cultural actors and are identified within the body of ethnographic interviews. Once domains have been identified, the analyst identifies semantic relationships among folk terms introduced during interviews with informants.

The next step involves the identification of relationships

between the units, developing taxonomies. Here our goal is to
identify cultural themes common to the various members of the cultural group although not necessarily shared equally by the respective members. The taxonomic analysis is drawn directly from the
previous domain analysis.

A third level of analysis involved in the ethnographic method
is the componential analysis. This goes hand in hand with the use
of contrast questions previously discussed. Here we are able to
contrast different included terms, identifying differences among
them. Details which are not available can be obtained through
further interviews, both structural and contrast.

Phenomenology of PK Experimenters

Utilizing these steps we can begin to probe the phenomenology of successful PK experimenters. Due to limitations of space,
this discussion can only be an overview of a fragment of information which emerged in the course of ethnographic analysis. Specifically, it will consider some aspects of the general mental preparation that goes into PK experimentation, thus providing a useful
example of the methodology's value in psi research.

Various mental strategies are employed by all three informants to enhance experimental success. For example, there is a
need to develop positive expectations regarding experimental success. According to one informant: "Whenever I get ready to do
PK ... I am very positive that it will work. I want very much for
it to work."

The need for focused attention is extremely important; this
factor was articulated by each of the informants. To enhance
focus, various techniques are employed by the PK experimenters.
Each emphasized the need to concentrate attention on individual
trials during an experimental session, rather than on the experiment as a whole. The use of imagery strategies was articulated as
a means of enhancing focus. In the case of our initial informant,
the goal is to imagine himself as the experimental display, acting
out the display through physical exercise in order to increase his
involvement with the desired outcome. This strategy of physical
and mental preparation, carried out prior to an experiment, is reenacted just before a given experimental session. The act of
visualizing the desired outcome was noted by the other informants
as well.

The ability to focus on the task also involves a detachment of
ego involvement, although the degree of concentration to this detail differs among the respondents. The conceptualization of PK
experiments as a dynamic group process or ritual appears to be a
strategy for reducing ego involvement. Each of the three

experimenters interviewed does not see himself as the sole source of an effect.

A common approach to maintaining focus involves the introduction of novelty.

> Sometimes I move my hands and it perhaps gets my mind ... it enhances the focus.... There are a number of special techniques that I use. Sometimes I try a mantra. I have to watch so that none of the things become too automated.

A similar trend was noted by the other informants, although the strategies employed differed according to the individual testing procedure.

Discussion

Much more research must be undertaken to understand completely the dynamics at play in the minds and bodies of successful PK experimenters. The preceding discussion only scratches the surface of a rich and multifarious research domain--the phenomenology of psi experimenters. The data, while preliminary in our understanding of successful psi researchers, do serve to illustrate the usefulness of ethnographic method in our study of psi phenomena. This method is useful alone or as an adjunct to laboratory investigations. For example, it provides a systematic means of exploring a vast wealth of qualitative data, data which are often cast aside due to their unruly nature (i.e., what am I going to do with all this stuff?). Additionally, it is a method flexible enough to allow our data to shape the direction of our research rather than our forcing them through a preconceived methodological filter. As such, the integrity of the phenomena under study, in this case the phenomenology of successful PK experimenters, is maintained.

Many scientists fail to understand the value of phenomenological inquiry in our studies of consciousness, of which psi is clearly a part. One need not abandon experimental methods in order to gain phenomenological detail. The approach outlined in this paper is complementary, not adversarial, to experimental studies. We only stand to gain by looking inward in a manner which is responsive to our transitory nature yet systematic enough to accommodate our need for rigor! As a Mexican curandero so clearly expressed to a researcher studying folk healing practices:

> Many of these things you must experience, before you understand them. When you have experienced and understood them, you either will not need to ask questions, or your questions will be the kind that I can answer [Trotter and Chavira, <u>Curandismo: Mexican American Folk Healing</u>. Athens, GA: University of Georgia Press, p. 11].

THEORIES AND TESTS OF THEORIES

PSYCHOLOGY OF THE OTs: INTRODUCTION TO THE OBSERVATIONAL QUASI-MOTOR MODEL

Brian Millar (Mexicodreef 187, 3563 RL Utrecht, The
   Netherlands)*

    The observational theories (OTs) deal primarily with the "engineering" properties of combinations of components, such as random generators and psi sources. Psychology seems to have been discarded somewhere along the way. This paper brings psychology back into the mainstream of the OTs where it belongs. The Observational Quasi-Motor model outlined here fits snugly into the elastic framework of cognitive psychology.

    In the fundamental psi circuit, a psi source is connected to a random generator via a feedback channel. The feedback channel carries information about the outputs of the random generator to the psi source. The "magical" influence of the psi source biases the remote random generator in such a way that the psi-source-active input is stimulated more frequently. In general, the feedback channel is no simple transmission line but is an information-processing system which may conveniently be represented by a computer program.

    On its own, the psi source is a blind, insentient "machine" which acts to appease its primeval hunger for stimulation. The function of the feedback channel determines what effect the psi source has on the external world. If the psi source is likened to gunpowder, then the feedback channel is the gun which directs its effect onto a distant target.

    Given a psi source, one may construct a feedback channel to accomplish some desired goal. For example, one might wish to reduce the temperatures of a group of fever patients in New York. A feedback channel could be constructed on the following lines.

---

*Presented in absentia by Robert L. Morris (University of Edinburgh).

Temperature is measured automatically every few minutes. The current measurement is electrically compared with the previous one: if the temperature has dropped, a "fall" signal is formed; if it has risen or stayed the same, however, a "rise" indication is produced. These signals are transmitted over a telephone link to Paris. There they are decoded: on a "fall," a pulse is fed to the active input of the psi source, whereas a "rise" sends a pulse to the neutral input.

Some human beings apparently produce psi effects, but a human is no naked psi source. Rather, the brain of a psi subject contains such a device. Sensory input is subject to much processing before eventually reaching the psi source. In other words, there is an <u>internal</u> feedback channel in addition to the external one. It is the function of this internal channel that accounts for the intelligence of the psi effects exerted by human beings. The internal channel is, in effect, the user of the psi "gun." In particular, it is in the internal channel that explanation of the psychology of psi effects must be sought.

Cognitive psychology is characterized by its emphasis on the internal processes that mediate between stimulus and response. Conceptual models of parts of the human information-processing system are built and compared with experimental results. This approach treats the information-processing functions independently of their neurological substrate.

According to the Observational Quasi-Motor model, the part of the human information-processing system relevant to psi is that between the sensory inputs and the psi source. From the point of view of the central nervous system, the psi source is just another output organ, such as a hand. The processing involved in PK, then, is almost identical to that involved in quite ordinary perception/motor response. The latter has been subject to intensive examination, and much knowledge of the information processing involved has been accumulated. This can be applied directly to the psychological aspects of psi. The predictions obtained in this way are fairly general ones.

It is possible to go a step further, however, and look at perception/motor response and psi together in the same experiment. In this way it should ideally be feasible to predict the psi results of a particular subject from moment to moment under varied circumstances. The attempt is, in effect, to "bug" the output of the internal channel by tapping it off via a convenient existing output, such as the hand.

The effectiveness of this strategy is naturally dependent on how well the bugging can be carried out. Empirically, it seems that a great deal of control can be exerted over the "program" running in the internal channel just by asking the subject to do so. The subject is usually expected, for example, to be able to direct his or her PK onto the machine requested rather than one in Australia. He can often even voluntarily choose for "high aim" or "low aim." It is reasonable, then, to make the attempt to use the subject's own "software" to produce a high-fidelity external copy of the signal reaching the psi source. One may, then, try to tap into the internal channel by exploring different instruction sets given to the subject. Physiological measures may likewise be employed. Success in this search should result in perception/motor responses which are <u>monotonically</u> related to PK hitting. PK success under any kind of experimental manipulation can then be accurately predicted from the mirroring changes in ongoing measurements of perception/motor response.

The Observational Quasi-Motor model forms the basis for an entire research program in the psychology of psi effects, one that is firmly based on theory. This is in marked contrast to the current largely empirical state of the art in parapsychology.

TESTING THE INTUITIVE DATA SORTING MODEL WITH PSEUDORANDOM NUMBER GENERATORS: A PROPOSED METHOD

Dean I. Radin[†] and Edwin C. May (SRI International, 333 Ravenswood Ave., Menlo Park, CA 94025)

One premise of the Intuitive Data Sorting (IDS) model is that people can use some sort of informational mechanism to select the "right" time to respond in a random number generator (RNG) experiment (May et al., <u>RIP 1985</u>, pp. 119-120). The model postulates that in a successful psi experiment employing an RNG, the RNG is not perturbed by an energetic PK-like force but locally deviant subsequences are chosen or otherwise sorted out from naturally fluctuating random sequences.

A computer-based method was designed to test this premise using a pseudorandom number generator (PRNG), and the method was explored in an experiment with two selected subjects. The methodology was as follows: When the program was evoked, the computer initialized a PRNG, set up the screen for the feedback display, then waited for the subject to press a button. When the button was pressed, the program pseudorandomly chose one of nine sequence lengths, corresponding to bit streams of length 101, 201, 401, 701, 1001, 2001, 4001, 7001, or 10,001, as discussed in May et al.

Immediately after a random sequence length was chosen, a PRNG was initialized with the current value of the computer system clock (incrementing at a 100-Hz rate) taken modulus 20,000. If the resulting value was odd, one was added to make it even. This process provided one of 10,000 even numbers to seed the PRNG when the button was pressed, at the rate of 50 different seeds per second.

After the PRNG was initialized, the next N (where N was the sequence length for the current trial) pseudorandom bits were generated and summed. To prevent subjects from realizing that sequence length varied from trial to trial, a delay factor was built in so that every trial took the same amount of time. At this point, sequence length, the number of summed 1s (hits), and the PRNG seed number were saved in a data file, subjects received feedback on their trial in the form of a graphical representation of the absolute magnitude of a Z-score corresponding to the deviation from chance for the observed number of hits they obtained, and the next trial was ready to begin.

The key reason that a PRNG was used instead of a truly random number generator is that we could explicitly test for the presence of PK in the data by comparing the results recorded during the experiment with results later regenerated from the original data. If the two results were the same, we would have reason to believe that the random bit streams produced during the experiment remained unperturbed. We would also be reasonably confident that the computer system clock had not been affected, because computers are highly dependent on extremely stable timing, and any disruption of the clock would be likely to cause a system failure. Thus, if an experiment revealed no evidence of PK-like perturbations but there was statistical evidence of psi effects, this would suggest that an informational process had been responsible, as postulated by the IDS model.

The experimental protocol also involved eight planned analyses. The key analysis, testing the "right-timing" premise of the IDS model, was based on the fact that at each button press, a Z-score was created. Since each of the 10,000 possible seeds corresponded to a Z-score, a distribution of Z-scores could be examined for each of the nine random sequence lengths used in the experiment. A priori tests performed on these Z-score distributions showed that the expected mean of 0 and standard deviation of 1 were obtained; thus, under the null hypothesis of no psi ability a random sampling of Z-scores from these distributions should have resulted in variances nonsignificantly different from 1.0.

The essence of the IDS task was to select out the larger magnitude Z-scores from the tails of the normal Z-score distribution. This was tested by comparing the variance of the obtained Z-score distribution, one Z-score obtained per button press, against the chance expected variance of 1.0 (i.e., was the observed variance greater than 1.0?). Other analyses examined further aspects of the IDS model by determining if (1) the psi "effect size" was independent of the sequence length, (2) whether the nine sequence lengths were chosen uniformly at random by the computer program, (3) whether the selected seed numbers were uniformly chosen at random, (4) whether the recorded seeds were verified to be the same after being regenerated, and (5) whether the PRNG or some other aspect of the procedure might have been biased in some way. This last general test was performed by shifting the recorded responses in the "future" and the "past" by adding the equivalent of plus or minus one to five clock ticks (at 20 msec per tick) to the recorded seed numbers, then rerunning the analyses on the newly created results. If significant effects were obtained in the original data but <u>nonsignificant</u> effects were obtained after shifting the seed numbers, this would suggest that the observed psi effect was applied with an "accuracy" of 20 msec or better.

An exploratory study was performed with two selected subjects to evaluate the experimental procedure. Sun Microsystems Models 2-50 and 2-120 workstations were used for the test, and the program was written in the C language. A formal test was stated in advance to be 500 trials (i.e., button presses) in length. One subject completed the formal series; the other had completed 298 trials when this paper was prepared.

The primary results showed that the obtained Z-score distribution variances for both subjects were significantly larger than expected by chance (S1: Z variance = 1.188, N = 500, $p < .003$, one-tailed; S2: Z variance = 1.430, N = 298, $p < .00001$, one-tailed), in accordance with the postulated informational or "right-timing" ability. Other analyses revealed that the psi "effect size" was constant over the nine sequence lengths used in the experiment, and that the only times at which significant effects were observed were precisely at the times of the recorded button presses, suggesting that the psi ability was applied to an "accuracy" of at least 20 msec.

THE OUT-OF-BODY EXPERIENCE AS AN IMAGINAL JOURNEY: A STUDY FROM THE DEVELOPMENTAL PERSPECTIVE

Rex G. Stanford (St. John's University, Marillac Hall, Psych. Lab. SB15, Jamaica, NY 11439)*

This study examined whether adult reports of imagination-

---

*Presented in absentia by Debra H. Weiner (Institute for Parapsychology).

relevant experiences and pastimes during childhood (to about 12 years of age) relate to the reporting of having had at least one out-of-body experience (OBE) while awake, falling asleep, or dreaming. Granted that the fantasizing abilities associated with a profound response to hypnosis might also allow or even favor the occurrence of the OBE (Barber and Wilson, RIP 1981, 41-42; Palmer and Lieberman, RIP 1975, 102-106), OBErs as contrasted with non-OBErs might be more likely to have had as children the experiences and inclinations that Josephine R. Hilgard (Personality and Hypnosis: A Study of Imaginative Involvement, 2nd ed., U. of Chicago Press, 1979) found to be related to hypnotic susceptibility. She found that highly susceptible individuals are more likely to report reading as an activity in which they become deeply involved or absorbed in the emotional sense, and she noted that this type of reading involvement almost always developed prior to the beginning of adolescence. These considerations suggested that the greater the amount of time an individual spent before the age of 12 in reading as a pastime, the greater would be the likelihood that the individual would have the capacity for imaginative involvement that would be useful both to profound hypnotic response and to having an OBE. It also seemed likely, based on the work of Hilgard and of Barber and Wilson, that persons possessing the requisite fantasizing abilities for supporting the OBE might have been "loners" in early life, since being alone often might encourage the use of imagination and the inwardness of attention that favors imaginal experiences. It was thus expected that persons reporting the OBE would also report having spent less time playing with others as a child but more time spent playing imaginary games alone, in relating to transitional objects (stuffed animals or dolls seen as real individuals and to whom emotional attachment is strong), and in playing with imaginary playmate(s).

Following, again, the work of Hilgard (and others), there appears to be a positive relationship between variables like strictness of discipline or severity of punishment during childhood and measures like hypnotic susceptibility and spontaneous trancelike experiences. Hilgard and some others have interpreted these relationships in terms of children developing fantasy in order to block the pain or other consequences of severe punishment. If the OBE is, at least in part, a manifestation of fantasy, then the occurrence of the OBE might be related positively to (1) relative frequency of spanking, (2) relative frequency of deprivation as punishment, and (3) reports of having used the imagination to cope with punishment. The above expectations for correlations of OBE and developmental variables applied only to OBEs during wakefulness or while falling asleep, not for OBEs occurring in dreams. The dream state was thought to free the imagination sufficiently that the individual differences of interest here would play little, if any, role in OBE production.

Other developmental variables were included to obviate subjects' perception that the investigator was interested in a particular type of variable, but were examined in exploratory fashion. Two additional measures were examined as measures related to adult fantasy or imagination, namely the participant's report of the usual degree of vividness of sensory memories and the sense of realness of a verbally guided imaginary hot-air balloon trip experienced during the session. It was of interest to learn whether these two measures are related to reports of an OBE occurring during any particular state of consciousness.

Subjects were 50 undergraduate-age volunteers, mainly students, who participated without concrete benefits of any kind. Data from 3 of the 50 subjects were excluded prior to any knowledge of what the exclusion would do to outcomes. In two cases the subjects (both males) clearly did not take the study seriously, and in one case the subject made egregious errors in attempting to follow questionnaire instructions. Each of 10 students enrolled in a laboratory course in the Master's degree program in school psychology at St. John's University tested 5 subjects. Subjects were individually tested in a small cubicle and participated with informed consent relative to procedures; anonymity of data was guaranteed, both verbally and by procedures.

Each subject first participated in an imaginary hot-air balloon trip which was verbally guided by the experimenter's voice on an audiocassette. The experimenter vividly set the scene of boarding the balloon, preparing for launch, launching, and landing. There were two gaps during which the subject was to describe everything experienced during the trip. One gap represented the main course of the trip and lasted 4 minutes and 30 seconds; the other represented the descent and lasted 1 minute. Subsequent to the balloon trip, the subject responded to a questionnaire that was intended to measure the realness of the experience and that was carefully constructed to obviate demand characteristics. The realness score consisted of summed responses indicating a vivid, real trip.

The subject then responded to a series of questions related to developmental experiences and various imaginary experiences, including the OBE. Subjects ranked (separately for up to 12th birthday and beyond it to 18 years) the relative importance in their experience of several types of discipline and answered several other questions concerning the home atmosphere and relationships with parents. There followed an additional set of questions related to experience with transitional objects, use of imagination to cope with punishment, percentage of spare time devoted (through 12 years of age) to a series of activities, the OBE (see below), vividness of recall of physical memories, and favorite pastimes.

The OBE question read, "Have you ever had the experience of feeling that your mind or self was entirely separated from your physical body such that you saw your environment from a perspective that simply would not have been possible using the eyes of your physical body?" Subjects could answer "yes," "no," or "unsure." For positive respondents, other OBE questions concerning frequency and voluntariness of the experience were asked. They were also asked under what circumstance(s) this typically happens (or did happen, if it had happened only once): awake, in a dream, falling asleep, lying down, sitting, other posture, under general anesthesia, when fainting, while taking a drug, and during a religious exercise or meditation. (They could indicate more than one of these, as needed.)

Statistical analysis involved Spearman rank-order correlation. Reported percentage of spare time through age 12 that an individual spent reading or being read to correlated, as expected, with reporting an OBE while awake (r_s = +.427, 45 df, p = .002, two-tailed). Also, as expected, reported percentage of spare time through age 12 that an individual spent playing with others correlated negatively with reporting having an OBE while awake (r_s = -.387, 45 df, p = .008, two-tailed). The three other nondisciplinary variables discussed above did not correlate significantly with OBE while awake, nor did the three disciplinary variables. If the alpha level for statistical significance is adjusted for eight a priori expected effects that were examined for a given state of consciousness such that alpha = .05/8 = .00625, the reading correlation easily remains significant and the playing-with-others correlation, highly suggestive. For OBEs while falling asleep, the only one of the eight expected correlations that reached significance involved the percentage of spare time through age 12 that an individual spent playing with imaginary playmate(s) (r_s = +.433, 45 df, p < .002, two-tailed); this remains significant with the adjusted alpha. None of these eight variables correlated significantly with the reporting of OBE during dreaming, and this is in line with expectation.

None of the exploratory variables correlated with OBE occurrence in any of the three states of mind (at least with a two-tailed test and any kind of reasonable alpha involving correction for selection). Similarly, null results were found for the measures of the realness of balloon trip and the vividness of sensory memories as related to OBE occurrence.

Correlations were computed in order to learn how well the three "successful" developmental variables discussed above discriminated among OBErs in terms of the state of consciousness in which the OBE was reported to have occurred. Among OBErs (n = 23) the correlation between the reading variable and whether or not an OBE was reported as having occurred while awake was significant (r_s = +.606, 21 df, p = .002, two-tailed). Among OBErs the correlation between the playing-with-others variables and whether or not an OBE was reported as having occurred while awake was also significant (r_s = -.542, 21 df, p = .008, two-tailed). Likewise, the correlation between the imaginary-playmate variable and whether or not an OBE was reported as having occurred while falling asleep was significant (r_s = +.639, 21 df, p < .002, two-tailed). These correlations show the importance, when examining OBE correlates, of considering the reported state of consciousness of the OBE.

Part 2: Symposia

FIFTY YEARS OF THE JOURNAL
OF PARAPSYCHOLOGY*

PUBLICATION POLICY AND THE JOURNAL OF
PARAPSYCHOLOGY

Richard S. Broughton (Institute for Parapsychology, Box 6847,
    Durham, NC 27708)

Parapsychologists are particularly aware of publication policies of journals since it is frequently their work that challenges these policies or forces them into the open. The Journal of Parapsychology (JP) was born out of publication policies--those of other journals--and fifty years into the JP's history perhaps it is appropriate to examine how its own policies have evolved.

With a small team already working at Duke and reports coming from other researchers around the country, Rhine convinced William McDougall, then Chairman of the Duke Psychology Department, of the need for a separate specialist journal for parapsychology. McDougall convinced Duke University Press, and under the joint editorship of McDougall and Rhine the first issue of the Journal of Parapsychology appeared in March 1937.

In the opening editorial McDougall made it clear that the scope of the new journal would be the "more strictly experimental part of the whole field implied by psychical research as now pretty generally understood" (JP, 1937, p. 5). Though he expected that gradually much of psychical research would eventually be "invaded" by experimental methods, for the present only experimental studies would be admitted to the JP.

Thus was born the Journal of Parapsychology. It had the twin purposes of improving communication among scientists inter-

─────────────

*Organized and chaired by K. Ramakrishna Rao (Institute for Parapsychology).

ested in the emerging field and of defining the boundaries and setting reporting standards for the field.

Although initially well supplied with material, the JP quickly found itself short of quality material. Rhine complained of this to Gardner Murphy, who had never been too sympathetic to the idea of a specialist parapsychology journal and who was not impressed with the early JP. This led to negotiations late in 1938 which resulted in Murphy, Bernard Riess, and Ernest Taves in New York taking over the editorship of the JP. Part of the arrangement was that Murphy could shift the emphasis to extremely thorough experimental reports (he felt earlier JP reports had been too superficial) and that he could try an experiment with published peer commentary that grew out of suggestions made at the 1938 American Psychological Association meeting.

At first, Murphy's experiment went well but as the war reduced the ranks of academics and as the enthusiasm of the board of reviewers who supplied the comments waned, it became obvious that the experiment was faltering. It was no surprise that in 1942 the JP returned to Duke with Rhine as editor.

The new JP would abandon the formal commentary system which Murphy had tried but instead it opened a section for notes and comments where "all comments by any reader should ... be given careful attention and the mark of special authority reserved for none" (JP, 1942, p. 2). Also, the JP would return to what Rhine felt was the best policy for advancing the field. Now there would be a wider range of subject matter and, in addition to the technical reports, there would be more general articles and reports.

It was in this third incarnation that the JP hit its stride and established a pattern which endured for several decades. With the publication two years earlier of Extrasensory Perception after 60 Years (Pratt, Rhine, Stuart, Smith, and Greenwood, Boston: Bruce Humphries, 1940), the JP no longer had to wage the battle for the scientific acceptance of parapsychology and could settle down to reporting research and fostering communication among interested researchers.

At the editorial level as well, the JP settled into a routine which was to prevail for a while. Upon its return to Duke the JP was managed by a collective editorship (Rhine, C.E. Stuart, and J.G. Pratt) who shared responsibility for editorial decisions. This collective editorship was augmented by special statistical editors who examined all papers that used statistics.

As the Journal's horizons expanded, so did the editorial responsibilities. The editors developed an informal network of advisors to assist in making decisions, and in 1948 the JP established a formal "Advisory Board" to help in this regard.

Thus, by the late 1940s the mold for the Journal of Parapsychology was cast both in terms of its editorial structure and its content. Its content both defined and mirrored contemporary parapsychology and included not only experimental reports but also theoretical and review articles, book reviews, and, from time to time, news and comment. But it never strayed from its main role as the organ for experimental parapsychology. In general, the JP editorial policy remained stable for the next three decades until the present editor took over.

Whatever explicit and implicit policies were operative during those decades, there seems little disagreement about the fact that they were right for the times. They enabled parapsychology to grow and prosper in a way that probably would not have happened were it not for the Journal's role in communicating and focusing the research.

There was one aspect of JP policy that did prove contentious and that eventually produced something of a cathartic crisis in the field. This was the policy of not publishing in full those reports of experiments that had failed to provide any significant evidence of psi.

Although this policy was announced in the pages of the Journal in 1950 (JP, 1950, p. 1), by the 1970s this announcement had been largely overlooked by newer researchers, and grumblings of "cover up" and "covert policy" punctuated discussions among researchers.

Continuing discontent among parapsychologists and a paper submitted to the JP in 1974 prompted Rhine to tackle the issue directly in an editorial in 1975 (JP, 1975, pp. 134-142). Rhine defended this policy with two points, one statistical and the other editorial. On the statistical point Rhine said, "... so far as the statistical tests of significance are concerned one experiment is independent of another, and the results do not need to be pooled. In other words, a nonsignificant experimental result does not affect the significance of another one independently designed" (p. 136). The editorial point was that parapsychology was not sufficiently advanced in being able to control its experiments to permit anything to be learned from failure and that the Journal could not waste precious space on such papers. Finally, Rhine pointed out that this policy was not meant to be misleading, since the JP had always maintained the means for reporting such failures in a shortened form.

As always, the pages of the JP were open to opposing opinions, of which there were many. In the March 1976 issue the debate continued, but in the end Rhine was not successful in convincing the majority of parapsychologists of the wisdom of this policy.

This policy has, of course, been retired. When Dr. K.R. Rao became one of the editors in 1977, he quietly moved the journal to a more formal use of outside referees. To be sure, the Journal had always made informal use of referees, but under Dr. Rao's guidance the editorial policy became one of reliance on the peer review system to determine whether a paper merited publication or not, irrespective of the outcome of statistical tests. It is with this policy that the Journal of Parapsychology enters the second half of its first century.

CONTROVERSY AND THE JP

John Palmer (Institute for Parapsychology, Box 6847,
    Durham, NC 27708)

During its 50 years of existence, the Journal of Parapsychology (JP) has hosted numerous controversies among parapsychologists and between parapsychologists and their external critics. The purpose of this paper is to provide a brief but relatively comprehensive historical overview of these controversies.

The editorship of Gardner Murphy (1939-1941) provided a built-in vehicle for controversy in that referees' critiques of experimental reports, followed by the authors' rebuttals, were published along with the reports. Several of these reports were by Rhine himself, who expressed in one of his replies his displeasure with the quality of the reviews.

The most controversial experiment of this early period was by James MacFarland, who compared subjects' calls to two target sequences, one of which was controlled by a psi-conducive experimenter and the other by a psi-inhibitory experimenter. The most serious critique was by John Kennedy, who found discrepancies in the calls as recorded by the two experimenters. Charles Stuart, who defended the research, was forced to concede motivated recording errors by the psi-conducive experimenter, but he showed that the errors were not sufficient to account for the significance. (A similar strategy was used recently by Charles Tart to defend his ESP-learning experiments.)

Many debates over the years have concerned statistical issues. In the 1930s and 1940s, the most prevalent topics of controversy were optional stopping and suppression of negative results. In 1940, when Willy Feller suggested (without evidence) that such suppression occurred in the book Extrasensory Perception After Sixty Years (Pratt, Rhine, Stuart, Smith, and Greenwood, Boston: Bruce Humphries, 1940), Joseph Greenwood and Stuart calculated that 170,000,000 chance trials would be necessary to reduce the data base to nonsignificance. (A similar strategy has recently been used by Charles Honorton to defend the statistical significance of the Ganzfeld data base against a challenge by Ray Hyman.) Another focal point of statistical controversy was the appropriateness for parapsychological data of the critical ratio as compared to parametric statistical tests. This issue came to a head in 1979 when Greenwood and Thomas Greville, who at that time were statistical consultants for the JP, debated Donald Burdick, the present consultant. Greenwood and Greville attacked the use of parametric tests and Burdick defended them.

The most heated controversies in the JP concerned allegations or insinuations of fraud on the part of subjects or experimenters. In 1955, George Price published a paper in Science using Hume's essay on miracles to justify a priori attribution of fraud to successful psi investigators and proposing that a committee of hostile skeptics set up a conclusive, fraudproof experiment. In that same year, the JP published abstracts of this article and the subsequent exchange of letters, along with other critical letters submitted directly to the JP. Rhine took a rather upbeat tack, noting that Price had conceded the inadequacy of previous critiques. S.G. Soal (somewhat ironically in light of recent developments) maintained that replication was more likely to settle the controversy than fraudproof experiments. Among the outsiders, Michael Scriven noted that if Price's committee ever affirmed psi, Price's conclusions would have to be that they had lied. Price's response was to suggest that the committee be enlarged!

In 1961, C.E.M. Hansel published two papers in the JP, based on Price's philosophical position, purporting to show how subject fraud could have accounted for the results of the Pearce-Pratt experiment and how experimenter fraud could have accounted for the results of the Pratt-Woodruff experiment. Rhine and Gaither Pratt defended the experiments. Thirteen years later, R.G. Medhurst and Christopher Scott resurrected and extended the critique of the Pratt-Woodruff experiment; Pratt and Woodruff defended the research.

Scriven raised the hackles of some parapsychologists when he used the occasion of a Parapsychological Association banquet address to suggest that parapsychology was flirting with extinction and that Hansel had raised legitimate questions about the experiments he criticized (although Scriven also stated that, on balance, the parapsychologists had successfully defended themselves). The address, along with the ensuing critical exchanges, were published in the JP in 1961 and 1962.

A different kind of fraud controversy involved the research of the Indian parapsychologist H.N. Banerjee. In 1964, K.R. Rao reported suspicious anomalies uncovered by Rao and Pratt in some of Banerjee's card-guessing data. Pratt and Ian Stevenson, on the other hand, accused Rao of alleging fraud without sufficient evidence and chastised Rao for not sharing his critique with Pratt and Banerjee in advance. Rao denied actually accusing Banerjee of fraud.

PK research began to generate some controversy in the JP in the 1950s. In 1958, Robert McConnell used the JP to respond to a critique of his dice experiments when the journal that had originally published the research denied him that opportunity. In a series of letters appearing in the late 1950s and early 1960s, Carroll Nash and Haakon Forwald debated the physical forces involved in the latter's PK placement experiments. More recent and exotic PK research that provoked critiques included an experiment by Bob Brier on PK in plants and macro-PK effects claimed in a Spiritualist context by a group calling itself SORRAT.

Process-oriented research has received relatively little critical attention in the JP. Perhaps the best example is an exchange in the late 1970s between Irvin Child and Hans and Shulamith Kreitler over the Kreitlers' research concerning the influence of telepathy on subliminal perception. Child maintained that some of the results are attributable to statistical regression artifact.

Last but not least, mention should be made of the ongoing debate in the JP between Hyman, an outside critic, and Honorton concerning the Ganzfeld data base. The controversy concerns both the overall significance of the data base and the attributability of the results to procedural flaws.

Louisa Rhine's innovative approach to the evaluation of spontaneous cases provided yet another topic of controversy in the JP. The main issue was whether all spontaneous telepathic and apparitional experiences could be attributed to percipient psi (as Rhine maintained) or whether some cases required an active role by a living or discarnate agent. The latter view was defended in the late 1950s by Hornell Hart and in 1970 by Stevenson. Hart, in particular, became increasingly upset at Rhine's refusal to acknowledge evidence that he felt supported the traditional viewpoint. Stevenson challenged the adequacy of the sampling procedures in Rhine's case collections. Earlier (in the late 1960s), Rhine and Stevenson had had another critical exchange over the interpretation of Stevenson's reincarnation cases.

The metaphysical implications of psi were always of importance to J.B. Rhine, and the JP frequently hosted controversies on these more philosophical issues. In 1961, the JP invited a series of papers on the question of whether psi is nonphysical. In my opinion, the issue proved to be primarily semantic; viz., whether the definition of physics should be restricted to present-day physics. In 1983, this issue reappeared in a different guise when I.W. Mabbett and Gerd Hövelmann debated the definition of the term paranormal. Hövelmann said that to define it as unexplainable by science (as suggested by Mabbett) was unnecessarily metaphysical; Mabbett argued that Hövelmann's problem vanishes if science is defined as including a possible future science. In 1958 and 1974, respectively, physicists J.M.J. Kooy and M. Ruderfer speculated about possible physical explanations of psi, only to have their views challenged by C.T.K. Chari.

The long-standing debate between the British philosophers C.W.K. Mundle and Antony Flew concerning the logical status of the concept of backward causality achieved representation in the JP in the early 1950s. An attempt by Bob Brier to resolve the issue was attacked in a book review by Flew in 1975 and defended by John Beloff.

J.B. Rhine's position that psi research had established clairvoyance but not telepathy was the exact reverse of the position traditionally held by most British parapsychologists. In 1946, Rhine excerpted, integrated, and responded to a number of their arguments which they had expressed in letters to him. To their assertion that clairvoyance is incomprehensible, Rhine responded that "incomprehensible" simply means "paranormal." Rhine also found the evidence for telepathy from the Soal research and mediumship investigations less than compelling.

In the early 1970s, Robert Thouless proposed that telepathy could be claimed as established if one defined it operationally rather than metaphysically. Ironically, his position was actually more extreme than Rhine's, since he maintained that telepathy in the latter sense was unprovable in principle. Thouless also defended his cipher test as potentially providing good if not conclusive evidence for survival, but Rhine seemed to feel that only conclusive evidence was worth seeking and is unobtainable by present methods.

Finally, some mention should be made of the role of book reviews in stimulating controversy in the JP. Perhaps the most extensive exchange of this type occurred in 1975 and concerned the quality of the papers in and the appropriate authorship of the anthology Psychic Exploration (New York: G.P. Putnam's Sons, 1974) by John White and/or astronaut Edgar Mitchell (depending on your point of view). Gaither Pratt was the principal critic of the book.

Whether or not the above controversies have settled anything, they have brought important issues to readers' attention. Let the debates continue!

J.B. RHINE IN THE JOURNAL OF PARAPSYCHOLOGY

H. Kanthamani (Institute for Parapsychology, Box 6847, Durham, NC 27708)

We are gathered here to observe the fiftieth anniversary of the Journal of Parapsychology (JP). The half-century of the history of the field is thus firmly captured in print, as well as in spirit, between the covers of many a volume--198 issues, to be exact--thus far. While much of the published work came from research in the U.S., the Journal was by no means restricted to American work only. Many articles from other parts of the world were not only accepted but were actively solicited. Therefore, an examination of the Journal of Parapsychology at once becomes an examination of the field as a whole.

As many parapsychologists will appreciate, the Journal of Parapsychology used to be synonymous with its famous editor, Dr. J.B. Rhine. It occurs to me that one cannot refer to the Journal without in the same breath mentioning Dr. Rhine. If such an automatic association is perceived by many in the field, it is so because J.B. virtually fathered and nurtured the Journal with such love, care, and devotion and fought many battles for its scientific credibility.

I will now turn to the main focus of this presentation, which is J.B. Rhine as the editor of the JP. Dr. Rhine remained in some capacity with the Journal for no less than four decades, from the journal's inception in 1937 to handing over the reins formally in 1977. These long years as the editor of a journal which recorded the scientific efforts made by a sparsely distributed group of scholars engaged in pioneering work, put him in a unique position indeed. As one reads the editorials penned by J.B., it is hard to miss the drama and the pathos that surrounded the emergence of the field. I am not familiar with a similar situation in which "the leader" of a field also served as the editor of its chief organ for such a long period of time. While we could come up with many disadvantages of such a protracted editorial tenure in terms of its effect on the healthy growth of a journal, in the case of the JP, however, the advantages outweighed the disadvantages. Parapsychology in its fledgling and unstable status could not have survived without long-term commitment of its chief pioneers. The Journal of Parapsychology served not only as a professional periodical but also as the main organ for "a scientific movement," for that was how parapsychology could survive, especially in the earlier decades.

J.B.'s editorials were clearly intended for a variety of audiences: contemporary and future; sympathetic and not so sympathetic; knowledgeable and not so knowledgeable. J.B., it would seem, was his own historian. For the very nature of his undertaking was historical and it was as if it were best for him to make a straightforward account of it, even as history was being made. The sheer volume of his writings, the detailed chronicling of the "journey," and the consistency in his basic theme would endear him to any subsequent historian.

Out of the many editorials that Dr. Rhine had written for the Journal of Parapsychology, the earlier ones basically dealt with issues relating to Journal policy and articles appearing within a particular number. Later, the editorials addressed specific topics of broader interest to the workers in the field and the general readership. While these topics were highly diverse, some general classification is possible, as follows. The topics that prompted more than one editorial over the decades were: the survival question; the nonphysicality of psi; religion and parapsychology; PK; telepathy; comparative science; university and professional issues; statistical issues; spontaneous experiences; criticism and controversy; funding; and repeatability. (It should be noted that our sample is restricted only to editorials titled as such, for Dr. Rhine expressed his opinions through other columns, such as "News and Comments," as well.) Although the editorials do not reflect any steady and continuing themes that could be reflective of the various concerns over the decades, one can discern some shifts in general focus. For instance, in the forties psychokinesis drew significant attention. The question of parapsychology emerging as a profession was also on the forefront. The forties also saw many editorials dealing with Dr. Rhine's "nonphysicality of psi." Toward the end of the decade, in 1948, the first editorial on spontaneous experiences appeared. In the early fifties there were several editorials that involved systematic comparisons of the new scientific field with other, more established disciplines, which included general psychology, psychiatry, biology, and physics. More importantly, the fifties also witnessed editorials addressed increasingly to refuting criticism and containing controversy. Thus, it is not entirely accurate to describe the fifties as "happy days," as far as the field of parapsychology was concerned.

With the advent of the sixties, criticism and controversy only heated up some more, thanks to well-meaning C.E.M. Hansel. In 1967, one editorial described the negative consequences of increased public interest in psi phenomena. Funding, the perennial problem, also received some editorial space. It was not until 1970 that an editorial discussed the questions of repeatability and reliability, which certainly did not put the matter to rest. A couple of editorials in the early seventies were devoted to the "Apollo test" of ESP in space. A significant case of experimenter fraud, detected in 1974, led to a spate of comments regarding the vulnerability of phenomena and findings and related security issues. It may be mentioned that beginning in the early seventies, the JP ceased publishing titled editorials, although Dr. Rhine continued to air his views through the "Comments" section. In 1977, Dr. Rhine relinquished his editorial duties, and to mark the occasion he wrote an article entitled "A Backward Look," covering his lifelong association with the field.

This hasty review does not cover the host of other articles J.B. wrote for the JP. One can single out any of the significant issues, depending upon one's own interest and the significance attached to the issue, for further examination. Dr. Rhine had attempted to integrate parapsychology with many other major disciplines, such as psychology, philosophy, biology, physics, and medicine, with the hope that such interconnection would benefit all those concerned. It is this interdisciplinary aspect that is well represented in the Journal of Parapsychology during the last 50 years, and it is bound to increase in the future.

PSI AND SYSTEMS THEORY*

PSI AND SYSTEMS THEORY

William G. Roll (Dept. of Psychology, West Georgia College, Carrollton, GA 30118; and Psychical Research Foundation)

Psychical research began as a revolt against the materialistic image of human nature projected by the physical sciences. When a group of scholars came together at Cambridge University 100 years ago to form the Society for Psychical Research (SPR) and thereby the discipline we now know as parapsychology, they hoped to paint a more optimistic picture. Their basic colors were the Cartesian white and black, the distinction between mind and matter, and they hoped to show the reality of mind as clearly as physical scientists had demonstrated the reality of matter.

Where Descartes had been content to leave the exploration of mind to religion and philosophy, psi researchers adopted their methodology from the physical sciences themselves. In seeking to establish an experimental science, they chose the model that lay closest at hand, that of behavioral psychology. But this in turn was a reflection of the outmoded Newtonian view of the physical world as a collection of separate entities, mechanically connected, the very image that psi researchers hoped to replace. Our experimental procedures were thus based on the assumption that the participants in a psi test, such as the ESP or PK subject and the ESP or PK targets with which the subject attempted to interact, could be regarded as distinct entities which connected at the precise time and place demanded by the test conditions and, moreover, connected without interference from other potential psi sources or targets. In particular, it was assumed that psi processes were independent of physical time and space, although the test conditions were always defined in terms of temporal and spatial coordinates and although psi occurrences in natural settings suggested that psi processes are interwoven into the physical context where they appear. This linear approach to what we are now beginning to see as a global state of affairs resulted in only intermittent psi effects

---

*Organized and chaired by William G. Roll (West Georgia College).

in the laboratory and to doubts whether these effects were real, however abundant they seemed under natural conditions.

While experimental parapsychology was trying to find a footing in a methodology that was based on a world view which denied the very possibility of psi, the physical sciences were beginning to point to connections between objects (Bell's theorem) and between objects and human observers that were suggestive of the types of occurrences to which psi researchers had drawn attention. Physics, the archenemy of parapsychology, now seemed to provide a philosophical shelter where psi occurrences could bloom.

Whatever their relation to the physical world, psi occurrences concern living systems and are therefore also a matter for the science that deals with such systems, namely biology. Even when we consider the possibility of life after death, we are concerned with living systems. In the early days of the SPR, however, the main offender against the dignity of humankind was biology, with its reduction of consciousness and free will to the mechanisms of the physical organism and its struggle for survival. But biology, also, is no longer the closed science it once seemed to be. Organismic systems theory offers a promising framework for exploring psi. According to this view, psi processes may be conceptualized as operating within the same living system rather than between entities that are essentially separate. Psi systems may be seen as a further step on the familiar organismic hierarchy. On each level, lower subunits are integrated into a larger functional whole with the emergence of new supervening principles. Atoms are arranged into molecules, these into cells, and so on until we reach the organism ruled by the central nervous system and individual consciousness. The psi level may be neither omniscient nor omnipotent. It appears that psi may link individuals and objects that have been in recent or frequent physical contact (viz. Bell's theorem), such as close family and friends and their physical surroundings. It also appears that psi may contribute to the well-being and survival of this group-environment. ESP in natural settings often concerns injury or death to significant individuals and may serve a similar function with respect to the psi system as the body's pain sensors serve the body. Precognitive impressions of threatening events may help avert them, and retrocognitive (psychometric) sensitivity to "haunted" areas, where someone has recently met a violent accident or death, may help the percipient avoid dangerous places. Haunted houses may have more to do with survival in this world than in the next.

This perspective holds several promises, including (1) increased understanding and predictability of psi occurrences, (2) relating psi to other processes in nature, but (3) without reducing psi to these other processes, (4) understanding psychic forms of consciousness, (5) establishing the foundations for ethical systems that go beyond individual self-interest, (6) finding a place for free will, and (7) relating psi to other transpersonal or "spiritual" systems.

(1) If psi interactions occur within a system that includes subsystems in addition to those involved in the manifest psi exchange, such as the sender and percipient in an ESP study, then the capacity to understand and predict psi should increase by taking the full system into account. This system would not be restricted to the living individuals concerned but would include their physical environments, present as well as past, and thereby "memorylike" and "emotionlike" features that may be embedded in this environment. It would also include any teleological principles that direct this system, presumably towards its survival, expansion, and well-being.

(2) As the Cartesian wall between mind and matter crumbles, features of one are found in the other. We already know that physical objects can act as sources and receivers of psi activity (clairvoyance and psychokinesis). We now also see that the histories and probable futures of physical objects may in some sense be part of these objects (Bohm's implicate order, four-dimensional theories of spacetime) and that these extensions may be accessible to psi, particularly with respect to events in the recent past and near future.

If psi processes are conceptualized as operating within one of the levels of the organismic hierarchy, we should expect psi to link up with processes on other levels of this hierarchy, and we should expect psi to show similar or analogous features as processes on other levels. For instance, ESP may be analogous to receptivity to afferent or incoming nervous traffic in the individual organism and PK to efferent or outgoing traffic. With respect to interactions between levels, ESP may link up with the parasympathetic system in the individual and PK with the sympathetic system.

(3) According to systems theory, descriptions of the psi system would not contradict descriptions of lower-level systems. For instance, ESP between mother and son, even across thousands of miles, should not contradict descriptions of the inanimate order. Though psi processes interact with physical and physiological processes, systems theory does not imply that psi can be reduced to lower-level processes. With each new level in the organismic hierarchy, new forms of relationships are introduced which have to be studied and understood in their own terms.

(4) On the psi level, the supervening principle may be reflected in characteristic forms of consciousness and self-consciousness. Psi awareness may encompass the past and probable future course of events and psi self-awareness may include the group-environment to which the person belongs. (5) These types of consciousness may lead to values and ethical systems

that are protective of the system and its well-being. Self-awareness would here become awareness of the other and self-interest would become the interests of the group-environment. (6) When it is recognized that we are not at the sway of the mechanisms of the lower levels, there is room for voluntary action. Free will becomes the capacity to respond or not respond to the goals associated with any of the levels within the limitations set by the processes that govern these levels.

(7) Beyond psi systems we glimpse larger systems that are yet beyond the reach of science but that the travelers of the great religions have spoken about and that transpersonal psychology is now exploring. Here the group consciousness and group values of psi systems may be transformed into a larger consciousness and into planetary or universal value systems.

In the following pages Hoyt Edge outlines the philosophical context of systems theory, and Jeffrey Munson explores the interpersonal aspects of psi from a systems-theoretical point of view.

SYSTEMS THEORY: PHILOSOPHICAL ASSUMPTIONS AND IMPLICATIONS FOR PARAPSYCHOLOGY

Hoyt L. Edge (Dept. of Philosophy, Rollins College, Winter
    Park, FL 32789)

In Western science two traditions have been dominant. The first--a person-centered science--takes the person as the model of reality and explains everything in mental terms. Aristotelian physics did this. The second tradition--a rock-centered science--is exemplified in the impersonal approach of the natural sciences since the seventeenth century and can be characterized as holding three beliefs: (1) causation is linear and unidirectional and is understood in terms of dependent and independent variables; (2) general laws can in principle be found; and (3) this view excludes teleology. The second approach to science solved an important problem in the seventeenth century--how to separate science from the authority of the church--and has been enormously successful solving a number of problems by taking the atomistic, mechanistic model of explanation used to explain physical objects and applying it to all phenomena.

But each of these approaches is inadequate. The first yields an anthropomorphism, while the latter one results in what can be called a mechanomorphism. What is needed now is a new approach to science, a Hegelian synthesis of the two earlier views which takes the good points of each and raises the synthesis to a higher level. Systems theory attempts such a synthesis in that it retains the teleology of the first approach but it agrees with the second approach that the teleology is not mind centered; rather, systems are natural processes. A discussion of the analogies of "team spirit" and "mosaic" help point to the distinction between structural and functional elements.

Five methodological implications for parapsychology come from this systems approach: (1) We must pay more attention to the interaction among elements of the field. The concept of causation changes from a stimulus-response model to one that is multidirectional and multifaceted. In fact, we may want to substitute the term "coproduction" for "causation" in our discussions. If there is more interaction in our experimental fields, we may want to pay more attention, for instance, to the influence of the participant on the agent; other kinds of interaction will become equally important. (2) We will attend more to temporal elements, not only to the histories of the participants but also to possible periodicities in the production of psi phenomena. (3) We will lay greater stress on induction, since our traditional models of explanation have been based on linear causal modes. At this stage in our research, we may want to do more exploratory studies and to use multidimensional matrices to analyze interactions more often than we have traditionally thought necessary. (4) Since one major reason for the development of experimental laboratories has been to create (largely artificial) situations in which dependent and independent variables could be easily isolated and manipulated, we will either have to work more in naturalistic settings or pay more attention to making our experimental conditions naturalistic. (5) Finally, in a systems approach we will need a convergence of measures.

INTERPERSONAL SYSTEMS AND PARAPSYCHOLOGY

R. Jeffrey Munson (Institute for Parapsychology, Box 6847, Durham, NC 27708)

How can general systems theory (GST) and its derivative, interactional psychology, help parapsychology understand the interaction of psi and interpersonal systems? One way is by providing descriptive and conceptual tools for a more complete and effective picture of interpersonal situations manifesting psi. More comprehensive descriptions of psi events may reveal unrecognized relationships among relevant factors. Also, through the processes of abstraction and comparison to other analogous systems, similarities and differences are cast into relief. Attempts to reconcile or explain them may reveal unrecognized possibilities for understanding psi. At the very least our current view of psi may be strengthened by having clear analogs with other systems of more certain character.

It should be noted, of course, that the relation between psi and systems theory should be expected to be dialectical or mutually informative. After all, considering the overlay and incompleteness of both fields, it is perfectly possible that parapsychology may offer information that would change or refine GST, as well as vice versa.

By far the most obvious interpersonal system of relevance to parapsychology involves experimenters and subjects. While earlier formulations of the experimental situation viewed the researcher as objective and separate, we now understand the experiment as a system comprising one or more experimenters, one or more subjects, any experimental tools, the context, and the interaction of these parts. Naturally, these terms often require extensive elaboration, especially when they concern participants' motivations, attitudes, relationships, interactions, and other factors. When psi appears in data, attribution can no longer confidently focus only on the subjects or experimenters. Instead, the experiment must be viewed as a spatial, temporal, and psychological whole: what Schwarz (Psychic Nexus, New York: Van Nostrand Reinhold, 1980) called the "psychic nexus." This is nothing less than a psi system.

Observational theories in parapsychology reflect the application of GST in the face of systemic interactions. First, the mutual influence between human consciousness and a physical entity or event in the process of observation constitutes such a systemic interaction. Neither the consciousness (in the form of observation) nor the physical event can be understood apart from each other. This concern becomes more obviously interpersonal with the divergence problem. Specifically, the possibility of the influence of multiple observers on psi events raises questions about the impact of the observers' relations, their motivations, attitudes, knowledge of each other, and other factors.

The interpersonal system formed by the scientist and the subject has a direct analog in the psychotherapeutic context. In this case the subjective quality of the relationship between the psychologist and the client is emphasized in looking at psi. There has been considerable discussion in the past about the manifestation of psi in the therapeutic situation. Not only is it reasonably certain that it occurs but it seems definitely tied to the client's psychodynamics, including their relationships to significant others. Moreover, a number of psychiatrists have linked it to the analyst's dynamics as well. Eisenbud (Psychoanalytic Quarterly, 1946, 32-87) maintained that he found psi in therapy to be connected to psychological material that was repressed by both the client and the analyst. It is as though the analyst and the client are simultaneously responding to the same affectively charged material as a single unit. What emerges is psi in the form of a transpersonal event. Danziger, a systems theorist, remarked in his examination of circular causality in interpersonal systems that "two individuals in interaction are simultaneously the causes and the effects of each other's behavior" (Interpersonal Communication, New York: Pergamon Press, 1976, p. 181). Chrzanowski also supported this overlap of systems theory and parapsychology when he observed that the holistic view of the therapy relation and its effects "changes the concept of transference by viewing it as a two-way phenomenon in a field, rather than as an intrapsychic, self-generated form of behavior ..." (Implications of Interpersonal Theory, 1976, 135-136). Ehrenwald, in turn, developed his theory of the mother-child symbiotic relationship as the "cradle of ESP" (The ESP Experience, New York: Basic Books, 1978, 14-27). He maintained that because of the lack of ego distinctions in this relationship (which would otherwise tend to separate people from each other), coupled with dependency needs and the lack of sensory communication capabilities, ESP is facilitated. Ehrenwald generalized from this situation to other analogous relationships and held that the similarity in the configuration of comparable factors likewise facilitates psi. This fits in well not only with findings from the clinical context on the relation between therapist and client but also with much of the anecdotal case material. Parent-child relationships, or close relationships that have similar structural features, are often present in psi-event contexts. (This also implicitly recognizes GST's important revelatory process of comparing isomorphisms, or systems with similarities of structure and function.)

Cases of recurrent spontaneous psychokinesis (RSPK) provide good examples of psi events amenable to systems-theoretic descriptions. This possibility is already implicit in current parapsychological mythology, which views the events as existing in and influenced by some more or less identifiable social system, such as a family or business. Even when a particular focal person is recognizable, the interpersonal context for that person remains important in the best description of RSPK. Consequently, RSPK research may want to borrow from the work of interactional psychologists. For instance, Sullivan (The Interpersonal Theory of Psychiatry, New York: Norton, 1953, 110-111) defined human personality as "the relatively enduring pattern of recurrent interpersonal situations which characterize a human life." Thus, in order to understand the genesis of RSPK the description of foci should include not only that person's relations to local others but those relations over time. This should be emphasized, because in no way can RSPK foci (and, hence, RSPK itself) be understood apart from the dynamic relationships involved.

Moreover, current parapsychological mythology holds that RSPK reflects disordered intrapsychic or interpersonal conditions. Interactional psychology states that this will manifest as disordered communication. This is interesting for several reasons. First, it suggests that we should expect to see poorly developed, deviant, or destructive processes in the normal (sensory) communication channels of RSPK systems. This is, in fact, what is apparent in many poltergeist situations. Second, it suggests that RSPK itself may be viewed as manifestations of disordered communication. That RSPK can be considered as communication at all follows in part from the current difficulty in distinguishing information and action (ESP and PK). Furthermore, by maintaining that these PK effects follow upon psychosocial disorder, they can be thought of as symptoms, and symptoms are often considered communications.

From the interpersonal point of view, however, these communications reflect attempts to establish or negotiate the terms of relationships. The destructive or disturbing paranormal events often seem to reflect unacceptable feelings of aggression or anger. That is, the feelings are intended for significant others, but their delivery is blocked by the person's relationships with those significant others which will not tolerate the revelation of the feelings. The feelings require expression, but they are too threatening to be owned by anyone in the group. The result is that they must be projected and indeed they are, far away to the outer world. There it seems that they do not have to be owned, even while they are expressed. Notice here that GST allows the relativization of psychological and physical space, which in turn allows a more comprehensive structural pattern to be described. The power of this description even gains strength by some findings that otherwise are often viewed as weakening the credibility of poltergeist cases, such as those in which RSPK agents have been caught in fraud. We know that when dealing with unconscious impulses that influence a client's behavior a psychologist often engages the client in some process of consciousness raising. If the technique is successful, the client will begin to recognize the source of the behavior and will accept ownership of both the impulses and the behavior. When the parapsychologist intervenes in a poltergeist case he or she educates the relevant group about psi and redirects attention to include the group as one possible etiological factor. Thus, the consciousness of the group immediately begins to rise. Where there is an RSPK agent, the ownership of the projected impulses thus tends to return home, as it were, as the projection diminishes. The fraud, then, is only fraud in the sense that the effects are not paranormal. Instead, the agent tossing the objects represents a step in the process of consciousness raising and the owning of impulsive behaviors or communication acts. The fact that sometimes the agents are unconscious of throwing the objects while at other times they are perfectly aware of doing so only recognizes a fine distinction in the process of consciousness raising.

Here is another way of using the technique of comparing isomorphic structures to understand RSPK as a system. First of all, stability and hierarchies are fundamental features of systems, and their nature and evolution are of major interest to systems theorists. Bertalanffy (<u>British J. for the Philosophy of Science</u>, 1950, 135-165) suggested that the number of elements of a system and the degree of interaction among them were important determinants of the stability of the system. Gardner and Ashby (Nature, 1970, 784) used the Monte Carlo method to test the relation between stability and connectance. Connectance is the relation by which one entity influences another. To be fully connected means that a change in any element will have an immediate effect on every other element in the system. In this case, the elements were randomly assembled and the sample size, n, and the connectance were gradually increased until the elements were fully connected. The system's stability was assessed for changing sample sizes and degrees of interaction. The authors found that "all large complex dynamic systems may be expected to show the property of being stable up to a critical level of connectance, and then, as the connectance increases, to go suddenly unstable" (p. 784). They found that as n increased, the probability curve quickly changed to a step function. In an extension of this work which vastly increased the range of sample sizes, May (Nature, 1972, 413-414) also found a sharp transition to instability when a critical value of connectance/complexity was reached. In 1975 (J. of Theoretical Biology, 1-11) McMurtric also used the Monte Carlo method to replicate these findings. More importantly, he found that introducing even a crude hierarchy (where each level interacted only with the levels directly above and below it) had a stabilizing effect on the system.

These findings can be compared to some features and possibilities in poltergeist systems. First, interpersonal systems can tolerate only so much closeness before they start to degrade. Some RSPK systems have exhibited characteristics of overinvolvement, such as an overprotected child or one who has remained at home too long. Degradation in the system's hierarchy may be connected to the paranormal events. I observed a family in therapy which claimed to have experienced a poltergeist, and their most notable feature was a pattern of Oedipal-like relationships. These were not only overconnected but broke down natural parent-child hierarchy levels. The parallel with the step-function pattern of system breakdown is implicit in the abrupt nature of RSPK. Perhaps poltergeist events occur precisely because the interpersonal system reaches a critical level of connectance and/or hierarchy degradation.

There have been a number of psychometric tools designed to assess interpersonal behavior. These could be of use to parapsychologists who wish to evaluate responses of subjects to experiments and relationships in spontaneous cases or clinical settings. Leary (Interpersonal Diagnosis of Personality, New York: Ronald, 1957) developed the Interpersonal Check List, a self-reported adjective checklist providing 16 scoring categories of interpersonal behaviors. Findings from this scale were used to develop the Interpersonal Behavior Inventory used by observers to rate another person's interpersonal behaviors. Kiesler and his colleagues (e.g., The Impact Message Inventory, Richmond, VA: Commonwealth University, 1975 and 1976) developed the Impact Message Inventory. This tool measures the complementary responses given to communicated attempts to mold behavior or relationships. Benjamin (Psychological Review, 1974, 392-425; J. of Consulting and Clinical Psychology, 1977, 391-406; J. of Abnormal Psychology, 1979, 303-319) developed the Structural Analysis of Social Behavior, which is based around the axes of affiliation and interdependence and assesses both interpersonal behaviors and intrapersonal attitudes.

I would like to leave you with a last general application of general systems theory to parapsychology, and this has to do with the functioning of psi for larger social groups. There has been some interest in the cultural influences on psi, such as broad belief structures and their tendency to predispose paranormal incidents. Given the success of sheep/goat studies, this possibility should be given more attention.

On a different tack Eugene Marais, in his book The Soul of the White Ant (Harmondsworth: Penguin, 1970), hovered around the issue of how primitive social structures manifest psi as well as depend on it. He maintained that a giant termite colony is actually like a single organism, with an exoskeleton, a nerve center or brain, a dynamic flow of information and energy, and an intelligence that suggests a single emergent mind manifesting telepathically.

On a still higher level of systems interaction, Eisenbud (JASPR, 1976, 35-53) suggested that ecological homeostasis may be maintained through psi processes. He gave as an example evidence that some animals behave in a manner that is manifestly self-destructive on an individual level but serves to promote interspecies balance by aiding the survival of predator groups.

These are some thoughts on the relation between psi and interpersonal psychology. It appears that parapsychology can derive great benefits from attending to what general systems theory has to offer it, and solutions to problems in the interpersonal domain are not the least of them.

Part 3: Roundtables

IDS VERSUS PK: TESTING DIFFERING INTERPRETATIONS OF THE DATA*

INTRODUCTION

Richard S. Broughton (Institute for Parapsychology, Box 6847, Durham, NC 27708)

When Helmut Schmidt first used his random number generator (RNG) for PK research, he launched parapsychology in a whole new research direction--micro-PK. Although Schmidt was not the first to try PK on atomic systems--several attempts had been made during the preceding decade--his design possessed a simplicity that made replication very easy. The results he obtained made replication a necessity. Today, micro-PK is the substrate upon which a great deal of our research is based, and that research has provided parapsychology with some of its most robust findings.

But is it PK? At last year's convention, Edwin May and his colleagues from SRI International presented a model which appeared to challenge seriously the idea that RNG results are being "caused" by the subjects. Instead they argue persuasively that a precognition model, which they term Intuitive Data Sorting (IDS), can best account for virtually all of the binary RNG data to which they could get access (over 300 experiments).

Certainly, it was recognized very early that RNG data exemplified a certain symmetry between PK and precognition, and it could be argued that it was impossible to distinguish the two in RNG experiments. But that is hardly a very satisfying state of affairs. As the SRI team indicated, on a practical level it would be nice to know whether subjects are causing the future or just knowing it.

---
*Organized and chaired by Richard S. Broughton (Institute for Parapsychology).

Much of the micro-PK research has been called PK simply because we were telling our subjects "to make something happen." Unlike good, old-fashioned PK, RNG PK produces no physical evidence of something being affected. The evidence is purely statistical. What the SRI team has shown is that their IDS model--precognition--fits the data equally well. In fact, it seems to fit them better than a PK model because, on examination, the data appear to constrain any PK interpretation to a purely goal-oriented one with some rather odd characteristics.

Many of us find the IDS model very exciting, partly because it might be right, but mostly because it might be wrong. The exciting part is that in this case the developers of the model have shown us some ways in which we can prove them wrong--if we can. In effect, the SRI team is issuing a challenge to all experimental parapsychologists working in micro-PK. They are saying, in effect, "We think the IDS model makes the most sense of the data and if you don't think so, show us some data that do not fit."

This panel will ask some questions and address some issues in an effort to show what is at stake in this challenge and to help clarify what needs to be done by working experimenters to help meet the challenge. Do the data fit the model as well as the SRI group thinks they do? How should we design experiments to test the model, and what sorts of data will it take to falsify IDS? Can we ever hope to rule out goal-oriented PK?

RECENT ADVANCES IN THE IDS MODEL

Edwin C. May,[†] G. Scott Hubbard, and Beverly S. Humphrey (SRI International, 333 Ravenswood Ave., Menlo Park, CA 94025)

Conceptually, the Intuitive Data Sorting (IDS) model suggests that decision-making processes include a precognitive component. We will review the IDS model as applied to random number generator (RNG) data and describe its predictions for specific experiments. In the most general case (mean and variance shift) we are able to demonstrate a theoretical difference between causal (PK) and informational (precognition) processes. Although the model may not be able to separate these processes in practice, it does suggest protocols that would be necessary to resolve the issue. Preliminary data from pseudorandom-number-generator experiments, application of IDS to the historical RNG data base, and general circumstantial arguments from specific experiments provide compelling evidence in favor of an informational process as the basic mechanism underlying RNG experimental results.

EXPLORATORY TEST OF THE IDS MODEL

Dean I. Radin (AT&T Bell Laboratories)*

The Intuitive Data Sorting (IDS) model is based on the premise that it is possible to optimize future results by choosing favorable times to act in the present. In conventional parapsychological terms, IDS may be called a precognition model. IDS makes two main predictions about psi performance that can be tested with pseudorandom number generators (PRNG).

Imagine an experiment in which an individual presses a button. This action causes a computer program to set the value of the system clock to a seed number, which in turn is used to initialize a PRNG. The PRNG generates a fixed sequence of pseudorandom bits, and a Z-score is formed for the resulting number of hits (say, 1s) in that sequence.

The first IDS prediction is that the individuals will be able to press the button to select out, in effect, Z-scores from the tails of the normal distribution (actually, the normal approximation to the binomial distribution) of hits. This can be evaluated with a variance test in which the observed Z-score variance for a series of trials is tested against the expected variance of 1.0.

The second prediction is that the observed psi effect will be constant over varying sequence lengths. That is, on average, the Z-score obtained with a sequence of pseudorandom bits will tend to be the same regardless of whether the Z-score was formed from 100, 1000, or 10,000 pseudorandom bits. This prediction can be tested by comparing the observed and theoretical slopes and intercepts of linear-regression lines formed from pairs of points, where each (x,y) pair consists (in log-log space) of the sequence length and the absolute value of the deviation between observed and expected proportions of hits for that sequence length. IDS predicts that the theoretical and observed slopes will not differ but that the corresponding intercepts will, with the observed intercept being higher than the theoretical intercept.

These predictions were confirmed in an exploratory experiment (see pp. 109-111) with two selected individuals, both of whom had been successful in previous computer-based psi tests. Both produced significantly larger variances than expected by chance ($p < .005$ and $p < .00002$) and both produced nonsignificant slopes and significant ($p < .005$) intercepts in the predicted direction.

---

*Current address: Human Information Processing Group, Green Hall, Princeton University, Princeton, NJ 08544.

A variety of planned control tests checked the PRNG and procedural and analytic methods and found them to be in accordance with chance expectation.

COMMENTS ON THE INTUITIVE DATA SORTING HYPOTHESIS

Evan Harris Walker (Box 69, Aberdeen, MD 21001)

May, Radin, Hubbard, Humphrey, and Utts (Proceedings of the Presented Papers of the 28th Annual Parapsychological Association Convention, Tufts University, Medford, MA, August, 1985) have provided a significant analysis of the extensive random number generator (RNG) PK literature and have proposed some possible interpretations of the systematic trends they find. Before we draw final conclusions, however, several points must be investigated in more detail. Examination of the May et al. report shows that simulated data have been mixed with experimental data to obtain the linear relationship between the excess hit rate $|\Delta P|$ and the number of trials per run, $\underline{n}$, on a log-log plot of the data. This may produce artifactual agreement between the "data" and the proposed Intuitive Data Sorting (IDS) hypothesis. In addition, high values of $\underline{n}$ in RNG experiments are often achieved simply by running the RNG at higher sampling rates. An experimental run of a million trials may require no more experimental time and no more effort by either the subject or the experimenter than a run of a hundred trials. As a result, finding that two such experiments yield the same statistical significance would not be surprising. However, a plot of log $|\Delta P|$ versus log $\underline{n}$ would yield a linear fit with a -0.5 slope. Thus, we would appear to find a correlation between two parameters of the experiment despite the fact that the RNG sampling rate had no effect on the pertinent measures of the experiment.

Examination of the IDS hypothesis suggests that it does not account well for the experimental data. In proposing the IDS hypothesis, May et al. state: "Using psi-acquired information, individuals are able to select locally deviant subsequences from a longer random sequence" (p. 249). The question is, however, how long are those subsequences? It is not reasonable to hypothesize these sequences to be exactly the run length. A computer simulation of the IDS hypothesis, assuming constant subsequence length, yields results deviating significantly from the data. The only hypothesis that fits the data is that of goal-directed targeting. But if we conclude that the data indicate a goal-oriented mechanism, we should look to an observational-theoretic explanation, since goal-directed targeting is a salient feature of observational theory (OT). To

test the OT explanation I have modeled observer state selection
based on a state-vector interpretation of the RNG experiments.
Assuming only that state selection depends on the time-independent
"feedback" for a favorable versus an unfavorable run outcome, the
computer simulation reproduces all the characteristics of the RNG
PK data as spelled out by May et al. The data best support a
quantum-mechanical theory of psi.

STRIVING TOWARD A MODEL

George P. Hansen (Psychophysical Research Laboratories,
    301 College Rd. East, Princeton, NJ 08540)

In an unpublished paper titled "On the Structure of 'Electronic PK'," Mr. W.E. Cox anticipated many of the issues now discussed as Intuitive Data Sorting (IDS). In that paper, he suggested an experiment which would address the sequence length problem. He also suggested that precognition might best account for psi effects involving electronic random number generators (RNG); however, PK might best describe psi effects on mechanical systems such as tumbling dice. There is some tentative evidence (e.g., Forwald, JP, 1961, 1-12; Braud, JASPR, 1980, 297-318) that the strength of the psi effect depends upon the physical characteristics of the system being influenced. This would seem to argue against an IDS interpretation of such cases.

Within the last year, there have been many discussions of the IDS model. Those with which I am familiar include informal groups at last year's convention, a miniconference at Psychophysical Research Laboratories (PRL), and communications among members of PRL, Princeton Engineering Anomalies Research, and SRI International. There has been confusion at all levels of discussion. At the conceptual level, there are contrasting views of PK. Proponents of IDS seem to view PK somewhat akin to a classical force; observational-theoretic notions are largely unacknowledged. There is talk of a PK "mechanism" and an IDS "mechanism"; it seems to me that there are some hidden assumptions behind this choice of terms, but I am not sure. There have been contradictory usages of the term "goal oriented" within the IDS debate. Even the handling and presentation of the data have been ambiguous. The appropriate method of aggregating data has not been described.

Given this confusion, outside observers of the discussion should realize that the IDS modeling process is in a state of flux. The model cannot yet specify full falsifiability criteria, but clearly there is movement in that direction. The model is evolving, and I don't think that proponents should be forced to repudiate the entire notion even if some later experiments contradict it. Likewise, critics should not be expected to accept the entire thing. We should expect changes and modifications of the ideas and positions of those working with the model.

These discussions have had a number of benefits. For instance, new ideas for experiments have been generated, there has been further development of the idea of complexity, and the modeling process has produced novel approaches to analyzing data.

To avoid confusion in the future, I recommend that discussions begin at the level of specific experimental designs. This should make it easier to see differences in assumptions and to facilitate identifying and clarifying them. One of the most recent, precisely described experiments that bears on the IDS hypothesis was presented by Zoltan Vassy at the 1985 PA convention (RIP 1985, 81-84). His design could be extended to involve a true RNG.

ON SOME STATISTICAL IMPLICATIONS OF THE IDS HYPOTHESIS

Zoltan Vassy (Psychophysical Research Laboratories,
    301 College Rd. East, Princeton, NJ 08540)

The core of the Intuitive Data Sorting (IDS) model is the "selection hypothesis": There is a long random number sequence with the usual statistical properties of random sequences; then some psi source selects from it shorter subsequences with an increased frequency of the preferred number.

The IDS proponents sometimes make an additional assumption that in a large number of experiments there are approximately as many hitting sequences as missing ones. This way the overall Z-score has a zero expected value, while its variance will increase compared to the chance case. This can be called the "sorting" hypothesis. It is clearly not a necessary consequence of the hypothesis of data selection. There have been experiments with strictly one preferred direction of effort, and in many of these the results actually were significantly in that direction, with definitely not an overall Z-score of zero. I don't think the IDS proponents want to exclude this kind of experiment from the region of validity of their model, so the "sorting" assumption is neither theoretically necessary nor practically useful.

A further assumption often made by IDS proponents is that the number of hits in the chosen subsequences continues to obey the binomial distribution. This assumption again does not follow from either the selection or the sorting hypothesis. (I have written a technical note with a simple counterexample and can give a copy of it to anyone who is interested in the details.) The situation is similar with a still further assumption of the IDS proponents, namely, that the expected value and the variance of the Z-score are independent of the sequence length. They have found such independence in their meta-analysis of the existing literature of RNG experiments. Again, this assumption does not follow from either the selection hypothesis or the sorting hypothesis. The expected value and the variance of the Z-score do not depend on the sequence length <u>only</u> if the hit probability depends on it in a very special way, and that special way is no more characteristic of intuitive data selection than of PK. (Details can be found in the technical note mentioned above.)

To sum up: In my opinion the statistical considerations made by the IDS proponents to validate their model really cannot be used for that purpose. I agree, however, that from a physical point of view IDS seems to be a more parsimonious working hypothesis than is PK. In the so-called micro-PK experiments the physical process to be influenced sometimes varied greatly from one experiment to another, yet these differences were not reflected in the results. This indeed points to the existence of some common process which has nothing to do with the systems themselves but belongs to the psi source or sources participating in the experiment. Although we should not expect that Nature works always in the way most parsimonious to us, this argument definitely makes the IDS hypothesis worthy of further elaboration and empirical study.

AN INTERACTIVE SYSTEM MODEL FOR ANOMALOUS DATA

Roger D. Nelson (Princeton Engineering Anomalies Research, School of Engineering/Applied Science, Princeton University, Princeton, NJ 08544)

The Intuitive Data Sorting (IDS) model proposes that precognition is used to determine the opportune moment for initiating a trial in a random event generator (REG) experiment such that the stream of random events is invaded while its values deviate from its mean and thus contribute to the generation of the desired result. A testable corollary is that the magnitude of the deviation must depend on the number of fundamental events (usually binary) produced and counted in a trial initiated by a single button push.

The general psychokinesis (PK) model proposes a direct intervention that changes in some way the process that yields a score in the REG experiment. That is, the effort exerted during the trial is thought to affect the device and alter its outcome according to intention.

Here the results of the Princeton Engineering Anomalies Research (PEAR) program will be considered, where relevant, to the following points of discussion:

(1) IDS depends on precognitive selection of an appropriate trial initiation time; PEAR data from a hardware pseudorandom source suggest that time of incursion may be the effective mechanism.

(2) IDS prediction is distinguishable from statistical regression to the mean in large samples only by a shift of the distribution mean which is, according to the model, inversely proportional to the square root of the number of events in a trial. PEAR data suggest that a maximum of 1 or 2 percent of total variance is attributable to the experimental effects. This, if generally true, indicates that the log-linear IDS model and its alternatives cannot be statistically distinguished, because the quality of fit for linear regressions is driven almost entirely by random noise.

(3) In the PEAR data base, results based on a pseudorandom source are at least as strong as REG results, in contrast to the reasonable predictions of PK models.

(4) PK models also appear to be falsified by distance experiments. The effects in the developing PEAR data base are complex but appear not to be attenuated in the expected manner as a function of distance. However, no persuasive argument requires the inverse-square physical model to apply.

A viable alternative to these approaches is an Interactive System Model (ISM), wherein the human operator and physical apparatus are considered as a single system. Such a perspective can have broad application to REG-type experiments and serve as well to model information-transfer experiments. An instructive expression of this point of view can be found in the Quantum Mechanical Model of Consciousness developed by Jahn and Dunne (Technical Note PEAR 83005.1, Princeton Engineering Anomalies Research, School of Engineering/Applied Science, Princeton University, Princeton, NJ 08544, June 1984 [revised]).

(1) ISM proposes that the person and machine can become a single system whose characteristics may appear anomalous from the perspective of the separated components.

(2) Characteristics of the Interactive System are determined by nonlinear (wave-mechanical) superposition of characteristics of the operator and the machine and also reflect a matrix of environmental factors.

(3) The Interactive System is not fully characterized in the physical spacetime metric; it must be defined in the consciousness domain.

WHAT RESEARCH SHOULD WE BE DOING?*

ON THE SCIENTIFIC STUDY OF OTHER WORLDS

Charles T. Tart (Dept. of Psychology, University of
  California, Davis CA 95616)

A major instigating force behind psychical research was the desire to test the essential claims of religion. One aspect of that is to investigate objectively the reality (or lack of it) of ostensibly independently existing "nonphysical" worlds (NPWs).

The most common contact with ostensible NPWs is during out-of-the-body experiences (OBEs). The more lucid quality of OBE consciousness (compared to dream consciousness) inclines the OBEr to take the perceived NPW reality as indicating its independent existence. Considering such an NPW independently real is especially likely if: (1) it is stable and not changed by arbitrary acts of will on the OBEr's part, as can happen in lucid dreams; (2) repeated OBE visits to the NPW show it to have consistent, lawful properties; and (3) the characteristics of the NPW seem to validate previous beliefs of the OBEr.

NPWs, compared to lucid-dream worlds, are reported to have a solidity, stability, and lawfulness that resists the OBEr's mental desires. If you want an object to disappear from the NPW scene, wishing is not enough; you will have to pick it up and carry it away. The possession of lawful properties in a way apparently independent of the experiencer's wishes leads to the ascription of independent reality to the world in both ordinary waking life experiences and NPW experiences.

Such experienced phenomenal independence and lawfulness of NPWs could be accounted for by retaining the hypothesis that the NPWs are still subjective creations and that there are simply more rigid psychological processes (automated habits) underlying their apparent consistency and independence. Some NPWs are probably

---

*Organized and chaired by Keith Harary (Institute for Advanced Psychology).

adequately accounted for by such a hypothesis. But suppose some NPWs really are independently existing realities, not subjective creations of the experiencers' minds. How would we discriminate such NPWs from purely subjective ones?

Assuming we develop a technology for producing consistent OBE excursions to NPWs or can locate people capable of doing this through their own natural talents, we may look for consistency of descriptions from independent observers as a test of the NPWs' reality. If their descriptions of a particular NPW, call it NPW-A, were coherent and consistent in major details and not significantly contradictory on important details, we would provisionally grant at least partial independent reality status to NPW-A.

Several factors will influence how much likelihood we will grant to NPW-A's independent existence. First, we know that interior experiences can be shaped by belief and suggestion, so we must ask: Is the nature of NPW-A significantly different from what would be expected, given overt cultural beliefs held by our OBErs about such ostensible worlds? Second, we must consider the influence of implicit cultural beliefs. If we have a control group of people from the same culture fantasize about having an OBE and visiting NPW-A (with minimal directions for getting there), how different are their fantasy productions from the reports given by the OBErs who claim to have actually been there?

Third, people influence each other, so we would want to establish strongly that our several OBErs have not been influencing each other during normal, physical-world contact. Ideally, they should not know who each other are. If normal contact is effectively ruled out, the more difficult problem of ruling out psychic influences on each other, influences which might lead to consistent subjective constructions, arises.

The proposed line of research will not be an easy one, running against current scientific prejudice as it does, but it will produce data highly germane to questions about the nature of humanity, our place in the universe, and the possibility of some kind of survival of death.

QUESTIONING OUR ASSUMPTIONS ABOUT THE MIND

Keith Harary (Institute for Advanced Psychology,
    1550 California St., San Francisco, CA 94109)

There are fads in psi research just as there are in mainstream culture. Some trends, such as the focus on survival research that emerged with the James Kidd legacy in the early 1970s, are stimulated by the availability of funding for particular lines of research. Others, such as the card-guessing experiments of the Rhine generation, emerge out of a desire to make psi research findings palatable in traditional academic circles. More current trends, such as the continuing focus on Ganzfeld and remote-viewing studies, seem to emerge out of our desire to conduct more and more repeatable experiments.

The good thing about following fads is that they can provide a general focus for research in a field that has limited resources. But following fads may also limit our creativity and lead us to make incorrect assumptions about the nature of the process we're studying.

In order to make progress in psi research we must continually question our assumptions about the mind. A common assumption underlying much of our research is that psychic functioning is limited to living organisms. The foundations of much of our research also rest upon crucial assumptions about the nature of randomness. We determine that an individual appears to have functioned psychically because the results of a given experiment seem to "beat the odds." But we have yet to study the possible role of psi in influencing the most basic physical processes.

If psi is an inherent part of so-called random interactions, creating a level of organization that we don't consciously perceive but which influences us, the origins of psychic functioning in organisms may lie within those apparent "random" interactions. We may not be creating psychic interactions so much as perceiving information that is somehow psychically present in our environment and awareness at a subliminal level.

We should be carrying out research aimed at developing a better understanding of what we mean by randomness. Specifically, we should search for hidden evidence of underlying organization in what appear to us to be random processes. A simple series of experiments would compare individual streams of randomly generated target selections for possible correlations. A more sophisticated approach would use a random generator to select "viewer" responses to a series of Ganzfeld or remote-viewing targets, then blind judge these responses in the traditional manner for such experiments.

The key would be to initiate the random process in a manner that couldn't be overtly influenced by living organisms. Although such a condition might be impossible to achieve in a practical sense, an organism's potential influence upon initiating the random process could still be limited. We may be surprised to find that a properly programmed computer is as capable of performing certain types of psychic functioning as we are.

ON MIRACLES AND MODERN SHAMANISM

D. Scott Rogo (John F. Kennedy University, 12 Altarinda Rd., Orinda, CA 95463)

Psi research has traditionally dichotomized itself into two areas of study: experimental laboratory research and field investigations. It is my view that psi researchers today have not explored the dramatic possibilities offered by this second area of study. Field studies have usually encompassed a very limited range of investigations--i.e., trying to verify the real-life psychic experiences reported to us from the general public or tracking down and studying hauntings and poltergeists. The range of paranormal events that occur in real life goes considerably beyond these limited phenomena.

The first area of study that should be of concern to psi researchers are those paranormal effects that occur specifically within a religious context. These events are traditionally called "miracles," although they probably represent an extension of many of the phenomena currently studied in psi research. Although Everard Feilding, a chief investigator for the Society for Psychical Research, investigated a case of a "bleeding picture" of Christ shortly after the turn of the century, no other psi researcher has taken up the challenge of such cases. Cases of weeping statues, bleeding pictures, and collectively perceived apparitions of a religious nature are reported by the press all the time. Despite this fact, psi researchers continually seem to ignore these reports. For instance, in 1968, reports hit the press of an apparition appearing over a church in Zeitoun, Egypt. This apparition, which was presumed to be the Virgin Mary, was reportedly seen by thousands of witnesses and photographed repeatedly. No mention of these apparitions, which appeared nightly for months, was ever made in the literature of psi research. These appearances certainly must have represented some sort of paranormal event and should have been of utmost interest to the field. Related phenomena are currently being reported in Yugoslavia.

The second area of interest to me personally is shamanism. Psi researchers have recently become interested in anthropology and how field investigations conducted within technologically undeveloped cultures can help us to understand psi. However, the study of shamanism proper--the miracle workers of these cultures--has generally not been pursued on a pure level. It seems odd that with few exceptions (e.g., Giesler, JASPR, 289-330; JASPR, 1985, 113-166), psi researchers since Ronald and Lyndon Rose in the early 1950s have not been interested in seeking out these special people. Yet there are indications in the literature that some shamans may well still possess the powers traditionally attributed to them. During the early 1970s, a film crew from Germany claimed that they had successfully filmed an African shaman levitating. I have been trying to track down more information on this case. More recently, an anthropologist was able to witness a Sioux yuwipi ceremony--which closely matches in procedure a typical Victorian seance. He allegedly witnessed psychic lights, raps, and telekinesis.

I am not suggesting that we should abandon our traditional areas of concern. But there is considerable evidence that paranormal events are occurring in the world before us that go beyond the limited range of phenomena studied in conventional psi research. Psi researchers should at least be surveying these more bizarre effects.

HUMAN PERCEPTUAL MODALITIES AND REMOTE VOLITIONAL INTERACTION

Elizabeth A. Rauscher (Parapsychology Division, Tecnic Research Laboratories, 64 Santa Margarita, San Leandro, CA 94579)

In order to suggest new methodologies and techniques for examining psi, we must first examine the conceptual basis for much of our current research. The results of some of our recent studies particularly indicate the need to examine issues related to the observer/participant and mind/body concepts.

In quantum measurement theory, physicists have shown that the observer interacts with so-called external reality. We might even begin to consider whether the observer creates reality!

When we define observer or participant we also define that which is observed and that with which the observer participates. We define self and objective reality, the domains of the internal and external.

If we cut ourselves, the natural process of healing occurs and the cut, if it is relatively small, soon heals. A mysterious process we consider internal, i.e. healing, repairs our body, which we perceive as part of "us."

Dr. Beverly Rubik and I recently conducted three major studies of an alleged psychic healer's ability to affect intentionally the properties of remote sterile cultures of bacteria. In these experiments, which are well documented elsewhere, experimental bacterial cultures "treated" by Dr. Olga Worrall showed a significant increase in movement and growth rates relative to control cultures. In short, the ability to influence a supposedly external element appeared to overcome the distinction between internal and external reality.

Keith Harary's concept of "psi as nature" is a picture of reality in which psi is an integral part of nature. Three dominant views of the basis of reality are the mechanistic view wherein all is seen as material, the mind/body duality (with various proportions of mind and body), or the spiritual view. In this latter view most of reality is nonphysical and some small part is "condensed" out as matter. This latter view can hold that consciousness is a dominant force. In this view, psi can be considered as a fundamental property of consciousness.

If we hold this view, which may be consistent with Harary's perspective, then psi is ever present in all conscious activities and endeavors. If this is the case, we cannot truly have a control experiment for psi and, in a sense, all experiments then measure "relative psi" which is present in all human endeavors. In this case, controls and targets are distinguished by researchers who guide a subject's intention to affect the targets maximally and the controls minimally. However, no experiment is devoid of experimenters, hence consciousness and hence psi! Such a model must be considered when conducting an experiment such as the one with Olga Worrall.

In remote-perception experiments, no control runs are possible, as one cannot have a situation in which there is no target. The beacon cannot be nowhere, having no experience, even when sleeping--unless they are dead and there is no survival! The concept of a control group depends on the idea that such a group will obey the laws of statistical randomness. Conversely, the weight of evidence for an experimental effect is based upon the extent of significant deviation from this definition of randomness. This weight of evidence applies to psi data as well as to nonpsi data. But some data are so striking that statistical analysis seems irrelevant.

If the above picture is more valid than the mind/body dualistic view or the mechanistic view, we must design our experiments accordingly. Let us consider one such issue related to quantum measurement and psychokinesis. Much formalism and discussion have been made about the problem of quantum measurement. It's clear, at least microscopically by the Heisenberg Uncertainty Principle, that all measurements affect the system being measured in such a manner that we cannot "see as though we did not look." The experiment we conduct determines the results we get. If we look at the diffraction of light, we see wavelike properties, and if we examine the photoelectric effect, we observe the particle nature of light. From physical and experimental results there appears to be a correlation of the observer and the observed, the inner mind and the outer world.

We define this inner/outer picture in such terms as subjective/objective and mind/body. Is this conceptual division part of our problem in understanding psi phenomena?

STUDYING CHANNELING*

THE STUDY OF CHANNELING

Arthur Hastings (Institute of Transpersonal Psychology, 250 Oak Grove Ave., Menlo Park, CA 94025)

Channeling is a contemporary term for the process in which a person transmits messages from a presumed discarnate source external to his or her consciousness--as for example through automatic writing, trance speaking, or reporting mental dictation. Often the source identifies itself as a being from a nonphysical reality, such as an angel or deity, a composite entity, an advanced being, or a formerly incarnate person. Mediumship, prophecy, and revelation have been used in other contexts for this phenomenon; its occurrences in the past have been mostly with oracular utterances or religious teachings. Several thematic categories emerged in my survey of channeling: Spiritual teachings include the Koran (Mohammed), Book of Mormon (Smith), Oahspe: A New Bible (Newbrough), Aquarian Gospel of Jesus the Christ (Levi), Scripts of Cleophas (Cummins), and works by Alice Bailey; literature: writings of Patience Worth (Curran), Jonathan Livingston Seagull (Bach), and The Mystery of Edwin Drood (James); physics: The Unobstructed Universe (White) and The Nine (Puharich); personal and spiritual development: At the Feet of the Master (Krishnamurti), Seth Speaks (Roberts), Messages from Michael (Yarbro), and A Course in Miracles (Anonymous); new age transformation: Revelations (Spangler) and Starseed Transmissions (Raphael); cosmology: Urantia Book (Anonymous); arts: harp music (Andrews) and painting (Gasparetto).

Channeled material is experienced as coming from outside the individual's self, appearing to be an independent personality. Theoretical models, however, also include the possibilities of subpersonalities, a personification of archetypes of the deep self, multiple personality or dissociative states, and role playing. The personality, knowledge, and attitudes of the person who is channeling

---
*Organized and chaired by Arthur Hastings (Institute of Transpersonal Psychology).

affect the content and style of the transmission. In addition, the
channeled material is clearly tuned to the culture and themes of the
time. For example, the psychological-growth emphases of Seth,
Michael, and A Course in Miracles are new facets of channeled
material. Another recent development is the message that a transformation of consciousness is coming and human beings are being
prepared and assisted by many discarnate beings (Spangler,
Raphael). Some of the sources say they are responsible for UFOs.
Scientific or technical information is sometimes transmitted, though
not usually of a useful quality. Though a source may claim a particular identity, there are often inconsistencies internally or with
external facts, and such representations may be for convenience,
metaphor, or effect. Some of the transmitted messages are trivial
or mediocre; other material is sophisticated and sensitive and is a
contribution to spiritual literature, personal understanding, and
social change. Many individuals currently find important personal
meaning and insight in the channeled literature or in personal interaction with channeled sources.

Studies of channeling phenomena are relevant to the nature
of personality, depth psychology, models of nonphysical realities,
and transpersonal processes. The content is relevant to social
themes and movements, spiritual teachings, and human potential.
The increasing incidence of persons who are channeling and the
public interest in the phenomena should encourage further study of
the process.

THE CASE OF PATIENCE WORTH

Stephen E. Braude (Dept. of Philosophy, Univ. of Maryland,
    Baltimore County; Baltimore, MD 21228)

Beginning in the summer of 1913, a St. Louis housewife
named Pearl Curran began to receive cryptic but elegant message
fragments on the Ouija board. Pearl had only an eighth-grade
education and had never traveled abroad (and apparently had no
desire to do so). Her interest in reading was minimal and seldom
extended to anything more demanding than women's magazines and
the occasional light novel. Her only notable ability seemed to be
musical, and even that was quite modest.

The personality apparently manifesting through Pearl on the
Ouija board, and eventually through automatic writing, called herself Patience Worth and claimed to be the spirit of a seventeenth-
century English woman. Patience wrote thousands of poems and
several novels of an unusual and often exceptional literary quality.
The entire Patience Worth communications fill 29 volumes in the

Missouri Historical Society in St. Louis and include her poems, novels, conversations, and pithy aphorisms. The communications lasted for about 25 years, but most of the major work was done in the first 12 to 15 years.

As in many cases of ostensible mediumship, Pearl and Patience had markedly different personalities. The two most exceptional aspects of the case are (1) Patience's unprecedented literary abilities, unlike those of any other writer, and (2) the unusual dialect preferred by Patience. Regarding (1), Patience's writings flowed spontaneously, without correction or revision (or decline in quality), and as fast as the scribes could take them down. This was true even in cases in which Patience was asked to extemporize poems on subjects chosen by sitters or accomplish various compositional stunts (e.g., to make each line of a poem begin with a different letter of the alphabet, from A to Z, omitting X). Regarding (2), Patience made extensive use of English words belonging to the seventeenth century and sometimes several centuries earlier. Some dialect words were tracked down by scholars only after they appeared in the Patience Worth scripts. Moreover, the scripts often exhibited an unusually heavy reliance on Anglo-Saxon roots, apparently unprecedented in English literature, giving the works a unique rhythm and style. Some of Patience's writings were more relentlessly archaic than others, but even her more modern writing had a quaint and distinctive quality consistent throughout all her works.

Is Patience Worth the result of a dissociative capacity of Pearl? In principle, Patience could be considered as the creation of extraordinary cognitive (and maybe psi) abilities unleashed in a state of dissociation--i.e., a nonpathological form of multiple personality. Nothing we know about the limits of human cognition or psi (especially under conducive dissociative conditions) forbids this approach. Or was Patience a discarnate entity temporarily possessing Pearl's body? The evidence does not favor one interpretation rather than the other, especially since no firm evidence was ever discovered for the existence of a real Patience Worth. At present, the case remains a psychic and psychological mystery, as well as a source of some outstanding literature.

STATISTICAL METHODS FOR DISPUTED AUTHORSHIP APPLIED TO CHANNELING

Jerry Solfvin (John F. Kennedy University, 12 Altarinda Rd., Orinda, CA 95463)

The study of "channeling" has primarily focused on determining the veridicality of the information that "comes through the channel." If the information is accurate, and if there were no "normal" means for the medium ("channel") to have gotten it, we at least support the view that a "parapsychological" communication has occurred. However, the study of channeling begs for new approaches, and I would like to outline one that was suggested many years ago and which is being resurrected by Josephine Coffey, a graduate student at John F. Kennedy University, because it seems to be particularly promising.

In the early 1970s, Ian Stevenson brought to Edward Kelly's attention the interesting case of The Mystery of Edwin Drood, Charles Dickens' last--unfinished--novel. Since Dickens was widely read in his own time, and since it was known that he was in the process of writing the novel at the time of his death, there was considerable interest within the literary community in completing the novel. Dickens had left no notes nor had he confided his plan for the ending. As a result, a number of writers of the time attempted to complete the novel in Dickensian style. Amongst the several versions of The Mystery of Edwin Drood that were printed, one of them comes from a "medium" in Brattleboro, Vermont, who claimed to have channeled the completion of the novel from (the deceased) Dickens himself. From a methodological point of view, there could be no more ideal set of circumstances for "controlled" investigation of mediumship than this fortuitous sequence of events.

The next piece of this puzzle fell into place in the 1960s at Harvard University, when a well-known statistician, Fred Mosteller, was asked by a history professor if there was any way in which statistics could be used to help identify the authors of a number of the Federalist Papers. It was known with near certainty that all of the disputed documents were written by either John Jay or Thomas Jefferson, but their styles were so similar that scholars were unable to decide who wrote which of the pamphlets. Mosteller set to work, assisted by colleagues, and produced the first statistical study of disputed authorship based on such dependent variables as word counts and length of sentences and paragraphs, items too subtle to catch the eye of the human reader but tailor-made for computer analysis.

In 1973, Ed Kelly and I, with Ian Stevenson's advice and encouragement, proposed a "disputed authorship" study of the completion of Dickens' last novel, using the procedures that Mosteller had pioneered with the Federalist Papers. The situation is ideal because

(1) there is a readily available "control" in the form of Dickens' voluminous premortem writings;

(2) there is an additional "control" in the form of several attempts by professional writers to imitate Dickens' style;

(3) there are other writings by the conscious "imitators" to make variability estimates for whatever dependent variables are ultimately used in this study.

It would be marvelous to discover writings that were produced by the "channel" in his "normal" waking state but even without them, we are presented with a unique historical opportunity for exploring channeling phenomena from a new and exciting perspective. While it is unlikely that such a study will provide us with ironclad proof that the deceased Dickens was the real author of the channeled version of the novel, there is far more to be gained by this study. Whatever the results show, it is certain that this study will pioneer a new methodology which may prove useful for contemporary studies of channeling and, perhaps, for scholars and scientists in other fields as well.

HEALING THROUGH SPIRITS: AN EXPERIENTIAL ACCOUNT OF DISOBSESSION IN THE BRAZILIAN SPIRITIST TRADITION

Matthew C. Bronson (Babel Inverted Group, 31318 Carroll Ave., Hayward, CA 94544)

Central to the spiritist tradition of Brazil is the idea that many physical and mental disorders are the result of the intervention of a spirit entity or entities no longer focused in the physical plane. The person who is negatively affected by this fixation on him or her is said to be "obsessed" by the offending spirits and the recommended treatment is "disobsession" therapy.

The basic set-up for a disobsession proceeding is to convene several mediums, one or two directors, cleaners, and other assistants. The patients need not be present. A guiding spirit is often consulted through one of the mediums to determine the protocol and order of treatment. The name of the patient and other vital information is read, and the director invites any spirit associated with the patient to incorporate into one of the mediums.

Once the director establishes verbal contact with the spirit, the process of "orientation" or "indoctrination" begins, wherein the director, with the possible assistance of "guiding spirits" who incorporate into other mediums, gets it to recognize its discarnate state, release the patient, and take its "proper place in progression." A single disobsession case usually spans several sessions.

I was serving as a translator last winter for Edson Queiroz, a well-known spiritist healer who had come to the U.S. to teach mediumship and spiritist healing techniques. One evening, he asked me if I would serve as an "intermediary," which I agreed to do. He had been to a counseling session for cancer patients that day and had noticed with his clairvoyant vision that there was a vampiric, skeletal entity obsessing one of the patients with a large, cancerous face tumor.

He proposed that I would act as a medium for this entity. The patient was not present at this session. After I released my fear and my usual awareness stepped into the background, I became aware of a terrible hunger and heard myself wailing pitifully. Eventually, under the guidance of a director, the spirit's story came out in a creaky, whiny voice definitely not my own. It seems that she had left her daughter (the same spirit as the patient) in a hut during a severe storm which had cut off her village from food supplies. She went looking for food but came back to find her daughter dead of exposure and hunger and vowed never to leave her again--hence the obsession. She responded to the director's instructions and allowed herself to be led into the light.

The next day, everyone noted an improvement in the demeanor and appearance of the patient. A psychodrama session built around the spirit's story was pursued with some intensity by the patient and a great emotional catharsis resulted. This was a case, in spiritist terms, of using the physical (the medium's body--mine) to heal the spiritual (the obsessing spirit) which, in turn, heals the physical (the patient's body and psyche).

EARLY FINDINGS ON THE NATURE OF CHANNELED DISCOURSE

Dan Hawkmoon Alford (Babel Inverted Group, 31318 Carroll Ave., Hayward, CA 94544, and California Institute of Integral Studies)

In our preliminary investigations into about eight Bay Area channels (or mediums), we find the following modes of communication active to a greater or lesser degree in each individual, such that the proposed structure accounts for most phenomena observed to date in all individuals. The first three modes are seen as pattern interruptions in the normal speaker/listener model.

(1) <u>Activation of Trance-Talk Mode</u>: Most channeled information is couched in what can only be called trance-talk, its object being motivation (looking at old information from a new perspective) rather than new information. Many phenomena of the powerful speaking called clairparlance (such as power metaphors, repetition, etc.) are present in channeled discourse. A question to be asked here is: How effective and coherent is the stream of trance-talk coming from the channel?

(2) <u>Xenoglossic Effects</u>: From the word for "foreign tongue," "xenoglossy" refers to speech effects of a different dialect or language which "bleed through" into the discourse, reminiscent to a greater or lesser degree of another time and place (depending on Mode 5), thus strengthening the dramatic manifestation of a separate being. A question to ask here is: How integrated and authentic are the effects exhibited in suggesting a different time and place?

(3) <u>Glossolalic Effects</u>: From the word for a semanticsless "speaking in tongues," "glossolalia" refers to the often seemingly meaningless repetitions of sounds/words that seldom advance the communication ("as such," "as so," "indeed," etc.), and often downright impede it. These may serve as yet unexplained functions in the totality of the channeling phenomenon. A question to ask here is: How frequent and disturbing are these effects in discourse?

(4) <u>Genuine Intuitive Hits</u>: From time to time, genuine intuitive information seems to be blended into the trance-talk; such hits can be present independent of the other modes being discussed, so a channel must not be judged solely on the basis of whether intuitive information comes through or not. A question to ask here is whether any new information was present in addition to trance-talk.

(5) <u>Congruence</u>: Finally, we must examine the overall integrity and congruence of the channeling performance including and accompanying the speech stream. This is subjectively measured by a sense of power and appropriateness felt afterwards concerning some channels but not others. Questions to ask here are: How convincing is the performance? How empowering or disempowering was the event?

We realize that these are but first thoughts, formed at the beginning of our research and subject to change. Channeling is an ancient linguistic phenomenon, seemingly universal, which has not benefited from modern research techniques. We take no stand as to the ultimate identification of the "entities" being channeled, whether living entities as such or concretized metaphors. But we must sound caution regarding the growth of cults around channeled "entities," governed as they are by hidden assumptions that the beings are intelligent, benign, and endowed with advanced perspective over that of human beings.

PSYCHOLOGICAL RESISTANCE IN RESEARCH ON CHANNELING: A DISCUSSION OF THE CHANNELING PANEL

Charles T. Tart (Dept. of Psychology, University of California, Davis, CA 95616)

The socially appropriate frame of mind for listening to papers on channeling (a currently fashionable name for possession) is a cool, impersonal, intellectual one. We PA members are a brilliant and open-minded group of intellectuals, aren't we? How interesting that one's consciousness and ego can temporarily disappear and be replaced by an ostensible higher entity who has teachings for the world or by an ostensible hate-filled, revenge-seeking ghost of someone who passed away in great torment. Fascinating philosophical and scientific questions are raised about the nature of personal identity, the altered states of consciousness involved in ostensible channeling/possession, the ontological status of the ostensible possessing entities, the degree to which such entities show evidence for psi processes, and how best to design research to study this phenomenon.

Listening to and thinking about the papers in this panel I experienced the above frame of mind. It is intellectually challenging. I also noticed that on an emotional level I was, as we say in California, quite freaked out! Some *thing* is going to push me aside and take over my body? My thoughts and feelings will be subordinated to those of another *entity*? Labeling such things and entities "ostensible" may fool my intellect, but not my feelings! Regardless of what my intellect says, my feelings say "No way!"

Judging by the widespread nervous laughter and nods that greeted the above remarks in my discussion of this panel's presentations, such negative feelings toward channeling/possession may be fairly common in the parapsychological community, even if normally only partially acknowledged or not acknowledged at all. These kinds of feelings could subtly bias and distort research on this phenomenon. Particularly, if such negative feelings in oneself are not consciously acknowledged and dealt with, they are liable to be projected onto "subjects" who show channeling/possession. This can amplify pathological elements already present in the experimenter/subject dichotomy, an important problem area (JASPR, 1977, 81-101): "This subject is susceptible to possession by the irrational, he is not like I." Further, it lends credence to a widespread implicit assumption that only special, different people can channel. Perhaps most of us could channel to some degree (for better or worse) if we dealt with our fears around this issue. Fear of possession is one special form of a general fear of psi. These issues must be faced or future research will be sabotaged (JP, 1982, 313-320; JASPR, 1984, 133-143).

I believe our personal feelings about channeling/possession can be positively resolved, so we can become better researchers as well as growing personally. This will involve various degrees of personal psychological work, though, and will not be accomplished by suppressing our feelings and pretending our approach to this subject is purely intellectual.

PSI AND MENTAL HEALTH*

NOTES ON CLINICAL PARAPSYCHOLOGY

William G. Roll (Dept. of Psychology, West Georgia College, Carrollton, GA 30118; and Psychical Research Foundation)

Surveys and casual inquiry suggest that a large proportion of the population have had experiences that may be of parapsychological origin and that are disturbing to the individuals or families concerned and cause them to seek or attempt to seek professional advice about these experiences. There is currently no professional help available for such individuals, and they may have recourse only to therapists who dismiss ostensible psychic experiences out of hand. If the client has had convincing psi experiences, it does not help a therapeutic relationship if the therapist denies the very possibility of them. The other route is to go to a medium or self-styled "parapsychologist" who often lacks the training and capacity to enable their clients to gain understanding of the psychological and interpersonal dynamics of which the psi incidents may be an expression. The involvement of such advisors may even exacerbate the problems, since their psi abilities, real or supposed, may impress the client and lead to deeper problems, including over-dependence on the psychic or imagined encounters with demons and occult forces.

The question is whether professionally trained parapsychologists will do any better. In the course of my research into psi disturbances such as recurrent spontaneous psychokinesis (RSPK) I have been able to tell the families that there is no demon in their house but "only RSPK" and that such incidents typically cease after a few months. But when it comes to the further question of counseling the people, I could only advise them to see a therapist and hope that they would find someone with a mind open to the possibility of psi and with sufficient insight to see the dynamics behind the occurrences. But such therapists are rare, and all too often the family's problems remain, though their expression may change from psi to more familiar symptoms. This is a disturbing

---

*Organized and chaired by William G. Roll (West Georgia College).

situation. It has not been helped by the negative attitude to psi found in some academic and scientific circles or by the attitude of some parapsychologists that basic research into psi lags too far behind to think of practical applications. I disagree with this view because I have found over the past few years that I could aid the families involved in apparent psi disturbances.

Another fact makes it timely to consider a profession of clinical parapsychology. We now know that psi effects are not discontinuous with other natural occurrences. In particular, psi processes appear to operate within an extension of a familiar biological system: the family and its physical surroundings. Psi seems to link individuals and objects that have been in frequent physical contact and that are joined by affective and historical ties, such as close family and friends and their physical environment. A psi system can then be viewed as a further step in the familiar organismic hierarchy, and psi disturbances can be viewed as perturbations of that system.

A clinical parapsychologist would then be an individual trained in traditional modes of therapy and with an understanding of parapsychological processes. It is time to show that parapsychology is not restricted to the laboratory and conference hall but that it has a place, and a deeply rooted place, in the real world. This being the case, it is also time to respond to the many students and others who are deeply committed to parapsychology but who are forced to abandon the field because there is no professional practice at the end of their studies.

PSI AND THERAPEUTIC INSIGHT

Jeannie Lagle Stewart (Psychical Research Foundation and
    Parapsychological Services Institute, 1502 Maple St.,
    Carrollton, GA 30117)

In the historical Memories, Dreams, and Reflections (New York: Pantheon, 1963) Carl Jung tells of a tremendous struggle in his life which involved very elaborate psychological and parapsychological phenomena. In his account, he reports talking to "spirits" and communicating with fantasy entities; he speaks of his dreams and visions and of his house being "haunted." These events represented "symbols" rather than "symptoms," symbols from "the unconscious" that reflected the workings of the psyche. As he struggled with integrating his inner world with the outer world, he and his family began to feel "haunted." One daughter reported seeing an apparition of a woman; another daughter related that twice in the night her blanket had been snatched away; and his son had an anxiety dream that contained several symbols which Jung had been experiencing in his own dreams and fantasies. The whole family heard the doorbell ringing, and Jung saw it move, but no one was in sight of the door. He writes, "the whole house was filled as if there were a crowd present, crammed full of spirits." It was at this point he poured out his pseudonymous work, Septem Sermones and Mortuos.

Jung took on a work that "should at almost every step of my experiment have run into the same psychic material which is the stuff of psychosis and is found in the insane." His is the territory, the same razor's edge, that I feel is before us in seeking to understand more fully the psychical world. The intensity of the challenge probably depends a great deal on how much we are personally willing to experience consciously, or "bring to light," our inner and outer worlds.

On a number of cases involving individuals reporting feelings of possession and haunting as well as poltergeist activity, William Roll and I have used in combination hypnosis and seance-room and gestalt procedures to facilitate integration and release of what the family has experienced as an entity or entities. At these times either of us may respond as a medium apparently receiving information that neither of us knew before the session. Ostensible RSPK effects have also been elicited, seemingly as the entity's response to a question. At times, the entity is embodied by a member of the group and speaks to the group through him or her. The apparently telepathically derived information provides valuable diagnostic material as well as therapeutic insight or gestalt for the client. Through integration or giving up of the possessing elements, relief is found in the form of insight. Follow-up shows the individual maintaining and increasing mental health and freedom from the problem.

Writers more contemporary than Jung have reported the occurrence of psi in psychoanalysis and psychotherapy (J. Eisenbud, Psi and Psychoanalysis, New York: Grune and Stratton, 1970; E. Mintz, The Psychic Thread, New York: Human Science Press, 1983), providing valuable therapeutic material. Jung summarizes his experience in these words:

> The experience has to be taken for what it was, or as it seems to have been. No doubt it was connected with the state of emotion I was in at the time, and which was favorable to parapsychological phenomena. It was an unconscious constellation of whose peculiar atmosphere I recognized as the numen of an archetype. "It walks abroad! It's in the air!" The intellect, of course, would like to arrogate to itself some scientific, physical knowledge of the affair, and preferably, to write the whole thing off as a violation of the rules. But, what a dreary world it would be if the rules were not violated sometimes.

ON THE MENTAL HEALTH OF PARAPSYCHOLOGY AND PARAPSYCHOLOGISTS

Charles T. Tart (Dept. of Psychology, University of California, Davis, CA 95616)

Abraham Maslow, the founder of humanistic psychology, postulated an important principle as a result of his study of mature, creative, and fulfilled adults. This was the need to express the talents that one naturally has if one is to grow toward full self-actualization. If one does not express such inherent talents, one will not only feel unfulfilled, one's adjustment at lower levels can be undermined.

I believe that many of us working in the field today, as well as our founders, were motivated by some degree of personal spiritual and humanitarian needs to enter our field.

While we know too little to speak about it yet with the scientific precision we would like to have, we recognize that (1) there is some sort of spiritual reality to man; (2) current materialistic ideas of man deny these needs; (3) this denial causes a great deal of suffering through the attitudes created; (4) a wholesale acceptance of everything labeled "psychical" or "spiritual" is not an acceptable solution, for these labels embrace too much nonsense and pathology; but that (5) properly applied scientific method can at least partially separate the spiritual wheat from the spiritual chaff, leading to both better science and greater human happiness.

Maslow also pointed out that needs operate in a hierarchical fashion, with unsatisfied lower needs often inhibiting or distorting higher ones. Parapsychologists are normal human beings, not abstract idealists, and so we want to be socially accepted by our society; especially by the people defined as so important, the scientific establishment. This would bring social advantages and practical material advantages for doing further research.

It is not healthy to deny any needs, but too often today I see parapsychologists denying their higher needs in the service of their lower ones. We have forgotten why we are here. I have certainly fallen into this forgetfulness many times. The operating attitude becomes: "Forget the spiritual inspiration, act like a conventional aspiritual or antispiritual scientist in order to get the social acceptance and material support that would result."

This is not an emotionally neutral forgetting. Because part of the rejection of parapsychology stems from semi- or unconscious fears, psi phenomena and parapsychologists threaten many conventional scientists, so in our quest for fulfillment of the lower need of social acceptance we go too far in forgetting the noble and spiritual aspirations of our quest. This becomes a personal forgetting and a cognitive and emotional denial, not just an expedient social gesture.

I think it is time for individual parapsychologists and the field as a whole to reexamine why we are in this field and to acknowledge and act from our highest aspirations instead of denying them. Unconscious denial is not healthy. Our individual and collective mental health will benefit from this honesty, as will our research results.

THE NEED FOR A HERMENEUTIC METHODOLOGY IN
APPLIED CLINICAL PARAPSYCHOLOGY

Oscar Miro-Quesada S. (Parapsychological Services Institute,
    1502 Maple St., Carrollton, GA 30117, and Emory
    University)

Of special relevance to the practice of clinical parapsychology is that the therapist be able to enter into and sustain an unbiased, unadulterated mode of communication with the psi system revealed through the client's disturbance. Aside from having one's own psi abilities and corresponding transpersonal intuitive capacity--or, as Arthur Koestler so aptly put it, "man's intuitive intimations of deeper levels of reality"--well developed, this form of psi encounter requires of the therapist to be open minded, ideologically flexible, empathetic, highly attentive to the conscious and unconscious polarities at play ("dialectic mindfulness"), ready to participate in the client's world view, and able to cultivate the necessary passivity of mind that comes with practice in meditation. Applied in a systematic and professionally sound ethical manner these characteristics, combined with a thorough and practical knowledge of parapsychological research, clinical psychology, neurophysiology, and, ideally, transcultural psychiatry, provide the parapsychological clinician with the means to understand as well as to manage the diachronic causes and synchronic relationships that constitute the client's chief complaint.

Three cases labeled as "possession" by the clients illustrate how the above formulated holistic clinical orientation, applied within a cross-cultural hermeneutic model, affords both client and therapist a state-specific methodology. This, in turn, facilitates an experiential objective interpretation of the transformative intentionality obscured by the variegated phenomenology of the transpersonal or parapsychological disturbances. It is therefore possible to reveal the salient <u>pattern</u> and <u>meaning</u> (purpose)--unmanifest to the material senses--behind the disturbing and unbalanced release of the client's once dormant psi faculties and, consequently, to arrive at a comprehensive clinical approach relative to the client's inner call to abandon the security of a familiar ego-syntonic personality, now in polar opposition to the autonomous yearnings of the collective unconscious.

It is an important proviso for the practicing clinical parapsychologist to embrace consciously the paradox that <u>change</u> (transpersonal growth) is most likely to occur when the client's right <u>not to</u> change is first fully accepted. Moreover, in the psychotherapeutic context psi functions permit a self-generating communication with "archetypal gestalten" created by the transit of certain supervening levels of psi consciousness through an already existing hierarchy of a higher order of operative intelligence constitutive of what may be termed the client's human/technical and sensori/experiential body. It appears this self-regulating process is directed by a faculty of the mind (nonphysical part of the brain) that is homeostatically aware of any psychic imbalances and somatic aberrations which it autonomously seeks to remedy with its own resources. At times, though, this may be beyond its capacity, in which case a measure of external assistance may be required. But if this is to be effective, it must be such as to assist, not override, the innate intelligence of the client's mind/body.

RESONANCE AND PSYCHOTHERAPY

Virginia A. Larson

In dissertation research entitled <u>An Exploration of the Nature of Resonance in Psychotherapy</u>, 130 questionnaires were sent out to two sample pools to demonstrate that there exists a population of psychotherapists who have experienced "resonance," which was delineated as a very intense level of rapport occurring between therapist and client during psychotherapy. This kind of experience was distinguished from more typical rapport by a high level of experiential intensity when therapist and client momentarily interact as one nonverbal system echoing the other emotionally, physically, cognitively, and/or spiritually, frequently suggestive of extrasensory communication. The concept of resonance, borrowed from physics, was utilized here as a metaphor to illuminate subtle nonverbal, communicative systemic exchanges which may function as healing mechanisms during psychotherapy. One implication of this exploratory study is that altered states of consciousness may increase the propensity toward resonance experiences.

Of the 130 research questionnaires returned, 34% (44 psychotherapists) reported they had experienced psychotherapeutic resonance with clients more than once during therapy. Of 31 psychotherapists who were interviewed (these were therapists in the sample who stated they had experienced resonance more than once with clients and were willing to be interviewed if kept anonymous by coded number), 97% or 30 interviewees specifically stated that their psychotherapeutic resonance experiences had beneficial effects by creating safety and trust so that difficult psychological issues were able to be addressed. A grouping of 24 interviewees (77% of 31 interviewed) reported that they used their total body as an instrument to keep in contact with their own experiential process and/or hypothesize about their client's emotional experience.

Interviewee 11 described: "One resonance experience occurred when suddenly I became able to say the client's precise words and the client, my exact words."

Interviewee 14 noted: "Suddenly there was a moment of feeling separate yet being very connected. The energy changed as if there was an alchemy or a movement into a strong vibration frequency like meeting and understanding."

Interviewee 15 affirmed: "Everything I verbalized seemed relevant. At this moment the client seemed simultaneously far away and very close, as if there were two levels concurrently occurring when I could express an exact description of the client's experience."

Interviewee 17 reported: "Suddenly my heart began beating very fast and I expressed to the client, 'I'm wondering if you're feeling scared.' The client immediately answered yes and related feeling very understood, not isolated, and very emotional."

Interviewee 22 stated: "There had been deep eye contact; then there was a sudden feeling in my stomach when I experienced being part of the client's experience."

The researcher's goal was to illuminate and describe a wide spectrum of systemic communicative transmissions emerging during psychotherapy interactions, since these subtle transmissions may be psychotherapeutic healing mechanisms. Many of the anecdotal reports from the interviewed therapists suggested the presence of parapsychological phenomena.

CROSS-CULTURAL APPROACHES TO MULTIPLE PERSONALITY
DISORDER: E.C. MENDES AND "PSICO-SINTESE"

Stanley Krippner (Saybrook Institute, 1772 Vallejo St.,
    San Francisco, CA 94123)

Eliezer C. Mendes is a former surgeon who heads a therapeutic community near São Paulo and has organized such communities in four other cities. He specializes in treating epileptics, schizophrenics, and cases of multiple personality disorder (MPD) resistant to conventional therapy. Inspired by Kardec's writings, Mendes' basic assumption is that many of these individuals are psychically sensitive and that the development of their sensitivity may reduce their symptoms.

According to Mendes, MPDs can often be understood in terms of hypersensitivity to past lives. To diagnose a case of MPD Mendes relies on mediums. Mendes has found that mediums are often able to evoke alter personalities with more facility and to understand them better than do most psychotherapists. The mediums place the client in an altered state of consciousness, typically through music and movement. While the clients dance, their changing movements, voice, and facial expressions are observed, and the mediums record in writing their observations concerning each personality that manifests itself.

In the case of MPDs who represent former lifetimes, the goal of therapy is a merging of personalities by bringing them into what Mendes calls the "psychological center." This merging first occurs emotionally as linkages are formed between personalities. Mendes claims that later personalities typically emphasize one of four styles: emotional, instinctive, intellectual, or spiritual. These styles roughly correspond to the Jungian typology of feeling, sensing, thinking, and intuiting.

Clients are told that the rate of their integration is dependent upon them and their own efforts to effect a "psico-sintese" of their various personalities. However, if there is an intrusion of a malevolent personality--from a past life or from another source--exorcism rather than merging is advised.

Another alternative is taken in the instance of those clients who become mediums and may retain one or more alter personalities to assist them in their profession. Mendes discussed one case in which a medium would allow a French personality from a former life to take control. This personality purportedly spoke French and was able to obtain cultural information which supposedly was not available to the host personality.

Of the more than 20,000 clients Mendes had seen by the time

of my interview in February 1985, over 1,000 were diagnosed as epileptic and about 300 manifested MPD. Most of the remainder were said to be schizophrenic.

Mendes claims to be able to rehabilitate 70% of his MPD cases, the average length of treatment being about three years. He purports to have an 85% success rate with epileptics, many of whom are trained to control their seizures by becoming mediums and incorporating spirits. With schizophrenic clients, Mendes claims only a 15% success rate.

Whatever else may be said, there is an urgent need for cross-cultural research on MPD, epilepsy, and dissociated states to distill the common denominators underlying successful treatment and to determine what role, if any, psi may play in treatment.

CLINICAL ETHICS IN PSI RESEARCH*

INTRODUCTION: ETHICAL CONCERNS WITH CLINICAL SERVICES IN PARAPSYCHOLOGY

R. Jeffrey Munson (Institute for Parapsychology, Box 6847, Durham, NC 27708)

This panel will explore the parapsychology/clinical psychology interface from philosophical, empirical, clinical, professional, and legal perspectives to clarify potential ethical problems and solutions.

Parapsychologists are drawn into the clinical domain because: (1) psychodynamic influences on psi require empirical clarification. Such research requires clinical development of hypotheses, methodologies, and procedures for handling subjects. Dealing with subjects sometimes reveals people in need of psychological intervention. (2) Similarly, parapsychologists are often approached by lay people seeking validation of their beliefs or experiences. These also may suggest psychological problems requiring intervention. (3) Sometimes parapsychologists are approached specifically for counseling services because of ostensible psi cases.

Parapsychologists are obligated to attend to problems of services because their specialized knowledge (including future research findings clarifying psi/psychology relations) puts them in a position to improve standards of care in certain cases. The problem in these cases is that researchers are not mandated to provide services. Moreover, there are potential conflicts between the purposes of research (wanting to elicit psi) and services (wanting often to eliminate psi). Definitions of professional domains and the priorities of duties are required here.

Interactional influences on the genesis and character of psi require that researchers and therapists pay close attention to their role in the creation of psi. Possible psychological conflicts for these professionals may be generated by contrasting motivations and intentions.

---

*Organized and chaired by R. Jeffrey Munson (Institute for Parapsychology).

The ethical obligation to develop new and effective treatment forms conflicts with the need to prohibit procedures based on questionable grounds. Parapsychology is in a difficult position here because of the controversial nature of its subject matter and because some factors that may predispose psi are informed by different cultures whose ethical foundations conflict with one another.

These and other problems must be examined in order to guarantee professional and ethical services to clients in need.

CHANGING ETHICAL PERSPECTIVES AND PARAPSYCHOLOGY

Hoyt L. Edge (Dept. of Philosophy, Rollins College,
   Winter Park, FL 32789)

Significant changes in our understanding of ethics have been made in the last two decades. I will mention three of these changes and suggest some of their implications for parapsychology.

(1) A transition from principles to virtues. Ethics traditionally has been patterned on a view of science which has been called the hypothetico-deductive model in which one deduces from a general principle (law) how an object must behave. Likewise, it was assumed that in ethics one must be able to deduce from a general principle how a person ought to act. Thus, ethics consisted of a discipline that, like science, searched for general principles from which one could deduce the right thing to do. Just as this understanding of science has been questioned, so our view of ethics is changing. Now, rather than concerning ourselves with principles, one thinks of morality as being concerned with exemplifying virtues, such as being compassionate and understanding.

(2) A transition from ethical decisions being based purely on rational processes to a view where ethical action arises naturally from a certain kind of person. This means that ethics is inextricably bound to teleology--to a view of what it means to be a person and to what it means to fulfill ourselves as human beings.

(3) A transition from taking the civil end of the spectrum as the paradigm of ethics to accepting the intimate as more important. An ethics based on civil interactions accepts the contract model of ethics as paradigmatic, but the fact that our culture is entering into marriage contracts is a reductio ad absurdum of this view. Rather than taking the abstract, contractual point of view as encompassing morality, ethical thinking is reemphasizing the intimacy of personal relationships as more paradigmatic.

Several implications for parapsychology follow. First, in

relation to subjects, we should not think of our moral obligations to our subjects in some sort of contractual or legalistic way for two reasons: (1) the legal is mainly prohibitive and says more about what we may not do than what we ought to do, and (2) contracts and legal obligations are on the civil end of the spectrum, not on the intimate.

Secondly, there is a tension between the methodology of science and our ethical obligations toward experimental participants. The traditional self-perception of science as value neutral and objective has implied that experimenters should eschew the personal and the intimate. Even if we engage "subjects" in a friendly manner, the reason for doing this may be more for manipulative reasons (we get better results under this condition) than ethical--but manipulation has never been a moral category. It is a mistake to think that morality is adequately expressed vis-a-vis our participants through prescription, either through consent forms or methodology. In other words, we need to concentrate on character--not on how I should act in this circumstance, but on how I should be as a person.

THE ETHICS OF CLINICALLY RELEVANT SITUATIONS ENCOUNTERED IN RESEARCH

Rex G. Stanford (St. John's University, Marillac Hall, Psychology Laboratory, SB-15, Jamaica, NY 11439)

The following circumstances in studies may be of special concern:

(1) ESP tests are often given in contexts that invite and encourage participants to abandon, albeit temporarily, some of their usual reality testing and to give free rein to their more imaginative and fanciful inclinations. Attention to and free verbal expression of fleeting thoughts, images, and other mentation are eagerly sought by the experimenter. Though such exercises cause no harm to psychologically stable persons, these somewhat regressive modes of thinking might pose dangers for others by, for example, weakening what ego psychologists would term an already weak ego boundary. These observations may be especially true of free-response ESP tests given in settings such as hypnosis or Ganzfeld. Some form of screening should be used in such studies; options include standard psychological testing, interviews prior to any testing, and the use of pretesting questionnaires that include questions likely to detect individuals at risk in such work. Some laboratories combine the latter two approaches. Such screening procedures should always be done in ways that do not threaten the self-esteem of

persons not found acceptable for a particular study. Prescreening promises of participation in a particular study should generally be avoided. Alternate studies can sometimes be arranged if this seems desirable.

(2) If participation in a study enhances the belief that one has psychic powers or is subject to psychic influences, certain individuals might be harmed by participation, especially those inclined to delusional thinking. Often the latter types of individuals talk very freely and can be detected at an early stage. Nonetheless, screening, as discussed above, can be very useful.

(3) The person who emerges from a parapsychological study with the freshly developed perception that he or she has a particular psi ability--whether or not this perception is correct--may have some difficult adjustments to make emotionally, cognitively, and possibly socially (if this perception is made known to others). Precautions should be taken to insure that participants do not misconstrue or overinterpret the feedback given in a psi study. Special procedures such as hypnosis or Ganzfeld may have a protective value for some participants. If a participant believes that such a procedure enables a psi experience that he or she would not ordinarily experience and that would not continue to happen outside that setting, the impact of psi experience in that setting might be less disruptive. If a researcher clearly identifies special talent or trains it in an individual, that investigator might do well to provide opportunities for counseling and support and should monitor the participant's adjustment to the circumstances created by the study.

ETHICAL STRUCTURE IN CLINICAL APPLICATIONS OF PARAPSYCHOLOGY

James A. Hall (8125 Westchester Dr., Ste. 244, Dallas, TX 75225)

Parapsychology is not a clinical science. Rather, it may be related to clinical applications in psychiatry, psychology, psychoanalysis, or pastoral counseling in a manner analogous to the relation of biochemistry to clinical applications in the practice of medicine.

Some patients present with complaints ostensibly related to psi phenomena, others present apparent psi phenomena in the course of psychotherapeutic treatment. Like all clinical phenomena, psi events occurring during psychotherapy must be subsumed into the general purposes of treatment and cannot, in that context, be used to explore evidence for psi.

In clinical situations it is necessary to attempt discrimination between psi and pseudo- or delusional psi experiences. Furthermore, either type of experience might seem to move toward either integration or disintegration of the patient's overall psychological health.

In the absence of a reliable test for psi, when presumed psi events occur during the course of clinical treatment their psi or nonpsi nature remains a matter of clinical judgment. This would not at all prevent the gathering of clinical descriptions of parapsychological events which might be used in the manner of Louisa Rhine's evaluation of the range and nature of spontaneously reported psi events.

The potential clinical applications of parapsychology clearly raise problems of ethics, malpractice, and legal vulnerability if such intervention is judged by the prevailing standards of ethical clinical conduct. For example, a patient's alleged psi experiences might be treated as such by a clinician. But should the patient subsequently develop clear signs of paranoid schizophrenia, the clinician might be held accountable for neglecting the delusional nature of the psi material, thereby unintentionally contributing to the enlargement of the patient's psychotic system.

With the present state of knowledge there are several avenues of approach, in my opinion, that the Parapsychological Association might consider if this body wishes to move toward clinical applications of psi research.

First, a standardized, self-administered test could be developed to elicit history of psi belief and experience prior to the beginning of psychotherapy. In addition to providing a framework within which subsequent psi reports could be judged, such a test eventually would provide research data about the incidence of psi belief and reported experiences within various patient populations, giving some clues as to the relationship between psi and the range of mental functioning. I foresee no ethical or legal problems in the application of such a test.

Second, the Parapsychological Association might provide guidelines to clinicians as to observations that might help to distinguish reported parapsychological events from experiences that are more evidential of psychological disorder. There should be no legal or ethical problem with such guidelines. In addition, the existence of such guidelines would be a protection to clinicians concerned with psi occurrences in psychotherapeutic practice.

Third, those parapsychologists who are also licensed practitioners in a mental health field could, under the auspices of the Parapsychological Association, form a committee or a branch of this association for the specialized purpose of acting as a referral source outside the field of mental health. Patients in whom psi experiences are a significant problem could be referred for consultation to such a committee or its designees in a manner analogous to referral for psychological testing, x-ray, sleep evaluation, or other traditional medical support systems.

Such a group would form its own ethical guidelines, under the direction of the Parapsychological Association. A practitioner referring a patient for such specialized evaluation would have a more easily defensible ethical stance than if an attempt were made to bring parapsychological evaluation within the ordinary range of practice of an established mental health profession.

THE PRACTICE OF CLINICAL PARAPSYCHOLOGY: ETHICAL CONSIDERATIONS AND TRAINING ISSUES

Maria Nemeth (1281 47th Avenue, Sacramento, CA 95831)

Interest in the practice of clinical parapsychology has given rise to ethical and training issues. I will use the practice of psychology in the state of California as a model to discuss clinical parapsychology as falling within the psychology licensing law.

All those calling themselves psychologists, with the exception of those working in exempt agencies, must be licensed to practice. Therefore, clinical parapsychologists would be required to receive the same education as general psychologists. They would be subject to all of the same regulations regarding the practice of psychology.

Is clinical parapsychology a distinct subspecialty like organizational, social, or counseling psychology? Is it, rather, an integral component of standard psychological training, like minority issues, child abuse, substance abuse, and human sexuality? Assuming a distinct base of knowledge, what do clinical parapsychologists do that differs significantly from the standard practice of clinical psychology? For example, given a patient in crisis, regardless of the subject matter, are there techniques for handling this that are specific to clinical parapsychology?

What are the legal and liability issues that surround practitioners? Are they at greater risk in the courtroom because of the nontraditional nature of the field? What are some possible issues regarding obtaining malpractice coverage and billing insurance companies?

This discussion will be from the perspective of a veteran member of California's Psychology Examining Committee, one of the largest licensing bodies in the United States.

DO WE DISCOVER AND/OR CREATE REALITY?*

EXPLORING OUR LIMITED PERCEPTIONS

Keith Harary (Institute for Advanced Psychology,
1550 California St., San Francisco, CA 94109)

Is psi research exploring the extent to which human awareness is capable of extending beyond the apparent boundaries of physical laws? If we define psychic functioning as paranormal, or as a violation of normal processes in nature, then psi itself becomes an anomaly. By approaching psi from this perspective we may subconsciously view nature as being in some way disorganized or chaotic, permitting the occasional subversion of natural processes through human intervention on an almost supernatural level.

It is possible, however, that psi research is uncovering as much about the limits of human awareness as it is about our untapped perceptual potential. Perhaps we have created psychic functioning out of our inherent inability to perceive clearly or to comprehend what is actually taking place in the world around us. Nature itself may be more organized, on an informational level, than we imagine or are capable of perceiving under ordinary conditions. Viewed from this perspective, psychic functioning may be described as an intermittent perception of organized information in nature by an imperfect observer.

Rather than violating physical laws, psychic functioning may violate only the usual limitations of our own perceptions. Instead of suggesting supernatural intervention, psi may be viewed as an information-organizing principle in nature which permeates everything.

It is possible that we are both creating psychic functioning and observing psi. If we could perceive nature clearly, we might have no need of a special term to refer to a part of nature's normal functioning that we don't usually perceive. The organizing principle

---

*Organized and chaired by Elizabeth A. Rauscher (Tecnic Research Laboratories).

which we call psi might, nonetheless, be present, but psychic functioning might become a part of that which we would refer to as ordinary perception.

DO WE CREATE OR DISCOVER REALITY?

William C. Gough (Foundation for Mind-Being Research,
    Los Altos, CA)

The Foundation for Mind-Being Research was established as a nonprofit organization six years ago to assist in the evolution of consciousness studies and to help bring this new field into wider recognition as a bona fide science. Through a series of meetings, workshops, reports, and research projects, the Foundation has explored approaches to an integrated model of consciousness with emphasis on the nature, power, and role of thought and the impact of one's world view upon perceived reality. The focusing theme of the Foundation's work during the past two years has been, respectively, a study of "patterns in the universe" and "interdimensional communication."

The Foundation has sought competent individuals who (1) are open to a multidisciplinary approach to knowledge, (2) recognize they are an integral part of any experiment, and (3) know and are prepared to extend their own level of consciousness. The approach has been to seek/merge knowledge from individuals trained in the traditional fields of the physical, biological, psychological, engineering, and medical sciences with persons talented and skilled in the parapsychological, psychic, metaphysical, shamanistic, and spiritual areas. My discussion will summarize the key conclusions of this six years of exploration. Emphasis will be upon the human process for formulating physical reality.

CAN WE UTILIZE OUR CURRENT RESEARCH AND EXPERIENCE
IN PARAPSYCHOLOGY AND THE PHYSICS OF CONSCIOUSNESS
TO ADDRESS THE ISSUE, "DO WE DISCOVER AND/OR CREATE
OUR OWN REALITY?"

Elizabeth A. Rauscher (Parapsychology Division, Tecnic Research
    Laboratories, 64 Santa Margarita, San Leandro, CA 94579)

This abstract presents some data, ideas, and models from science which may relate to psi phenomena and the issue of whether we discover or create our reality and/or experience of reality. We also need to consider that discovery and creation are not necessarily mutually exclusive and may be interwoven descriptions related to the manner in which life forms, particularly humans, create concepts and carry them out into goal-oriented actions and effects.

In examining whether we create and/or shape our reality, or at least our concept of reality, we should distinguish two issues. The first is that what we believe and conceive determines how we perceive reality; our knowledge and emotional state determine how we organize and analyze incoming information. An analogy might be made to relativity theory: although the laws of physics are invariant under translation (homogeneous Lorentz groups) and/or rotation (inhomogeneous Lorentz groups), observers from different inertial or noninertial frames of reference apparently observe different sequences of spacetime events.

The second issue involves the possibility that one's actions and interactions with one's environment will actually affect the reality we perceive. An analogy comes from the Heisenberg Uncertainty Principle. If one makes a measurement in the micro domain, the probe, usually a beam of particles or radiation, changes the position and momentum (or energy and time of measurement) of the particle being observed. All measurement produces an interaction of the probe system with the system being observed; hence, one cannot make an observation without disturbing the system being observed. John Bell's interconnectedness theorem may be relevant to the manner in which we can formulate the observer-observed connection.

GESP and PK are part of our perceptive and interactive modalities. Because they are related to and an extension of perception and remote matter interaction, they are more intrinsically related to our observation and measurement of what we perceive as physical processes. The relative aspect of the observer to the observed and the manner in which one interprets the observed may relate to a form of remote relationship of the observer to the observed. This relationship may very well involve a remote perception aspect and may also encompass phenomena related to Bell's interconnectedness properties of matter.

GESP as well as such phenomena as Bell's theorem may be subsumed under geometries involving more than four dimensions. An analogy to give credence to this idea for modeling psychic phenomena is that of people in two cars driving around a curve on a mountainside who are not able to see each other but are moving so as to see each other in their futures. An observer in a helicopter sees this process and can predict the future meeting and passing of the two cars. In a sense his higher, three-dimensional frame of reference allows him to "see into the future" of the people in two-dimensional space. Although this is a crude analogy, I have developed detailed multidimensional models which include remote perception and mental intervention in physical processes.

The success of some laws of physics in predicting experimental outcomes implies that there is underlying order in the universe. The idea that says we create our reality also says that random creation is apparently not allowed. Therefore, although we may create our reality, there are limits to the processes and forms we create. The less we affect our environment, the more our process of observation looks like discovery.

Is all that is conceivable real? In fact, does the concept of something create its existence? Some apparently precognitive events (e.g., Leonardo da Vinci's designs of submarines and parachutes) may have been the creation of a concept finalized through engineers and material scientists carrying the concept into action, so that these ideas were later perceived as reality. All devices, inventions, social structures, etc., proceed from concepts in which their structure and nature are shaped and formed into creations. These creations have physical, psychological, philosophical, paranormal, and spiritual dimensions.

We can examine the development of ideas and inventions in terms of timelike loops to the future as precognitions of what is later created and developed. (Again consider da Vinci's designs.) We can then examine in more detail how much of what is termed regular scientific research involves psychic phenomena. From my observations working with large particle accelerators, it seems that replicability is not insured. Some scientists are far better at "particle finding" than are others. In fact, some "psi-miss" and make few, if any, new discoveries and have difficulty replicating other scientists' work. Other researchers have a high success rate because they have a "knack" for doing science (and perhaps psi!).

DO WE DISCOVER OR CREATE REALITY?

Julian Isaacs (John F. Kennedy University, 12 Altarinda Road, Orinda, CA 95463)

As posed, the question set to this panel is ambiguous and of unlimited generality. Is it scientific or philosophical? This choice constrains the relevant facts and the admissability of possible answers.

Concerning the creation of reality, the most conservative interpretation might be that we each live within a personal reality created by our past experiences, attitudes, and beliefs, although sharing common assumptions across social, cultural, and ethnic groupings. This becomes of greater significance when it is realized that ultimately we choose our orientations towards events, and these choices potently determine the perceived reality. Even the hypotheses we bring to this present question are framed within the context of our experienced states of consciousness, psychological integration, and cognitive/emotional relationship with the world.

A stronger hypothesis, probably shared by most parapsychologists, is that in addition to our conscious, normal, physical interventions in the world, psi provides another, usually unconscious, possibly pervasive but frequently hidden input influencing the events of the world.

The radical thesis argues that we are responsible, unconsciously, for the actual generation and/or maintenance of the world. But if this is true, what kinds of evidence could be relevant to its proof? The geological record indicates that the world seems to have existed prior to the evolution of human beings; therefore, we seem not to be necessary for its existence on a global scale. A quite popular current view is that the data of particle physics demonstrate the creation of particles by the expectations of physicists. But so far, no controlled studies of this hypothesis have yet been conducted, and very great difficulties seem to face such attempts. The parapsychological data, although indicating that psi influence on the world is real, do not yet demonstrate that physical reality is mind dependent, although they have been interpreted as suggesting this. Finally, the teachings of the major mystical religions, as far as they may be relevant or trustworthy, seem to suggest, arguably, that we are at most co-creators, minor characters, rather than the directors of the show.

CO-CREATED REALITY

Robert-Peter F. Quider (John F. Kennedy University,
    12 Altarinda Rd., Orinda, CA 95463)

To many scientists, the question of whether we discover or create reality surely must seem like a ridiculous question to ask. But, with the development of quantum physics and the realization that the very act of observation influences what we observe, some scientists have even begun to question whether an objective reality actually exists for us to discover. In addition, from a perceptual psychological standpoint we know that our observations of reality do not necessarily represent an exact replica of what we believe to exist in objective reality. Thus, not only do we apparently influence

Do We Discover/Create Reality?

what we observe but we can never really be sure if what we do observe accurately represents what actually exists. To put it simply, objective reality cannot be objectively verified. And, it seems the only objective reality is a consensus of our subjective experiences of reality.

Given the above, one might wonder if there is a great truth to the mystic's statement that physical reality is an illusion. But, if it is an illusion, how could such an illusion so convincingly be created?

In my opinion, the answer may be found in an understanding of the phenomena of extrasensory perception (ESP) and psychokinesis (PK). For it is through the concept of ESP that we can conceive of the means by which every being on the planet could share in an agreed-upon "official" view of reality. And, it is through the concept of PK we can conceive of the means to manipulate whatever (i.e., if anything) exists in reality to conform to the official view.

In fact, science is an activity by which official views are created. In "discovering" reality scientific beliefs are created and/or changed which, in turn, affect the common man's beliefs and perceptions about reality. If psi does exist, it certainly seems possible that massively shared beliefs could be the "cause" of our actual experiences.

If we assume it is our beliefs that structure our experience of reality, then we must change them in order to see changes in our experience of reality. Having informally conducted this experiment, I have noticed that my experience of reality is intimately linked with my a priori beliefs about it. I have also noted, however, that reality does not always conform to my newly held beliefs. But if we are all interconnected through psi, as parapsychology suggests, would not our experience of reality be governed by more than our own personal beliefs and desires?

It is interesting to view parapsychology's struggle to make psi function consistently and effectively as being due to the masses' fear of accepting psi. But I would caution those who see this as a suggestion to go out and allay those fears, because I do not think we realize what "unleashing" psi could mean for our experience of reality. Rather, I do suggest we create a new "psiology" (i.e., the study of psi) which focuses more on our "use" of psi in everyday experience. Then, by learning how we create this "ordinary" reality we may prepare ourselves for co-creating a reality in which we have conscious use of psi.

ADDENDUM*

STAGE MAGIC: WHAT DO PARAPSYCHOLOGISTS NEED TO KNOW?**
SUMMARY

Loyd Auerbach (John F. Kennedy University,
12 Altarinda Rd., Orinda, CA 95463)

As a sequel to the 1983 panel of magicians and mentalists, "The Role of the Conjuror in Psychical Research " (RIP 1983, 120-121), this panel discussed the art of magic and mentalism, including the kinds of things one can best learn in magic, how the parapsychologist can best become familiar with "magical" know-how, and things to keep in mind when consulting magicians.

Participants included George Hansen of the Psychophysical Research Laboratories (member, International Brotherhood of Magicians), Marcello Truzzi of Eastern Michigan University (member, Psychic Entertainers Association [PEA]), James Rainho of Simplex Magic (magic dealer and member, PEA), Ray Goulet of Magic Art Studio (magic dealer and member, PEA), and Loyd Auerbach of John F. Kennedy University (member, Society of American Magicians [SAM]).

The session was a very informal discussion. What follows is a summary, written by Loyd Auerbach from audio tapes, of comments by Truzzi, Goulet, Rainho, and Auerbach. (Mr. Hansen's abstract is printed separately; see pp. 185-186.)

Marcello Truzzi

There is something we can call the "magician's fallacy," the tendency to believe that if one learns some tricks and the principles of magic, one cannot be fooled. There are some magicians who believe this, as well as at least one parapsychologist. But everyone can be fooled--magicians fool each other all the time! There are even those who can be considered "magicians' magicians." Getting involved in magic should make one modest, rather than arrogant, about one's own perceptions.

The state of the art in magic changes all the time. There

---
*This roundtable was presented at the 1985 Parapsychological Association convention; however, this summary was not received in time for inclusion in RIP 1985.
**Convened by Loyd Auerbach (John F. Kennedy University).

are magicians, like Slydini, who learned their art in isolation, which is precisely why they're so good. This holds for children as well, so one should not ask, "Where could they [children] have learned it?"--they could have learned it by themselves.

Parapsychologists should keep in mind that magicians will go to any length to bypass set conditions. Houdini and others got out of many prisons, after being placed under (the wardens') "control" conditions.

Magicians are always searching for the new. However, the new may be simpler than the old and therefore that much harder to observe. Simple moves, when complex ones are expected, are not seen. Ninety percent of magic may be useless knowledge, except as illustrations of some principle.

One can get a lot of information by becoming part of the magicians' circle of friends. Backstage information can be of great advantage to getting involved in magic and mentalism. One may meet people who can enlighten one about specific personalities.

Mentalists may be antagonistic to magicians and may hold back secrets for their own inner circles. The real state-of-the-art mentalism is held to a select few.

PEA members may not disclaim psi abilities, and may in fact do readings. Major mentalists, who may not be PEA members, have come to feel that magicians are the enemy who expose the mental effect, supposedly in the name of rationalism so that the public is not misled.

There is no area where knowledge of misdirection is not important. Parapsychologists shouldn't assume when dealing with computers that any problem must be in the microchip rather than at a gross level.

When consulting magicians, one needs to ask not about specific effects, but what to do to preclude a simulation, what controls are necessary. A magician can give you this. Contact the heads of the magicians' organizations for their suggestions of appropriate consultants or for their opinions of certain individuals. One can contact the PEA whenever a new "superstar" or other subject appears on the scene to see if that person is known to the PEA. Do not simply go to your local magician and ask for help, since he or she may not be knowledgeable enough, trust you enough, or be willing to help. Also, keep in mind that there must be no media attention. Treat the magician as a private consultant; neither of you should seek attention for the consultation.

Ray Goulet

Magicians, when put under conditions they are aware of--no matter what these conditions may be--are ready for them. When creating new effects, the magician looks for things that are relevant, for new methods or new ways to combine old methods. New methods often come about by accident or by going over and recombining old methods. Some effects may not be duplicated, but the methods may change when the effect is repeated. Remember: the mentalist doesn't want to be 100% correct.

When consulting magicians, remember that just as you may not know the magician, the magician doesn't know you. Being a magician, I won't divulge the secret. One needs to join a magicians' club to socialize with magicians; once they know you personally, they're more apt to tell you their modus operandi.

James Rainho

One must be humble, because one can always be fooled. As a magic dealer, I have had parapsychologists and psychologists complain that they'd love to learn magic but they haven't the time to practice and learn. One can more easily learn the principles than the tricks; one doesn't have to be a performer.

If you want to learn magic, remember that tricks are expensive often because one is paying for the secret. Catalog descriptions of effects are often missing something or are not completely true. The best way to learn magic is to get a good course, such as the Tarbell or the Mark Wilson courses.

As for consulting, remember that there are certain individuals who are egotistical and interested only in personal gain, but there are others who are ethical.

Loyd Auerbach

Knowing the psychology of magic is not the same thing as knowing how to perform single effects; there are entertainment and showmanship aspects that are very important.

To learn magic one can (1) go to magic shops and learn from the dealers; (2) attend conventions and witness close-up and stage shows, talk to dealers, and attend lectures; (3) observe close-up magicians in any context; or (4) read the catalogs. Magicians do give lessons, but this may be an expensive way to learn. Magicians can teach, given that there is a fine line between telling how a trick is done and teaching how to do it.

But no matter how much you learn, don't become immune to suspicion. When designing a new experiment, we may want to ask, "Is it Randi-proof?" Knowledge of magic can help point us to where the answer to that question may lie.

In parapsychology, the principles of magic apply everywhere, from experimental design to spontaneous cases or to someone merely reporting a psychic experience whose cause may be a misperception or misunderstanding of an ordinary event. In addition, one must learn that parsimony applies equally well in magic as in parapsychology.

It is also possible for psi to imitate magic. There are anecdotes among magicians and mentalists of information "coming through" during their acts and even cases in which apparatus was broken but worked anyway.

As for consulting magicians, my attempt to create a directory of magicians has met with only ten responses. According to Ray Corbin of SAM, members may not volunteer until a specific request comes in.

EXAMPLES OF A NEED FOR CONJURING KNOWLEDGE

George P. Hansen (Psychophysical Research Laboratories,
    301 College Rd. East, Princeton, NJ 08540)

At the 1976 PA convention, Martin Johnson arranged for a magician to perform. The magician was so effective that 10 to 20 parapsychologists suggested that he was using psychic means to accomplish his feats (EJP, Nov. 1976, 1-5). After such an incident, one might expect parapsychologists to educate themselves on magic; however, this seems not to be the case.

When scientists report observations and analyses in a professional journal, they imply that they have the technical competence to make such observations and the expertise to evaluate them. The evidence suggests that a number of psi researchers do not realize their limits of expertise in the area of conjuring. To illustrate the point, I will cite a number of articles in which researchers have commented on magic or detection of fraud, and I will give a magician's perspective on these comments. Because of limitations of space and because of the ethical guidelines of magicians, I will not describe specific methods of accomplishing effects. As a result, some of my comments might seem rather cryptic.

Haraldsson and Osis (JASPR, 1977, 33-43) reported observing

Sai Baba produce a number of ostensible PK effects. Part of the article reported observations made in order to detect fraud. To a reader knowledgeable in conjuring, the types of observations described would be unlikely to reveal fraud.

Eisenbud reported an investigation of Susie Cottrell who apparently used ESP to guess cards. Randi has explained a method involving a standard card trick which she might have used to control the experiment and manipulate the cards (The Skeptical Inquirer, Spring 1981, 68-71). The method is entirely consistent with Eisenbud's report.

Thalbourne and Shafer (RIP 1982, 62-64) discussed the use of a radio transmitter to circumvent security measures in a GESP experiment with feedback to the sender. They claimed that there should be semantic correspondences between the target and response if a transmitter were used. However, even a brief glance at some of the advertisements for these devices in magic periodicals would reveal that such correspondences would not necessarily be expected.

Giovetti (Theta, Summer 1984, 29-31) described her observations of an Italian medium. The descriptions were essentially identical to those of magic tricks. The article included no discussion of trickery or any alternative explanations. It is surprising to note that the editors of Theta are rather prominent members of the PA.

On the other side of the coin, Anderson (JASPR, 1985, 283-288) discussed behaviors of D.D. Home that he thought were suspicious. One of the behaviors would suggest to a layman that trickery might be used; however, to a magician, the opposite is suggested.

At the 1983 PA convention, there was another roundtable on magic. One would hope that this would have made researchers a bit more alert to the need for familiarity with that area and a bit more circumspect when commenting professionally. The articles by Giovetti and Anderson indicate that this has not happened.

Part 4: Invited Address

THERAPEUTIC TOUCH: REPORT OF RESEARCH IN PROGRESS*

Janet F. Quinn (College of Nursing, University of South
  Carolina, Columbia, SC 29208)

Background

Therapeutic Touch (TT) is a derivative of the laying-on of hands but does not take place within a religious context. TT was derived from the laying-on of hands by Dora Kunz and Dolores Krieger. During research studies on the laying-on of hands Kunz and Krieger had the opportunity to observe hours of healing by Oscar Estebany. Krieger began to practice the technique, receiving guidance and feedback from Kunz and Estebany, and became quite effective. Convinced that the ability to use Therapeutic Touch was a natural human potential and also aware of the role that touch plays in virtually every nursing act, Krieger and Kunz taught the newly evolved practice of Therapeutic Touch to a group of registered nurses in 1974. Since then, Therapeutic Touch has been taught to thousands of nurses and other health-care professionals in the United States and foreign countries. Workshops and formal courses in Therapeutic Touch have been offered on dozens of university campuses, and research on Therapeutic Touch is growing in quantity and quality.

Theoretical Framework

There are many frameworks within which one might examine a phenomenon such as Therapeutic Touch. However, when reviewing the literature in this area, one recognizes that a theory has been proposed. Although phrased differently by each of the investigators, the fundamental concept about which they speak is the same. The theory that they have proposed, which remains untested,

---

*This research is funded by the Department of Health and Human Services, Public Health Service, Division of Nursing Research, for the period September 1984-September 1987. © Janet F. Quinn.

suggests that when a person utilizes his or her intent to help or to heal a subject, an energy transfer takes place between them, stimulating the subject towards greater wellness. This conceptualization of people interacting with others in the environment via an energy exchange is one of the tenets of Nursing Science as developed by Martha Rogers (1970).

Within this conceptual system, people are viewed as four-dimensional, negentropic energy fields engaged in a continuous, mutual process with the four-dimensional, negentropic environmental energy field. "The human field extends beyond the discernable mass which we perceive as man" and is coextensive with the environmental energy field (Rogers, 1970, p. 90).

The view of person and environment as being inseparable and coextensive with the universe is a fundamental component of the major Eastern philosophies, while modern physicists are increasingly coming to the same conclusion. Guillemin (1968), in discussing quantum field theory states that "fields alone are real, ... they are the substance of the universe" (p. 175). However, there have been no investigations to date that measure interaction between individual human fields. The reality of such interaction is therefore taken as axiomatic.

Rogers postulates that all changes in the human field occur via a rhythmic flow of energy waves as the field engages in interaction with the environmental energy field. "Interaction between the human and environmental fields takes place across the conceptual boundaries of these two fields" (p. 90). Rogers defines the environmental field as "all that which is external to a given human field" (p. 97). By definition, then, when one person interacts with another, there is an interaction of fields as they become the immediate environment of each other. If a change then occurs within either person, it is considered to be an outcome of this field interaction. Quinn (1982) demonstrated that Therapeutic Touch done without physical contact between the practitioner and the subject could significantly decrease state anxiety. This study lends support to the theory of energy exchange as the basis for Therapeutic Touch (Quinn, 1984).

Purpose

The purpose of this project is to test the effectiveness of the nursing intervention of Therapeutic Touch in the reduction of anxiety in preoperative cardiac surgery patients. Specifically, this project seeks to determine the effect of Therapeutic Touch on anxiety, as measured by self-evaluation and two physiologic indices, immediately following treatment and one hour after treatment, in patients who will undergo open-heart surgery on the day following intervention. The following hypotheses are being tested:

(1) There will be a greater decrease from pretreatment scores in self-evaluated state anxiety scores immediately following treatment in subjects treated with Therapeutic Touch than in subjects treated with Mimic Therapeutic Touch or no treatment.

(2) There will be a greater decrease from pretreatment systolic blood pressure in systolic blood pressure immediately following treatment in subjects treated with Therapeutic Touch than in subjects treated with Mimic Therapeutic Touch or no treatment.

(3) There will be a greater decrease from pretreatment heart rate in heart rate immediately following treatment in subjects treated with Therapeutic Touch than in subjects treated with Mimic Therapeutic Touch or no treatment.

(4) There will be a greater decrease from pretreatment scores in self-evaluated state anxiety scores one hour after treatment in subjects who are treated with Therapeutic Touch than in subjects treated with Mimic Therapeutic Touch or no treatment.

(5) There will be a greater decrease from pretreatment systolic blood pressure in systolic blood pressure one hour after treatment in subjects treated with Therapeutic Touch than in subjects treated with Mimic Therapeutic Touch or no treatment.

(6) There will be a greater decrease from pretreatment heart rate in heart rate one hour after treatment in subjects who are treated with Therapeutic Touch than in subjects treated with Mimic Therapeutic Touch or no treatment.

Selected Literature Review

Research about Therapeutic Touch is built on the work of Bernard Grad, Sister Justa Smith, and Dolores Krieger. These researchers studied the phenomenon of laying-on of hands and all utilized Oscar Estebany as the healer. Laying-on of hands was found to increase the rate of wound healing in mice (Grad, Cadoret, and Paul, 1961; Grad, 1965); the rate of growth in plants (Grad, 1963, 1964); the rate of activity of the enzyme trypsin (Smith, 1972); and the level of human hemoglobin (Krieger, 1972, 1973, 1974).

Research to date indicates that Therapeutic Touch can increase human hemoglobin level (Krieger, 1975); induce physiologic relaxation (Krieger, Peper, and Ancoli, 1979), and decrease state anxiety (Heidt, 1981; Quinn, 1982). Studies directly related to this project will now be reviewed.

Heidt (1981) examined the effects of Therapeutic Touch on the anxiety of hospitalized cardiovascular patients. Building on the work of Krieger, Peper, and Ancoli (1979), which had indicated that Therapeutic Touch seems to elicit a state of physiologic relaxation, Heidt sought to measure its effect on psychologic anxiety/relaxation. She reasoned that physiologic relaxation is incompatible with psychologic anxiety and that if Therapeutic Touch could influence levels of physiologic relaxation, it should also influence one's subjective experience of anxiety. Three groups of 30 hospitalized, cardiovascular patients were utilized in this study, for a total of 90 subjects. All subjects completed the A-State Self-Evaluation Questionnaire (Spielberger, Gorsuch, and Lushene, 1970), and were then assigned to treatment group A, B, or C. Group A received Therapeutic Touch, which was defined as a derivative of the laying-on of hands that uses the hands to direct excess energies from a person in the role of healer to another for the purpose of helping or healing that individual. Group B received treatment by casual touch, which was defined as an intervention in which the nurse takes the subjects' apical and radial pulses and both pedal pulses. Group C received no touch, which was defined as an intervention in which the nurse sits beside the subjects and talks to the subject without touching.

Following the interventions, the A-State Self-Evaluation Questionnaire was readministered, and pretest-posttest means were computed. Comparison of pretest and posttest means in the Therapeutic Touch group revealed a difference which was statistically significant. Heidt's hypothesis that subjects treated with Therapeutic Touch would experience a reduction in state anxiety was supported. There was no significant decrease in state anxiety in either the casual-touch or no-touch groups.

In 1982, Quinn replicated Heidt's study with several differences. The focus of this study was the explication of the means by which the nursing intervention of Therapeutic Touch is effective. Specifically, this research was designed to test the theorem that Therapeutic Touch without physical contact would have the same effect as Therapeutic Touch with physical contact. This theorem was derived from the broader conceptual system developed by Rogers which suggests that the effects of Therapeutic Touch are outcomes of an energy exchange between two human energy fields. Since the effects on state anxiety of Therapeutic Touch with physical contact are known, state anxiety was utilized as a measure of the efficacy of Therapeutic Touch without physical contact. It was hypothesized that there would be a greater decrease in posttest state anxiety scores in subjects treated with Non-Contact Therapeutic Touch than in subjects treated with Mimic Therapeutic Touch.

A group of 60 cardiovascular patients completed the STAI self-evaluation questionnaire and were then randomly assigned to receive a Non-Contact Therapeutic Touch treatment or a Mimic Therapeutic Touch treatment. Both groups completed the questionnaire at the completion of the treatments. A partial correlation between treatment group and posttest scores, removing the effects of pretest score, yielded a significant correlation of 0.3321 with $p < .0005$, which indicated that the experimental group scores decreased significantly more than the control group scores. There was a highly significant mean decrease of 6.73 points (17%) in the anxiety scores of experimental subjects, while no significant difference occurred in the control groups.

The findings of this study are almost identical to those of Heidt. Heidt utilized a contact Therapeutic Touch intervention with her subjects, hospitalized on the same cardiovascular unit utilized in the Quinn study. When pretest-posttest differences in state anxiety, as measured by the STAI questionnaire, were computed for Heidt's group, a mean of 6.90 was obtained. Thus, the effects on state anxiety of Therapeutic Touch with contact and those of Therapeutic Touch without contact appear to be virtually identical. It appears that the variable of physical contact is not important in explaining the effectiveness of Therapeutic Touch. This finding supports the energy-exchange explanatory model of the effects of Therapeutic Touch. Furthermore, confidence in the effectiveness of Therapeutic Touch, with or without contact, in the reduction of state anxiety is increased by the similarity between the Quinn and Heidt findings.

Definition of Terms

Therapeutic Touch: An intervention which is a derivative of laying-on of hands in that it uses the hands to direct excess body energies from a person playing the role of healer to another person for the purpose of helping or healing the individual (Krieger, 1973). In treating a subject with Therapeutic Touch, the nurse

(1) asks the subject to turn onto his or her side in bed;

(2) stands facing the subject's back and centers herself by shifting her awareness from an external to an internal focus, thus becoming relaxed and calm;

(3) makes the intention mentally to therapeutically assist the subject;

(4) moves her hands over the body of the subject from head to feet, attuning to the condition of the subject by becoming aware of changes in sensory cues in her hands;

(5) redirects areas of accumulated tension in the subject's body by movement of the hands;

(6) concentrates her attention on the specific direction of these energies, using her hands as focal points;

(7) directs energy to the subject by placing the hands four to six inches from the subject's body, one in the area of the solar plexus (just below the waist) and one behind the subject's back, and leaves them in this area for approximately 120 seconds. Total time for this intervention is five minutes.

Mimic Therapeutic Touch: An intervention that imitates the movements of the nurse during Therapeutic Touch but during which there is no attempt to center, no intention to assist the subject, no attuning to the condition of the subject, and no direction of energy. In treating a client with Mimic Therapeutic Touch, the nurse

(1) asks the subject to turn onto his or her side in bed;

(2) stands facing the subject's back and makes the intention to imitate the movements of Therapeutic Touch;

(3) focuses her attention on mentally subtracting from 100 by 7s;

(4) moves her hands over the body of the subject from head to feet while continuing to subtract from 100 by 7s;

(5) returns to the subject's head and repeats step 3;

(6) places her hands four to six inches from the subject's body, one in the area of the solar plexus (just below the waist), and the other behind the subject's back, and begins to count backwards from 240;

(7) removes her hands when she has counted down to zero. Total time for this intervention is five minutes.

State Anxiety: A transitory emotional state or condition of the human organism that is characterized by subjective, consciously perceived feelings of tension and apprehension and heightened autonomic nervous system activity. State anxiety (A-States) may vary in intensity and fluctuate over time (Spielberger, 1966). Subjective state anxiety is being measured by the Self-Evaluation Questionnaire, STAI Form X-1, developed by Spielberger, Gorsuch, and Lushene (1970).

Heart Rate: The number of heart beats per minute as counted at the radial pulse site by the research assistant.

Systolic Blood Pressure: The whole number, in mm Hg, at which the first Korotkoff sound is heard following cuff deflation, as measured by an aneroid sphygmomanometer and stethoscope.

Intervention Groups

To determine the effects of Therapeutic Touch on preoperative anxiety, three groups are being utilized: the experimental group, which receives Therapeutic Touch as defined; a control group which receives Mimic Therapeutic Touch as defined; and a second control group which receives no treatment. The rationale for the two control groups is as follows.

Mimic Therapeutic Touch

It has been well established in the literature that patients may be assisted toward greater well-being when they perceive the presence of a health care professional as "helping." To control for this effect, a second intervention has been designed.

Therapeutic Touch has been described as a "healing meditation" (Peper and Ancoli, 1979). During the practice of Therapeutic Touch, the healer shifts his or her consciousness and becomes totally focused without effort upon the healing touch; no other thoughts enter awareness (Krieger, 1979, p. 36). This shift in consciousness is postulated to be the means by which the practitioner is able to attune to the client's condition and to direct energy.

To maintain ordinary consciousness, the nurse performs a mental operation known as "serial sevens," subtracting from 100 by 7. This is a well-known technique utilized in psychiatry to test patients' cognitive ability and capacity to sustain logical, rationale thought (Eisenman and Dubbert, 1978). Intervention by Mimic Therapeutic Touch thus has been designed to prevent the nurse from shifting her consciousness into the "healing meditation" while simultaneously mimicking the movements of the Therapeutic Touch process.

This control treatment was developed by Quinn in an earlier study (1982). Prior to the use of the intervention in that study, a videotape was made of nurses administering the experimental intervention and nurses administering the control intervention. A panel of 15 naive observers was provided with the operational definitions of each intervention. To establish the fidelity of the interventions, the videotape was shown to the observers, and they were asked to identify each of the observed interventions as Therapeutic Touch or the control intervention, or to indicate they did not know. If the observers were able to identify the interventions correctly, then the control intervention would require adaptation to make it appear more like the experimental intervention.

By chance alone, one would expect that a mean of 2 out of 6 interventions would be correctly identified (i.e., the probability of success on a single trial equals 1/3). With N = 15, the mean number of correctly identified interventions was 1.9. Thus, the panel of naive observers was unable to differentiate between the experimental intervention and the control intervention. This control treatment has now been utilized in at least three studies on Therapeutic Touch in three different graduate programs.

No-Treatment Group

One group of subjects will be measured on all dependent variables in the same time frame as the other two groups, but with no intervening treatment. This intervention is designed as further control for the effects of person, placebo effect, the Hawthorne effect, and chance differences between treatment groups.

Administration of Therapeutic Touch and Mimic Therapeutic Touch Interventions

The principal investigator administers both the real and the Mimic Therapeutic Touch interventions. Since the difference between the interventions, as defined, is the state of consciousness and intent of the practitioner during the intervention, one person can theoretically administer both interventions, provided that he or she is able to administer the "real" Therapeutic Touch. The investigator was taught Therapeutic Touch by its originator, Dr. Dolores Krieger, and has had over ten years of experience in practicing Therapeutic Touch. In addition, the investigator provided 4 of the 30 Therapeutic Touch treatments administered in an earlier study (Quinn, 1982). When the decreases in anxiety score obtained by the investigator were compared to those obtained by three other experienced Therapeutic Touch practitioners, no significant difference was found (p. 65). Thus, the investigator is qualified and capable of administering the experimental treatment of Therapeutic Touch.

In a previous study (Quinn, 1982), both interventions were administered by nurses other than the investigators. That design is superior to the design described herein. However, at the present time the investigator is the only nurse in the state known to practice Therapeutic Touch. Thus, unless treatments are provided by the investigator, the study could not be done.

The use of the investigator to administer both the experimental (Therapeutic Touch) and control (Mimic Therapeutic Touch) treatments contributes both strengths and weakness to the study design. There are two strengths of this method. First, the subjects are exposed to the same person. Any differences in posttest measures should not, therefore, be attributable to the subjects' varying responses to different attributes of the treatment nurse, such as general appearance, affect, voice, etc. Second, the research assistants as well as other patients and staff personnel are blind to which subjects receive which intervention. Since it is known that the investigator is the only local nurse who utilizes Therapeutic Touch, subjects' group assignment could be easily identified by the presence or absence of the investigator as the treatment nurse. This is the major reason for having the investigator administer both interventions rather than only the experimental intervention.

The necessity of utilizing the principal investigator to administer both interventions introduces a threat to the internal validity of the study. It is possible that the investigator could introduce bias by behaving in subtly different ways while interacting with each intervention group, even while following the protocols for each intervention. Several steps are being taken to minimize this threat.

The first precaution against the introduction of subtle differences between the treatments given to each group involves a change in the position of the investigator, vis-a-vis the subject, during treatment. In previous studies no attempt was made to limit face-to-face contact between the treatment nurse and the subject. Since it seems possible that the facial expression and amount of eye contact during treatment might influence outcomes and that there could be subtle, unconscious differences in these behaviors between the Therapeutic Touch and Mimic Therapeutic Touch groups, the investigator stands behind the subject during both treatments. Subjects are asked to stay in bed and turn onto whichever side is comfortable to them prior to treatment. The investigator simultaneously moves one hand over the front of the subject and one hand over the back, from head to foot. Thus, the subject will be between the hands of the investigator but will not be touched and will not be able to see the investigator. By having the experimenter stand behind the subject instead of face the subject, differences in her facial expression during each intervention become irrelevant.

The second precaution involves independent, blind judging of the two interventions prior to their use in the study. In a laboratory on campus, the investigator administered three Therapeutic Touch interventions and three Mimic Therapeutic Touch interventions, as defined in this study. These interventions were administered in random order. Seven naive observers in the laboratory were given definitions of each intervention. Following their observation of each intervention, they were asked to indicate which intervention they believed they just witnessed or to indicate that they did not know. The administration of the interventions was also videotaped. Forty-one naive observers viewed the interventions on videotape and completed the same procedure as the laboratory observers.

Analysis of the data revealed that the observers were unable to identify the interventions at a rate better than chance would allow. There were no differences in the rate of correct identifications between those who viewed the interventions live versus taped. Interestingly, the volunteer treatment subject, who was also blind to the sequence, correctly identified all interventions.

A final precaution against the introduction of investigator bias relates to the data collection procedure. All pre- and post-test measures are taken and recorded by research assistants who are blind to subjects' intervention group. Individual subject assignment is being recorded by the investigator in a separate data file. The investigator enters this information from a coded index card.

Although a doubleblind design can increase confidence in the internal validity of a study, it is not possible to construct such a design in this case. Since Therapeutic Touch involves the conscious use of self to help or to heal, the practitioner, by definition, knows that he or she is providing the intervention. This situation is not unique to studies on Therapeutic Touch but would apply to any study of any intervention that requires the practitioner to do something differently.

Limitations of the Operational Definition of the Independent Variable

The major distinctions between the Therapeutic Touch and Mimic Therapeutic Touch interventions are the state of consciousness and intent of the practitioner and the transfer of energy which takes place during Therapeutic Touch. At the present time, there are no appropriate measures available which can document either of these elements of the Therapeutic Touch process in a field-study setting.

Since Therapeutic Touch has been called a "healing meditation" (Peper and Ancoli, 1979), it would seem possible to utilize electroencephalography (EEG) during the Therapeutic Touch process to monitor the state of consciousness of the practitioner. This, in fact, has been done in a small laboratory utilizing one practitioner (Krieger, Peper, and Ancoli, 1979). At least two factors would preclude this method of measurement during clinical trials. First, the introduction into the clinical setting of the equipment required to monitor EEG patterns of the practitioner during Therapeutic Touch would be quite disruptive. Second, the monitoring of at least 100 interventions (50 Therapeutic Touch and 50 Mimic Therapeutic Touch) and then obtaining interpretation of each 5-minute EEG reading, would be extremely expensive.

A subjective measure of the practitioner's ability to do

Therapeutic Touch and thus alter his or her state of consciousness was developed at New York University as part of a nursing Research Emphasis Grant (Winstead-Fry, 1983). An expert in meditation interviewed Dr. Krieger and four other nurses experienced in Therapeutic Touch. From these data, a questionnaire (SETTS) was developed which contained 78 self-report items related to the subjective experience of doing Therapeutic Touch. The questionnaire was tested in a sample of 250 experienced and nonexperienced Therapeutic Touch practitioners. Data analysis revealed that the SETTS can distinguish between experienced and nonexperienced Therapeutic Touch practitioners with a reliability of .97.

As a measure of whether or not the investigator is experienced in Therapeutic Touch, the SETTS questionnaire could be completed by the investigator and analyzed. However, the investigator is not naive with respect to the tool. The investigator was one of the persons interviewed for the development of the tool and also reviewed the tool after its completion. Thus, the use of the tool in this instance would be inappropriate. In addition, this investigator is not convinced that one's performance on the questionnaire can predict one's performance of Therapeutic Touch. Subsequent work with the instrument might clarify this point.

At the present time, there are no measures known which can document energy exchange between two human fields. This assumption about the nature of Therapeutic Touch is a working hypothesis derived from the Rogerian conceptual system (Rogers, 1970) which remains to be tested (Quinn, 1984).

The lack of measures to document that a given practitioner is actually doing Therapeutic Touch is of concern to the researchers in this field and presents a problem which is ripe for further investigation. It would, however, seem premature to invest a large amount of time and money into research on the nature of the Therapeutic Touch process until the process has been adequately demonstrated to produce outcomes. If the Therapeutic Touch process, which as yet is poorly understood, can be shown to produce measurable outcomes through vigorous, controlled investigation, then future investigators will have a plethora of questions to explore. Some of the questions relative to the actual Therapeutic Touch process have been raised by Quinn (1982) and include: Can the process of "centering" be measured? Do all nurses administering Therapeutic Touch enter the same state of consciousness? Does the particular state of consciousness correlate with the outcomes of the treatment? Does amount of experience correlate with the state of consciousness of the practitioner and/or treatment outcome? All of these questions lend themselves to laboratory study rather than clinical field study.

Until the nature of Therapeutic Touch is better understood and measurable, perhaps the best indicators of whether or not a given person can do Therapeutic Touch are training and experience with the process. The investigator has a significant amount of both, as discussed. One final note would seem appropriate. If the nurse (in this case, the investigator) who is administering the Therapeutic Touch treatments is not doing Therapeutic Touch, the outcome of the study will not support the hypotheses that Therapeutic Touch has a positive outcome. Indeed, the administration of Mimic Therapeutic Touch treatment, as described earlier, produced no difference in anxiety. Thus, the risk is in the direction of falsely finding Therapeutic Touch to be noneffective rather than falsely supporting its effectiveness.

Method

The Sample

The sample for this study is composed of male and female subjects admitted to a private, nonprofit hospital the day before open-heart surgery. A minimum of 150 subjects will be included in the sample. Subjects who are unable to complete the English version of the Self-Evaluation Questionnaire are excluded from the sample.

Instruments

The Self-Evaluation Questionnaire (STAI) Form X-1 (Spielberger, Gorsuch, Lushene, 1970) is utilized to measure State Anxiety pre and post intervention in all groups. The A-State (State Anxiety) scale consists of 20 statements that ask the subject to indicate "how you feel right now, that is, at this moment." Subjects respond to such statements as "I feel calm"; "I feel anxious"; "I feel at ease"; "I am worried" by marking "not at all"; "somewhat"; "moderately so"; or "very much so" on the questionnaire. The scale is balanced for acquiescence set, with ten directly scored and ten reversed items. The STAI was originally developed as a research instrument for investigating anxiety in normal (nonpsychiatrically disturbed) adults. The tool has well-established reliability and validity.

Systolic Blood Pressure

Blood pressure is measure by a Tycos Aneroid sphygmomanometer and a Littman 2125 stethoscope. Calibration is checked at the start of each session by ascertaining that the needle of the gauge is at zero and within the "pointer-in-oval" accuracy range. The same stethoscope and sphygmomanometer are being utilized throughout the study.

Heart Rate

Heart rate is measured by manual palpation and counting of the radial pulse for one full minute.

All measurements on a given subject are taken by the same research assistant to eliminate variation in pre and post measures which might occur due to differences in sensitivity. The research assistants are registered nurses, who are thus well qualified to measure blood pressure and heart rate.

Procedure for Random Assignment to Groups

(1) The Principal Investigator (PI) prepares index cards for each data collection day in groups of thirty cards. Fifteen cards carry a designation of Therapeutic Touch and fifteen indicate Mimic Therapeutic Touch as the treatment to be administered to subjects enrolled in the study on a given day. An additional indication of which of the subjects (first or second of the day) is assigned to the no-treatment group appears on each card.

(2) Each card is placed in an opaque, unmarked envelope, and the envelope is sealed by the PI. The envelopes are shuffled and given to the research assistant (RA).

(3) The RA consecutively numbers the envelopes and brings one numbered envelope to the clinical site on each data collection day.

(4) The PI opens the envelope in a private location, notes the assigned treatments for the day, and records subjects' code numbers on the card as they are enrolled.

Procedure for Data Collection

The data collection procedures were designed to keep the data collector (research assistant) blind to the subjects' assigned treatment group.

(1) The PI and RA consult with the technician in charge of the surgery schedule for the purpose of identifying preoperative open-heart surgery patients.

(2) The name of each patient who meets the criteria is written in the data collection book in the order in which it is given by the technician.

(3) The PI solicits participation from potential subjects beginning with those patients housed on the uppermost hospital floor and working down through the hospital.

(4) An explanation of the research proposal is offered to each potential subject by the PI and willingness to participate determined.

(5) If the subject is willing to participate in the study, written consent is obtained.

(6) The RA takes the subject's blood pressure.

(7) The RA takes the subject's heart rate for one full minute.

(8) The RA provides brief instructions and administers the Self-Evaluation Questionnaire. She advises the subject that she will return in 10 minutes to pick up the completed questionnaire.

(9) When the RA instructs the PI that all pretest data have been collected, the PI administers the designated treatment after a brief explanation to the subject.

(10) When the PI informs the research assistant that the treatment has been completed, the RA returns to the subject's room and takes the heart rate and blood pressure. The Self-Evaluation Questionnaire is then readministered.

(11) The RA advises the subject that she will return in one hour to repeat the measurements.

(12) The RA compiles the demographic data.

(13) One hour after initial posttesting is completed, the RA takes the subject's heart rate and blood pressure and administers the Self-Evaluation Questionnaire for the final time.

(14) When all final measurements have been completed and entered in the subject's file, the PI provides the subject with the opportunity to ask questions and/or discuss the experience. The PI thanks the subject.

Data Analysis

Each of the six hypotheses will be tested using the Analysis of Covariance procedure (ANCOVA). Six separate one-way ANCOVAs will be performed. The pretreatment measures of state anxiety, blood pressure, and pulse will be used as the covariates for the analysis of covariance procedure. All hypotheses will be tested at the .05 level of significance.

The use of ANCOVA will increase the precision of the randomization procedure by statistically removing any preexisting differences on any of the dependent variables which may exist in the treatment groups prior to treatment (Wildt and Ahtola, 1978).

REFERENCES

Eisenman, E.J.P., and Dubbert, P.M. (1978). The mental health assessment interview. In B.A. Backer, P.M. Dubbert, and E.J.P. Eisenman, Psychiatric/mental health nursing: Contemporary readings (pp. 7-30). New York: D. Van Nostrand Co., Inc.

Grad, B. (1963). A telekinetic effect on plant growth. International Journal of Parapsychology, 5(2), 117-133.

Grad, B. (1964). A telekinetic effect on plant growth II. International Journal of Parapsychology, 6(4), 473-498.

Grad, B. (1965). Some biological effects of the "laying on of hands": A review of experiments with animals and plants. Journal of the American Society for Psychical Research, 59, 95-129.

Grad, B., Cadoret, R.J., and Paul, G.I. (1961). An unorthodox method of wound healing in mice. International Journal of Parapsychology, 3(2), 5-24.

Guillemin, V. (1968). The story of quantum physics. New York: Charles Scribner's Sons.

Heidt, P. (1981). Effect of therapeutic touch on anxiety level of hospitalized patients. Nursing Research, 30, 32-37.

Krieger, D. (1972). The response of in-vivo human hemoglobin to an active healing therapy by direct laying-on of hands. Human Dimensions, 1, 12-15.

Krieger, D. (1973). The relationship of touch, with the intent to help or heal, to subjects' in-vivo hemoglobin values: A study in personalized interaction. In Proceedings of the Ninth American Nurses' Association Research Conference. New York: American Nurses' Association.

Krieger, D. (1974). Healing by the laying-on of hands as a facilitator of bioenergetic change: The response of in-vivo human hemoglobin. Psychoenergetic Systems, 1, 121-129.

Krieger, D. (1975). Therapeutic Touch: The imprimatur of nursing. American Journal of Nursing, 75, 784-787.

Krieger, D. (1979). The therapeutic touch. Englewood Cliffs, NJ: Prentice-Hall.

Krieger, D., Peper, E., and Ancoli, S. (1979). Therapeutic Touch: Searching for evidence of physiological change. American Journal of Nursing, 79, 660-662.

Peper, E., and Ancoli, S. (1979). Two endpoints of an EEG continuum of meditation--alpha/theta and fast beta. In D. Krieger, The therapeutic touch. Englewood Cliffs, NJ: Prentice-Hall.

Quinn, J.F. (1982). An investigation of the effects of therapeutic touch done without physical contact on state anxiety of hospitalized cardiovascular patients. Doctoral Dissertation. New York University. Available through University Microfilms, Ann Arbor, Michigan.

Quinn, J.F. (1984). Therapeutic touch as energy exchange: Testing the theory. Advances in Nursing Science, 6, 42-49.

Rogers, M.E. (1970). An introduction to the theoretical basis of nursing. Philadelphia: F.A. Davis Company.

Smith, M.J. (1972). Paranormal effects on enzyme activity. Human Dimensions, 1, 15-19.

Spielberger, C.D. (1966). Anxiety and behavior. Volume 1. New York: Academic Press.

Spielberger, C.D., Gorsuch, R.L., and Lushene, R.E. (1970). STAI manual for the state-trait inventory. Palo Alto, CA: Consulting Psychologists Press, Inc.

Wildt, A.R., and Ahtola, O.T. (1978). Analysis of covariance. Beverly Hills, CA: Sage Publications.

Winstead-Fry, P. (1983). A report to the profession. New York: New York University, Division of Nursing.

Part 5: Presidential Address*

THOUGHTS ON THE ROLE OF MEANING IN PSI RESEARCH**

Debra H. Weiner (Institute for Parapsychology, Box 6847, Durham, NC 27708)[††]

I'd like to begin by describing how I came to think about the role of meaning and meaningfulness in psi research. Many of you will recognize in this description the conceptual history of parapsychology since the "paradigm shift" of 1976, the year that the experimenter effect was brought forcefully to our collective awareness by the nearly simultaneous publication of four important articles on the topic (Kennedy and Taddonio, 1976; Thouless, 1976; White, 1976a, 1976b). When you recognize that I was born into professional parapsychology the year the experimenter effect hit the journals, you may understand why it has dominated my thinking.

As most of you know, the idea that the experimenter plays a key role in the success of laboratory psi research was certainly not new 10 years ago; differences among experimenters' success rates had been observed since the beginning of the Duke research (Rhine, 1934). What was new in 1976 was the suggestion that this differential success was not caused by the experimenters' varying abilities to charm or motivate their subjects into outstanding performances, as had previously been believed, but by the experimenters' varying psi abilities. In other words, the new perspective was that successful parapsychological results may come about because of the experimenter's, not the subjects', psychic intervention. This was called the "psi-based experimenter effect" and is a manifestation of a larger issue called the "source-of-psi problem": the inability to pinpoint definitively the party (or parties) responsible for a certain psi effect.

---
*Chaired by Robert L. Morris (University of Edinburgh).
**Delivered August 7, 1986.
[††]I would like to thank Drs. Richard S. Broughton and John Palmer for their helpful comments on an earlier draft of this Address. I would also like to acknowledge my debt to the work of Drs. Walter von Lucadou and Klaus Kornwachs which inspired much of my thinking in this paper.

The psi-based experimenter effect has serious implications which were immediately grasped by parapsychologists.[1] In certain cases, such as when a person thought to be psychically gifted performs well in a variety of tests with different experimenters, we have some measure of confidence that the subject is indeed the psi source. However, in a large number of experiments, particularly those testing typical volunteers not selected for any evidence of psi talent, this confidence is weaker. This is a problem, of course, because if we cannot know for sure that the subjects are producing the effects, then in many cases we cannot interpret the results. For example, if the experimenter is actually the person psychically biasing a random event generator (REG) in a PK experiment, then a significant correlation between PK scores and, say, extraversion scores may have nothing to do with a genuine relationship between personality and psi performance but may merely be a psychically produced fulfillment--albeit an unintentional one--of the experimenter's desire to support his or her hypothesis.

In my research, I dealt with the source-of-psi problem in one of two ways. In some cases I, like may other parapsychologists, chose to ignore the problem and to go ahead to test correlates of psi performance among unselected subjects, justifying this decision on the basis that (1) I don't perceive myself as being particularly psychic, so didn't feel I had much to worry about; and (2) I believed that finding relationships between subjects' psi performances and some personal characteristic and/or situational condition that would replicate across experimenters would obviate the problem of psi-based experimenter effects. In other cases I, usually in collaboration with Dick J. Bierman, investigated the source-of-psi problem by testing a particular manifestation of it which we called the "future-observer effect." This hypothesis stems from the observational theories (e.g., Schmidt, 1975; Walker, 1975) which propose that psi effects on random events occur as a consequence of the observation of the outcomes of those events by conscious beings. The future-observer effect (or, more appropriately, the "later-observer effect" [Houtkooper, 1983]) refers to the possibility that persons, such as experimenters or analyzers, who observe these outcomes after the subjects have observed them might also have some influence. However, in recent years my thoughts on the source-of-psi problem have taken a different turn, and I have become interested in its conceptual underpinnings and in considering what these underpinnings say about how we parapsychologists do our work and think about psi. It is this latter, more theoretical approach that has led me to tonight's topic.

Conceptual Foundations of the Source-of-Psi Problem

The hypothesis that experimenters may be the psi sources in some of their research rests on the combination of a number of impressions about the psi process that we have developed over the past few decades of research. I will review these rather quickly, as I suspect they are already quite familiar to you. One impression is that psi is relatively immune to the effects of distance or temporal factors. The implication of this for the source-of-psi problem is that the fact that the experimenter is, say, thirty feet away from the REG when the subject is only two feet away does not make it less likely that the experimenter could have influenced the machine. Another impression is that psi is relatively immune to the effects of task complexity. "Task complexity" here refers to the number of steps required to successfully complete the psi task if it were being accomplished through normal means. For example, in the research technique known as "blind PK" (e.g., Osis, 1953), subjects are asked to influence the fall of dice to land with the target face upward. However, the subjects do not know which face, one through six, is the target; this information is hidden from them. The blind PK task can be modeled as a two-step process (Step 1: find out by ESP what the target face is; Step 2: use PK to make the dice land appropriately) as opposed to the standard one-step PK task. Despite the fact that blind PK entails a more complex task, subjects' success on it seems to be comparable to that on standard dice tasks.

Reviews of the PK literature by Stanford (1977) and Kennedy (1978) support the claim that PK is independent of task complexity, though a recent direct test of the claim suggests some modification of it (Vassy, 1986). Some (e.g., Braude, 1979b; Varvoglis, 1986) have argued that without knowing the limits of human information processing well enough to determine what is a "complex" task, a claim of psi's independence from task complexity is premature. These arguments notwithstanding, I think it is fair to say that at least within presently investigated levels of task complexity the parapsychological literature does not demonstrate a clear decline of success with increasing complexity.

The relevance of psi's apparent independence from task complexity for the source-of-psi problem is that a person cannot be ruled out as a potential psi source on the basis that his or her "task" in producing a particular result would be too complicated, would involve too many steps. For example, for our hypothetical experimenter studying a relationship between PK and extraversion scores to produce psychically a significant correlation, he or she would have to use ESP to discover the subjects' extraversion scores (since experimenters are typically kept blind to this information during the course of the study) and to use just enough PK influence on the REG to correspond to that subject's extraversion score. However, this is really no different from the blind PK task described above (use ESP to find the target and use PK to influence the random event to correspond to the target), so we have no reason for arguing on the basis of the complexity of the task that the experimenter could not have influenced the REG.

But the key element of the source-of-psi problem--and the one that has the most profound implications for the entire field of parapsychology--is that a person can use psi without being aware that he or she is doing so. After all, experimenters are not trying to psychically influence their results. To argue that they might be doing so unintentionally we must first determine if psi can be used without conscious intention.

Most of you are familiar with the literature on what has come to be known as "nonintentional psi." An example of a typical experiment is the nonintentional PK study of Stanford, Zenhausern, Taylor, and Dwyer (1975) in which scores on a distant random event generator determined whether or not subjects would be released from a boring task to participate in a more pleasant one. The researchers found that although subjects were not aware of the existence of the REG nor of the consequence of it for their immediate futures, significantly more subjects than would be expected on the basis of chance were released from the boring task. This line of research has been relatively successful and suggests that psi can be used unintentionally. (For a review of nonintentional ESP research, see Schechter, 1977.)

There is an amusing irony in the fact that research on nonintentional psi, which constitutes one of the principal foundations for the source-of-psi problem, is one of the few lines of research whose interpretation is not compromised by this problem! In a nonintentional psi experiment, no one--subject, experimenter, data checker, whoever--is engaging in conscious, purposive behavior relative to the task. So whether significant results are in reality due to subjects' nonintentional psi or the experimenter's nonintentional psi is irrelevant; the hypothesis that psi can occur in the absence of conscious intention is still supported.

Why this single factor should be of primary importance to the source-of-psi problem can be easily demonstrated in the following comparison. Let us assume that we live in a world where nonintentional psi is impossible. We design a PK experiment in which subjects are sealed in a cave 50 feet below the surface of the earth, with the PK device in a tower on a mountain top some 300 miles away. Suppose further that the PK task is not a simple one of biasing the REG output to produce more target than nontarget outcomes but rather involves the subject influencing the output to correspond to random firings of a cat's neuron being measured 100 miles away. Even under these challenging conditions, we would have no trouble--if nonintentional psi were impossible--in identifying the psi source: it is the person "wishing for hits" or otherwise engaged in some purposive behavior relative to the task. Contrast this hypothetical scenario to our present situation in parapsychology: with the possibility that psi can be used unintentionally, even the simplest experiment--a subject watching lights that glow when an REG hit is produced--cannot be unambiguously interpreted as subject psi.

With the possibility of nonintentional psi, then, we cannot know for sure that the operationally defined psi source is indeed the actual source. Therefore--and this is what makes the evidence for nonintentional psi so devastating for parapsychology--our conceptual link between an effect and source cannot be <u>defined</u> but must be <u>inferred</u>. Once an effect occurs, we make certain decisions about who we think produced that effect. Because parapsychologists often make these decisions implicitly, a study of them might provide a "royal road" into the assumptions underlying our concept of psi.

How Do We Link Source to Effect?

An examination of these decisions a few years ago led me to conclude that parapsychologists generally link the source to the effect through the concept of <u>benefit</u> or, more broadly, <u>motivation</u> (Weiner and Geller, 1984). In other words, parapsychologists seem to consider a person a possible psi source if that person would seem to benefit from a successful outcome and therefore would presumably be motivated to produce it, whether or not the person knew about the psi task at hand. Geller and I outlined some problems with this hypothesis and recently Varvoglis (1986) has added some others. However, I do not wish to review these arguments but rather to describe the reactions I received from other parapsychologists and how those reactions stimulated me to think about the roles of meaning and meaningfulness in psi research.

One of the problems in using the concept of benefit to determine who might be the psi source is that there is no logical basis for restricting attention to the potential benefit of significant results to just a few individuals (i.e., the subject or experimenter); one can propose ways in which significant results in psi experiments could theoretically benefit a variety of individuals. In our paper, we painted facetious scenarios: psi success is caused unintentionally by a high-school student who hates mathematics and is therefore motivated to create disturbing statistical anomalies; a significant reversal of an experimenter's pet hypothesis is caused unintentionally by the experimenter's family who wishes the experimenter would become frustrated with parapsychology and get a "real" job. Now, our purpose in offering these examples was not to suggest that disgruntled math students should seriously be considered potential psi sources but to stimulate parapsychologists to think about why we <u>don't</u> seriously entertain this possibility. Is it, as we asked in the paper, because parapsychologists actually <u>do not</u> believe that psi is independent of distance and therefore feel that the student is too far away from the laboratory to influence the results? Because the gratification of the student's desire would be too tangentially connected to the experimental outcome? What are our beliefs, our assumptions about psi, that make this example seem ludicrous?

We have not received any formal, published response to these questions[2] but informal comments from a few colleagues seemed to revolve around a similar theme: the math student is not a likely psi source because he or she is too conceptually remote from the experiment; the experiment is not meaningful to the student and the student is not meaningful to the experiment.

There are two rather distinct components of this statement. First, it says that parapsychologists' views of who may be a potential psi source are not necessarily based on who we think might benefit from the psi effect but rather on who we think might find the effect meaningful--a related but broader criterion. Secondly, it says that our view of who may be a potential psi source has to do with our conceptualization of the experiment and the role (or lack of it) someone plays in that conceptualization. What I hope to show here is (1) that these two components are intimately related, the first being a manifestation of the second; (2) that not only our determination of possible psi sources but our determination of what constitutes the psi event is based on personal frames of meaning that can vary from individual to individual; and (3) that in a certain sense the experimenter's frame of meaning, while private and subjective, takes on an objective reality and importance for the larger extrasubjective context.

Now that you have some sense of where we are headed, let us see how we get there. First, though, I need to digress a moment to clarify what I mean here by "meaning" and "meaningfulness."

Meaning has been studied and discussed by philosophers, cognitive psychologists, clinicians, anthropologists, sociolinguists, semioticians, phenomenologists, and a host of other students of human nature and society; I will not pretend to even try, in this short paper, to apply to parapsychology the fruits of their labors.[3] For the purposes of the present discussion, I will use the term "meaning" to denote a conceptual framework or understanding of an object, event, or concept, as in, for example, "this passage means such and such," though we need not restrict this usage to linguistic material. "Meaningfulness" will denote subjective valuation of an object, event, or concept (i.e., one's sense of its importance or value, as in the phrase "meaningful relationship"). Of course, these two concepts are not independent--for example, the definition of meaning implied in the phrase "What Freedom Means to Me" contains both cognitive and emotional dimensions--and some overlap of usage in the following discussion is unavoidable.

Meaningfulness: The Missing Link?

The view, then, that a psi source in a particular experiment is someone who would find the experimental outcome meaningful--personally important--is a broader view than one that considers only those persons who would seem to benefit from the outcome.

Of course, the concepts of benefit and meaningfulness are interrelated: if something benefits one, we expect it to be personally important and if something is particularly important (e.g., tests or challenges to someone with a high need for achievement) certain outcomes (e.g., success) will be especially beneficial. However, the concepts are not identical, and we can imagine ways in which one's perceptions of the meaningfulness of particular events would not map one-to-one against a measure of how much one would personally benefit from them.

This view of the source-effect link might suggest new theoretical analyses ("How is meaningfulness defined?") and new methologies ("How can we determine what is and is not meaningful to the experimenter or subject?"), both of which may be extremely useful. In fact, there have already been suggestions in the literature along these lines. However, for the present inquiry these new approaches beg the issue, for even before we ask these questions we have already implicitly decided who we are willing to consider as potential psi sources. We can just as easily ask how to measure the meaningfulness of our experimental results to our hypothetical math student, and thus we come back again, full circle, to the problem from which we started. It seems, then, that the more fundamental component of the problem is the second one described above: our view of who may be a potential psi source has to do with our conceptualization of the experiment. In other words, the hypothetical math student is excluded not because a successful outcome would not be personally important to him or her but because the student does not fit within the parapsychologist's mental structure of what constitutes the psi experiment. The conceptual link between this student and the REG results, quite simply, has no place within the parapsychologist's frame of meaning.

Meaning as the Sculptor of the Psi Experience

The idea that parapsychologists conceptually link the source to an effect on the basis of their personal frames of meaning has implications for <u>all</u> parapsychologists, experimentalists and field researchers alike, and not just for those trying to grapple with the source-of-psi problem. To appreciate this we need only look at what it is that we study.

Robert Morris (1980) hit the nail on the head when he wrote:

> If one examines the various anecdotes and experimental studies labeled as psychic by the parapsychological community, we find that in each case there is an observed organismic event or set of events that appears to resemble an environmental event or set of events in some meaningful way, meaningfulness determined by observer criteria [p. 1].

To avoid some confusion and to incorporate some of Morris's later statements (p. 4) into this discussion, let us replace "resemble" in the just-quoted passage with "correspond to." A sudden worried desire to call an old friend, for example, bears no physical or structural resemblance to the landslide occurring near the friend's house, but I think we would agree that the organismic event in some way corresponds meaningfully to the environmental event. Psi, then, is a meaningful correspondence between an "inner" event and an "outer" one that cannot be explained by normal sensorimotor mechanisms.

Calling psi a meaningful correspondence between organismic and environmental events may evoke the image of theories and models of psi that fit what Palmer (1980) has called the "correspondence paradigm." Some of these theories view psi as an acausal, synchronistic correspondence among events (e.g., Gatlin, 1977; Honneger, 1980; Jung, 1969) and others as a correspondence caused by direct action from one element or system to another (e.g., Braud, 1980, 1981; Stanford, 1978). But we need not restrict this discussion to these or any other particular set of theories. Whether we eventually find a cause for psi phenomena or decide that they are acausal is not really the point here. What is the point is that at the present level of development in parapsychology, all we can say for sure is that we see cases of an inexplicable correspondence between inner and outer--between dream and event, guess and target card, galvanic skin response and emotional stimulus experienced by another--and we classify these events as potentially "psychic" and take them under our purview. Therefore, the question of how we make this classification, how we decide what is meaningful (and even how we decide what is a correspondence) is important not only for the source-of-psi question but for the actual definition and identity of our field.

Morris acknowledged that the range of environmental events that can be thought to correspond to an organismic event is limited only by the observer's capacity to attribute meaning. Pointing out that this open-ended situation cannot be tolerated if we are to rule out chance correspondences, Morris makes his final definition of psi the "resemblance between the objective record of an inferred organismic event and the objective record of an environmental event that has been linked conceptually in advance to the organismic event by an external observer ...," such that the resemblance is not due to normal information channels or to chance (p. 4).

It was not Morris's intention to examine this conceptual linkage so he went on to discuss other points, but since it is our interest here to do this, let us continue the inquiry. First of all, and I believe that Dr. Morris would agree, the situation is not as straightforward as the phrase "linked conceptually in advance" may imply. After all, for years parapsychologists conceptually linked subjects to laboratory psi results. The paradigm shift to considering psi-based experimenter effects showed that this is not the only possible linkage that can be made.

Secondly, the idea that our frames of meaning determine who we are going to consider as possible psi sources can be extended to include our consideration of other elements of the psi event, indeed, to our entire mental construction of the event. Stephen Braude (1979a) made an astute observation in his critique of Lila Gatlin's (1977) information-theoretic approach to psi which is relevant here. He was discussing the famous anecdote of the mysteriously produced noises that emitted from a bookcase during an argument between Sigmund Freud and Carl Jung. These noises have frequently been interpreted as a synchronistic or psychokinetically produced event symbolic of the interpersonal conflict between the two men. But as Braude notes, "nothing intrinsic to the argument between Jung and Freud determines that the archetypal clash between them is the thing or element of the situation which the sounds symbolize. The decision to regard the clash as an element [of the event] is part of the overall decision to regard the sounds as symbolic of the clash" (p. 189). Braude goes on to point out that the noises could just as easily have been interpreted as symbolic of some other aspect of the event--gunshots fired outside or particularly explosive-sounding phonemes in the two men's speech. "Had we made these other comparisons instead," Braude writes, "the explosive words (say), rather than the clash, would have counted as elements" (p. 189).

It may seem that Braude was merely demonstrating the problem of multiple endpoints--of multiple opportunities to attribute meaning--that plagues the interpretation of spontaneous ESP experiences. However, he is really making another point: the determination of the structure of an event is not independent of the determination of its meaning. And this, I submit, is just as true for experimental work as for spontaneous-case research. An experimenter's conscious and subconscious decisions about what elements or events constitute the experiment arise hand-in-hand with another set of conscious and subconscious decisions about what the experiment means.

Meaning as the Sculptor of the Experiment: Part I

A simple example of this occurred when I was trying to understand a reversal of results obtained in a replication attempt (Weiner and Munson, 1981). The study Munson and I were replicating (Weiner, Haight, Marion, and Munson, 1980) had employed a competition between the sexes across three sessions of tests with elementary school children. That experiment had found a significant effect of the competition only in the last session, which we had attributed to increased subject/experimenter rapport and increased motivation created by rewards. However, the replication, which tested an identical population with the same tests and the same rewards, found a significant difference between boys' and girls' performance during the first session. In trying to make sense of this reversal, it struck me that there was one similarity between the last session of the first series and the first session of the second series that may explain why they were the ones in which the sex competition worked: these were the sessions in which subjects first encountered both male and female experimenters.

The point of this for the present discussion is that this similarity could not be known by anyone reading the experimental reports. The report of the first series stated that all testing had been done by JoMarie Haight, Melissa Marion, and myself: three females. What was not stated was that in the last session we had taken a new piece of equipment on its maiden run and the engineer who had assembled it, James Davis, wanted to be on hand to make sure that it worked properly. We introduced him to the children but he remained so much in the background that when it came time to write up the study, we didn't think to mention him. In other words, our public construction of the experiment, our selection of relevant events, did not include his presence. Similarly, to some extent our private mental construction of the experiment also did not include him. Certainly, we knew that he was there and if asked directly about it we would have acknowledged his presence, but he was of no greater import to us than, say, the arrangement of the room, which we also could have described. Given the results of the second series, perhaps his presence may have been important after all. Whether or not that is the case, however, an element of the situation that may have been psi effective was not included in the experimenters' conceptualization of the study because we did not, at the time, think it had meaning.

The number of events occurring to the experimenter, the subjects, and other participants during the six- or eight-month duration of an experiment is extremely large. The experimenter's mind naturally and automatically divides these events into foreground and background, experiment-relevant versus experiment-irrelevant events. Researchers' mental constructions of what they did and what occurred, then, is a set of selected observations and memories. This is how it must be; certainly, an experimenter cannot be expected to consider everything a part of the experiment. However, although we cannot include every element and every event, we can try to understand the process of selection. This selection must, it seems to me, be guided by the experimenter's frame of meaning and by a host of inarticulated assumptions about what types of elements constitute an experiment, what types of elements are relevant to the production of psi, and so on. It is important to recognize that this is true not only for our public presentation of our experiment, the journal report or convention report, but is equally true for our own personal memories and impressions of our work.

In short, an experimenter is something of a sculptor: out of a set of elements the researcher carves out an image--a "statue," if you will--of what the experiment was. The "chisel" for this process is the selection of items noted in the labbook or retained in one's memory, and the hand holding the chisel is guided by an implicit sense of what does (and does not) have meaning. We are very aware of how this problem of perceptual and memory selection can bias reports of spontaneous ESP experiences but, as Patric Giesler has pointed out to me in conversation, it is an illusion to assume they play no role in experimental work.

All of this is not to say that our experimental work is replete with opportunities for perceptual and memory biases to mascarade as psi effects. We have come a long way in developing and refining our methodology to rule out virtually all forms of nonparanormal interaction. I am speaking about the next, higher level of inquiry: having designed an experiment to preclude all normal explanations, how do we interpret the significant results we obtain? In looking at our experiment to see if psi occurred and, if so, why, we cannot help but see our work through the filters of our frames of meaning. We should not feel that this makes us any lesser as scientists; it is a fact of life in any scientific endeavor.

Parapsychology's "Rashomon": What Is the Real Experiment?

One implication of this is that the "official" description of the experiment (the one published in a journal) and even the experimenter's "unofficial" description (the one given during coffee-break or party anecdotes) is not the only description possible. Depending on their background, personality, and information about the experiment, the subjects may have a very different understanding and description of the experiment. This is obviously the case when subjects are purposely kept ignorant of certain features of the design, for example, the presence of hidden control trials or the fact that they are experiencing one condition whereas another subject experienced a different condition. Experimenters, who necessarily sit with a broader but more distant view of the experiment, cannot in all cases understand how subjects, who have a limited but more intimate view, might experience their participation. Even when subjects have full knowledge of the design and purpose of the research, which is sometimes the case in our field, we cannot always know how they are experiencing their participation, what _they_ believe, what _they_ decide is meaningful or irrelevant.

Consider the following quotation:

> There is certainly no reason to assume ... that the experimenter's delineation of a physical event and the subject's

perception of it are isomorphic. What represents an important dimension of the physical event for the experimenter may not even exist as part of effective stimulus for the subject. Similarly, the subject may perceive aspects of an experimental event which may have been ignored by, or are unknown to, the experimenter [Prokasy and Hall, 1963, p. 315].

This statement comes from an article on primary stimulus generation published in a mainstream psychological journal. We can imagine how much more it may pertain to parapsychological research, in which the tasks (e.g., "influencing" electronic equipment) and the topic matter itself are so much more unusual and controversial and are open to a wider variety of personally and culturally moderated meanings.

This point can be most clearly demonstrated when we look at subjects with very different frames of meaning from our own. Patric Giesler (1986a) described the reactions of Afro-Brazilian cultists he tested in remote-viewing and forced-choice ESP tests. Because these cultists were uneducated, the idea of doing something for the sake of "research" was very foreign to them. Many did not understand what was expected of them or, what for research purposes was worse, "understood" that Giesler was doing something "for school" and since "school" means "figuring things out," they decided--despite clear instructions to the contrary--that they were supposed to deduce logically where the outbounder had gone. Others, understanding the tests through their own frames of meaning, believed that the test was a magical induction Giesler was teaching the shaman. My favorite anecdote to demonstrate these subjects' very different perspective is of the remote-viewing percipient who "saw" the outbounder going to the airport, buying a ticket for France, flying there, spending three days buying books, and then returning to the cult center--all within a 15-minute trial!

Giesler, an anthropologist knowledgeable about the cultural and subcultural context to which he was introducing these tests, was certainly aware that such problems could arise and did what he could to minimize them (as he explains in his paper, there were good reasons for proceeding with the research despite them). Although most of us work with subjects of similar cultural, educational, and/or socioeconomic backgrounds as ourselves, which means that our assumptions about their understanding and meaning of their participation are likely to be generally correct, we do not know this for sure. The fact that our subjects do not go into trance during testing or believe that we are performing magic does not necessarily mean that they view the experiment as we think they do, only that the potential differences are more subtle.

Whether or not subjects' views of a psi experiment have anything to do with how the results turn out is not the point. We know from our introductory textbooks that one of the first steps of hypothesis testing--before we even consider results--is to describe what we have done. We should recognize when contemplating the literature that, as in the Japanese film classic Rashomon in which a crime is described in four different ways by four different individuals and the audience never knows what really happened, we have before us not so much experiments as descriptions of experiments. Perhaps the "real" experiment is some composite or interaction of all participants' descriptions.

Meaning as the Sculptor of an Experiment: Part II

The experimenter's view of his or her work, then, is an intellectual construction shaped by a personal frame of meaning and is only one of many possible such constructions. However, this does not deny that in a very real sense the experimenter's frame of meaning plays a role far superior to that of any other participant. This comes about, quite simply, because the experimenter's frame of meaning becomes manifest through the choices or actions the experimenter makes and thereby, in a certain sense, takes on an existence independent of the researcher's mind.

How can meaning take on an existence of its own? Let me demonstrate this concept with an example. I imagine that most of us, in the process of working on a paper, filling out tax forms, or in some other way dealing with a set of written materials, have had cause to organize the material spatially: that pile is Chapter 1 and this pile is Chapter 2; that pile consists of receipts for clearcut deductions; this pile consists of receipts for deductions I must discuss with the Internal Revenue Service. We sit with piles on our desks, piles whose spatial characteristics (e.g., "in upper lefthand corner") have meaning. Suppose (and I'm sure this has occurred all too often) some other creature--a pet, a child, a well-meaning friend--comes to the desk and without knowing that the divisions into piles and their spatial arrangement have meaning, walks on them, plays with them, or decides to do you a "favor" by cleaning up the mess, and proceeds to destroy the arrangement of the piles.

Of course the intruder did not understand the arrangement, so the separation of papers into piles had no meaning for them. But does it follow that the separation of papers into piles had no meaning at all? That it was only our opinion that they did and that the intruder has an equally legitimate opinion that they did not? Or can we say that it did have meaning but the intruder was not aware of it, did not perceive it? I am suggesting that the latter is the case. One way to sense this intuitively is to recognize that if we explained to our well-intentioned friend the meaning behind the arrangement, we would feel that we were merely correcting an error in their awareness or understanding, not that we were convincing them of the correctness of our opinion about the piles. In a similar way, the experimenter, by his or her actions in preparing and carrying out an experiment, creates meaning that can exist beyond the experimenter's personal frame of reference.

The statement that the experimenter, like the paper-pile organizer, creates meaning existing beyond the experimenter's mind raises a host of questions: Can we then say that the meaning exists in the object? Does the meaning continue to exist after the death of the last person who understands it? The fallacy here lies in our attempt to place "meaning" in a location, in either one's mind or in the object under consideration. I will not in this short talk attempt to tackle questions that have a long philosophical tradition. Instead, I wish simply to offer the concept of meaning that in some sense has reality within a larger extrasubjective context.

This concept allows for a slightly different perspective on the psi-based experimenter effect. When I first came to the Institute in 1976, James Kennedy, deep in the throes of contemplating experimenter effects and psi's independence of task complexity, would pose some simple but profound questions. For example, a few years earlier Martin Johnson (1973) had published a test of nonintentional psi during an academic examination in which, unbeknownst to subjects, the answers to certain exam questions had been written on a sheet sealed inside an envelope underneath the test form. (A cover story was given to keep the students unsuspicious about the presence of the envelope.) In this study, students obtained significantly higher scores on questions for which the answers were provided in this way than for the remaining questions. "Why," Kennedy would ask, "would subjects use psi to obtain just the answers inside the envelope when presumably not far away--certainly within the distance we know that psi can operate--there were books, the answer key, the professor, and a myriad of other sources for the correct answers to all questions?" To Kennedy, this sort of discrepancy between the apparent spatial restriction of psi in Johnson's experiment and the evidence in other research against spatial restrictions (at least at the distances in Johnson's study) suggested that Johnson's results were a psi-based experimenter effect.

Perhaps it may be useful to explore the discrepancy between Johnson's results and those of other parapsychological experiments by considering not the physical variable, distance, itself but the meaning of this variable within the experimental context. When Johnson attached the envelope to the answer sheet, he did more than bring certain answers physically closer to the students. He created a meaningful distinction between these answers and those of the remaining questions, just as the paper-pile organizer creates meaningful distinctions among the stacks on the desk. Perhaps, then, the subject (or whoever psi source may be) is responding more to the meaning of the experimenter's actions than to physical variables per se.

This speculation is reminiscent of some provocative questions raised by Schmeidler (1964) regarding what constitutes the target in ESP tests. In one of the first computerized ESP experiments, Schmeidler had obtained evidence that subjects had precognized computer-derived targets. In discussing her results she outlined the steps in which the subjects' written responses were coded into digits, keypunched onto tape, and translated into computer changes to be matched to the target computer changes. She then asked:

> How did the subjects do it? They did not aim at the computer changes directly; they made their choices in terms of stars, wavy lines, circles, crosses, and squares. Could a correspondence in meaning, mediated by digit and tape, have occurred? If so, could meanings be the ESP target, rather than words or specific shapes? But if so, what (in the classic phrase) is the meaning of meaning? [p. 11].

There is evidence that suggests that subjects do not respond to the meaning of the target, for example studies showing that successful psi responses (at least those of the special subjects being tested) resemble the target visually rather than semantically (e.g., Kelly, Kanthamani, Child, and Young, 1975; Puthoff and Targ, 1976; Sinclair, 1930). Similarly, there must be more going on in psi experiments than subjects simply responding to the meaning of an experimenter's actions. Otherwise, the experimenter's manipulations would always produce significant differences, and we would never see such "incidental" evidence of psi as linger effects, displacements, and the like. Still, it seems to me that on the whole the parapsychological literature more often shows factors of meaning taking precedence over structural or physical factors. And, as my last example will demonstrate, it sometimes seems that even the most simple factor can have profound effects, if that factor creates meaning.

The No-Healer Healing Study

A few years ago, Solfvin (1982) published an unusual study of psychic healing on mice inoculated with babesia rodhaini, the rodent equivalent of malaria.[4] Solfvin employed two manipulations. In one of them the assistants taking care of the animals were led to believe that some animals had received a high dosage and others a low dosage of babesia. Actually, all animals received the same dosage; Solfvin was manipulating the assistants' conscious expectations about the animals' health. Since this manipulation was not a purely parapsychological one (because the effects of such expectations could be manifested through subtle handling cues) I will not discuss it further here. What is more germane to the present discussion is Solfvin's second manipulation. He told the assistants that a "healer" working at a distance would attempt to cure half the mice of each dosage group, but the assistants were not told specifically which animals these were. In reality, there was no healer. Solfvin merely blindly and randomly divided photographs of the mice into two groups, putting one group inside an envelope labeled "H" (healed) and the other inside one labeled "NH" (not healed).

The amazing thing is that this manipulation worked:[5] mice whose photographs had been placed in the "H" envelope had significantly lower levels of disease, as determined by blind measurement of red blood cell count, than remaining mice.

On reading this report, my first thought was to send Solfvin ten dollars and a photograph of myself and ask him to put the picture in an envelope labeled "Healthy, Wise, and Successful"! But my second (unselfish) thought was to marvel that in this study the only thing that distinguished the experimental ("healed") animals from the control animals was the envelope in which their photographs were placed. There was no highly developed adept, no laying-on of hands, no ritual, no appeal to higher beings. The healed/not-healed manipulation was created solely by a simple clerical task, the sort of mundane chore that in other research might be relegated to an assistant. Yet no matter what pathway of agency we propose (e.g., Solfvin's or the assistants' nonintentional healing power) this simple task was the foundation for a result of life-enhancing biological consequence. What is it about this task that could have been important: the action itself or the meaning it created?

Conclusion

Some parapsychologists may greet this Address with an inward groan, thinking, "Parapsychology still has not yet come to definitive conclusions about the mind/body problem or life after death, and now we are being asked to consider another Big Philosophical Issue: Meaning." To those, let me suggest that we consider this positively, as a sign of the importance of the work we do. Much of my time in psi research is spent on relatively mundane questions: how best to devise a questionnaire, whether my data can be analyzed with parametric statistics, and so on. However, even though these mundane questions are uppermost in my consciousness, in reality I am--like the rest of us--just one step away from the most exciting and important questions of our existence: what is reality and who are we, as living conscious creatures, in it? Within the context of these larger questions, issues of meaning and meaningfulness assume a rightful and natural place. After all, it is these larger questions (certainly not the promise of riches and fame) that brought us into parapsychology. And therein, perhaps, lies the meaning of it for us all.

NOTES

1. For a succinct discussion of the implications of these effects for parapsychology as a whole, see Palmer (1985).

2. Michael Thalbourne (1985, August) has responded to other aspects of that paper.

3. There have been a number of interesting discussions of the role of meaning in parapsychology; to name just a few recent papers: Bohm, 1986; Braude, 1979a; Chari, 1967; Gatlin, 1977; Gielser, 1986b; Kreitler and Kreitler, 1974; Locke, 1980; Locke and Schlitz, 1983; and von Lucadou and Kornwachs, 1980.

4. The study I am citing is the second series in Solfvin's report. The interpretation of the first series is complicated by an unexpected problem of nonnormal distribution of scores.

5. In fact, it worked better than the nonparapsychological hypothesis, the manipulation of assistants' conscious expectations!

REFERENCES

Bohm, D.J. (1986). A new theory of the relationship of mind and matter. Journal of the American Society for Psychical Research, 80, 113-135.

Braud, W.G. (1980). Lability and inertia in conformance behavior. Journal of the American Society for Psychical Research, 74, 297-318.

Braud, W.G. (1981). Lability and inertia in psychic functioning. In B. Shapin and L. Coly (Eds.), Concepts and theories of parapsychology. New York: Parapsychology Foundation.

Braude, S.E. (1979a). Objections to an information-theoretic approach to synchronicity. Journal of the American Society for Psychical Research, 73, 179-193.

Braude, S.E. (1979b). The observational theories in parapsychology: A critique. Journal of the American Society for Psychical Research, 73, 349-366.

Chari, C.T.K. (1967). ESP and "semantic information." Journal of the American Society for Psychical Research, 61, 47-63.

Gatlin, L.L. (1977). Meaningful information creation: An alternative interpretation of the psi phenomenon. Journal of the American Society for Psychical Research, 71, 1-18.

Giesler, P.V. (1986a). GESP testing of shamanic cultists: Three studies and an evaluation of dramatic upsets during testing. Journal of Parapsychology, 50, 123-153.

Giesler, P.V. (1986b). Sociolinguistics and the psi-conducive social contexts of the laboratory and field settings: A speculative commentary. In D.H. Weiner and D.I. Radin (Eds.), Research in parapsychology 1985 (pp. 111-115). Metuchen, NJ: Scarecrow Press. (Abstract)

Honegger, B. (1980). Spontaneous waking-state psi as interhemispheric verbal communication: Is there another system? In W.G. Roll (Ed.), Research in parapsychology 1979 (pp. 19-21). Metuchen, NJ: Scarecrow Press. (Abstract)

Houtkooper, J.M. (1983). Observational theory: A research programme for paranormal phenomena. Lisse, Holland: Swets and Zeitlinger, B.V.

Johnson, M. (1973). A new technique of testing ESP in a real-life, high-motivational context. Journal of Parapsychology, 37, 210-217.

Jung, C.G. (1969). Synchronicity (2nd Ed). Princeton, NJ: Princeton University Press.

Kelly, E.F., Kanthamani, H., Child, I.L., and Young, F.W. (1975). On the relation between visual and ESP confusion structures in an exceptional ESP subject. Journal of the American Society for Psychical Research, 69, 1-31.

Kennedy, J.E. (1978). The role of task complexity in PK: A review. Journal of Parapsychology, 42, 89-122.

Kennedy, J.E., and Taddonio, J.L. (1976). Experimenter effects in parapsychological research. Journal of Parapsychology, 40, 1-33.

Kreitler, H., and Kreitler, S. (1974). ESP and cognition. Journal of Parapsychology, 38, 267-285.

Locke, R.G. (1980). Communication and imagery resonance: A theoretical approach to psychic healing. European Journal of Parapsychology, 3, 185-208.

Locke, R.G., and Schlitz, M.J. (1983). A phenomenological approach to experimental parapsychology. In W.G. Roll, J. Beloff, and R.A. White (Eds.), Research in parapsychology 1982 (pp. 238-240). Metuchen, NJ: Scarecrow Press. (Abstract)

Morris, R.L. (1980). Psi functioning within a simple communication model. In B. Shapin and L. Coly (Eds.), Communication and Parapsychology (pp. 1-19). New York: Parapsychology Foundation.

Osis, K. (1953). A test of the relationship between ESP and PK. Journal of Parapsychology, 17, 298-309.

Palmer, J. (1980). Parapsychology as a probabilistic science: Facing the implications. In W.G. Roll (Ed.), Research in parapsychology 1979 (pp. 189-215). Metuchen, NJ: Scarecrow Press.

Palmer, J. (1985). Psi research in the 1980s. Parapsychology Review, 16(2), 1-4.

Prokasy, W.F., and Hall, J.F. (1963). Primary stimulus generation. Psychological Review, 70, 310-322. Quoted in M.B. Creelman, The experimental investigation of meaning: A review of the literature. New York: Springer, 1966.

Puthoff, H., and Targ, R. (1976). A perceptual channel for information transfer over kilometer distances: Historical perspective and recent research. Proceedings of IEEE, 64, 329-354.

Rhine, J.B. (1934). Extrasensory perception. Boston, MA: Branden Press.

Schechter, E.I. (1977). Nonintentional ESP: A review and replication. Journal of the American Society for Psychical Research, 71, 337-374.

Schmeidler, G.R. (1964). An experiment on precognitive clairvoyance: Part I. The main results. Journal of Parapsychology, 28, 1-14.

Schmidt, H. (1975). Toward a mathematical theory of psi. Journal of the American Society for Psychical Research, 69, 301-319.

Sinclair, U. (1930). Mental radio. Monrovia, CA: Upton Sinclair.

Solfvin, G.F. (1982). Psi expectancy in psychic healing studies with malarial mice. European Journal of Parapsychology, 4, 159-197.

Stanford, R.G. (1977). Experimental psychokinesis: A review from diverse perspectives. In B.B. Wolman (Ed.), Handbook of parapsychology (pp. 324-381). New York: Van Nostrand Reinhold.

Stanford, R.G. (1978). Toward reinterpreting psi events.

Journal of the American Society for Psychical Research, 72, 197-214.

Stanford, R.G., Zenhausern, R., Taylor, A., and Dwyer, M.A. (1975). Psychokinesis as psi-mediated instrumental response. Journal of the American Society for Psychical Research, 69, 127-133.

Thalbourne, M.A. (1985, August). Some further thoughts on living without "ESP" and "PK." Paper presented at the 28th annual convention of the Parapsychological Association, Medford, MA.

Thouless, R.H. (1976). The effect of the experimenter's attitude on experimental results in parapsychology. Journal of the Society for Psychical Research, 48, 261-266.

Varvoglis, M.P. (1986). Goal-directed and observer-dependent PK: An evaluation of the conformance-behavior model and the observational theories. Journal of the American Society for Psychical Research, 80, 137-162.

Vassy, Z. (1986). Complexity dependence in precognitive timing: An experiment with pseudorandom number sequences. In D.H. Weiner and D.I. Radin (Eds.), Research in parapsychology 1985 (pp. 80-84). Metuchen, NJ: Scarecrow Press. (Abstract)

von Lucadou, W., and Kornwachs, K. (1980). Development of the system theoretic approach to psychokinesis. European Journal of Parapsychology, 3, 297-314.

Walker, E.H. (1975). Foundations of paraphysical and parapsychological phenomena. In L. Oteri (Ed.), Quantum physics and parapsychology (pp. 1-44). New York: Parapsychology Foundation.

Weiner, D.H., and Geller, J. (1984). Motivation as the universal container: Conceptual problems in parapsychology. Journal of Parapsychology, 48, 27-37.

Weiner, D.H., Haight, J.M., Marion, M.D., and Munson, R.J. (1980). The possible value of repeated visitation in group testing. In W.G. Roll (Ed.), Research in parapsychology 1979, (pp. 177-179). Metuchen, NJ: Scarecrow Press. (Abstract)

Weiner, D.H., and Munson, R.J. (1981). The importance of repeated visitation in group testing: A disconfirmation. Journal of Parapsychology, 45, 155-156. (Abstract)

White, R.A. (1976a). The influence of persons other than the experimenter on the subject's scores in psi experiments.

Journal of the American Society for Psychical Research, 70, 133-166.

White, R.A. (1976b). The limits of experimenter influence on psi test results: Can any be set? *Journal of the American Society for Psychical Research*, 70, 333-369.

NAME INDEX

Adams, M. H. 78, 82, 90-92
Adey, W. R. 79
Ahtola, O. T. 200
Alford, D. H. 157-58
Ancoli, S. 189-90, 193, 196
Anderson, R. I. 186
Ashby, W. R. 134
Auerbach, L. xi, 182, 184-85

Babu, S. 1-5
Bach, R. 152
Bailey, A. 152
Banerjee, H. N. 120-21
Banquet, J. P. 60
Barber, T. X. 112
Barker, P. xi
Barrington, M. R. 93
Baumann, S. 30-35
Bell, J. 178
Beloff, J. 122
Benjamin, L. S. 135
Berger, R. ix, 6-12, 75, 76
Bertalanffy, L. v. 133
Bierman, D. J. 17, 75, 204
Boerenkamp, H. G. 93
Bohm, D. J. 128, 219
Bosworth, J. L. 48, 51
Bowers, P. 43
Brame, E. G., Jr. 24-29
Braud, W. G. 48-51, 140, 210
Braude, S. E. 153-54, 205, 211, 219
Brier, R. 121, 122
Bronson, M. C. 156-57
Broughton, R. S. 62, 116-19, 136-37, 203
Bubenik, D. M. 80-81
Budner, S. 43
Burdick, D. S. 66, 120

Cadoret, R. J. 189
Camfferman, G. 93
Chari, C. T. K. 122, 219
Chavira, J. A. 106
Child, I. L. 40, 86, 102, 121, 217
Chrzanowski, G. 132
Coffey, J. 155
Corbin, R. 185
Cottrell, S. 186
Covey, M. K. 62, 66, 67, 73
Cox, W. E. 140
Crandall, J. E. 62-69, 69-71, 73-74, 76
Cummins, G. 152
Curran, P. 152, 153-54

Danziger, K. 131-32
Das, N. N. 60
Davis, J. 212
Dean, D. 24
Delanoy, D. 100-01
De Mattei, R. J. 24-29
Descartes, R. 126
Dey, N. D. 20-23
Dickens, C. 155-56
Dixon, W. J. 58
Don, N. S. 56-61
Dubbert, P. M. 193
Dunne, B. J. 2, 5, 8, 12-17, 41, 82-85, 143
Dutton, M. 63
Dwyer, M. A. 206

Ebon, M. 85
Edge, H. L. 129-30, 171-72
Ehrenwald, J. 132
Eisenbud, J. 131, 135, 163, 186

Eisenman, E. J. P. 193
Estebany, O. 187, 189

Feilding, E. 148
Feller, W. 119
Fisk, G. W. 52
Flew, A. 122
Foley, D. H. 58
Forbush, S. E. 81
Forwald, H. 121, 140
Franks, F. 24
Fraser-Smith, A. C. 80
Freud, S. 211
Friedman, H. 79-80

Gardner, M. R. 134
Gasparetto, L. 152
Gastaut, H. 60
Gatlin, L. L. 210, 211, 219
Geller, J. 207
Giesler, P. V. 148, 213, 214, 219
Giovetti, P. 186
Gorsuch, R. L. 190, 192, 198
Gough, W. C. 177
Goulet, R. 182, 184
Grad, B. 24, 189
Greenwood, J. A. 117, 119-20
Greville, T. N. E. 120
Guillemin, V. 188
Gurney, E. 90

Haight, J. M. 211-12
Hale, G. M. 27
Hall, J. A. 173-75
Hall, J. F. 214
Hansel, C. E. M. 120, 124
Hansen, G. P. ix, xi, 93-97, 140-41, 182, 185-86
Haraldsson, E. 185-86
Harary, K. 145, 146-47, 150, 176-77
Hart, H. 121
Hartwell, J. W. 56
Hasrudin, Sufi Mullah ix
Hastings, A. 152-53
Heidt, P. 189-91
Hilgard, J. R. 112

Hillyard, S. A. 61
Hiscock, M. 63
Hite, D. D. 62, 66
Hodgman, C. D. 57
Home, D. D. 186
Honegger, B. 210
Honorton, C. 6, 10, 36-39, 41, 60, 75, 76, 97, 120, 121
Horn, B. K. P. 98
Hornig, D. F. 28
Houtkooper, J. M. 204
Hövelmann, G. 122
Houdini, H. 183
Hubbard, S. ix, 55-56, 79-82, 137, 139
Hume, D. 120
Humphrey, B. S. 137, 139
Hyman, R. 93, 120, 121

Intner, S. M. 5
Isaacs, J. 179-80

Jahn, R. G. 2, 5, 8, 12-17, 41, 82, 143
James, T. P. 152
Jay, J. 155
Jefferson, T. 155
Johnson, M. 185, 216
Jung, C. G. 162-63, 210, 211

Kamiya, J. ix
Kanthamani, H. 66-73, 74, 123-25, 217
Kardec, A. 168
Keepin, W. N. xi, 5
Kelly, E. F. 60, 155, 217
Kennedy, J. E. 203, 205, 216
Kennedy, J. L. 119
Khilji, A. 66, 69-73, 74
Kidd, J. 147
Kiesler, D. J. 134
Koestler, A. 165
Kooy, J. M. J. 122
Kornwachs, K. 203, 219
Kreitler, H. 121, 219
Kreitler, S. 121, 219
Krieger, D. 187, 189-90, 191, 193, 194, 196, 197

Name Index

Krippner, S. 85-88, 168-69
Krishnamurti, J. 152
Kunz, D. 187

LaBerge, S. ix
Larson, V. A. 166-67
Leary, T. 134
Leonardo da Vinci 179
Levi 152
Levi, A. 40, 102
Lieberman, R. 112
Locke, R. G. 219
Lushene, R. E. 190, 192, 198

Mabbett, I. W. 122
MacFarland, J. 119
Madigan, S. A. 63
Maher, M. 39-42, 63
Maier, K. 63
Marais, E. 135
Maren, A. J. 97-99
Marion, M. D. 211-12
Maslow, A. 164
May, E. C. 79-82, 109-11, 136, 137, 139-40
May, R. M. 134
Mayaud, P. N. 86, 88
McAdam, D. W. 60
McConnell, R. A. 121
McDougall, W. 116
McMurtrie, R. E. 134
Mendes, E. C. 168-69
Medhurst, R. G. 120
Millar, B. 107-09
Milton, J. 100-03
Mintz, E. 163
Miro-Quesada S., O. 165-66
Mitchell, E. 122
Mohammed 152
Morris, C. 63
Morris, R. L. 60, 107, 203, 209-10
Mosteller, F. 155
Mundle, C. W. K. 122
Munson, R. J. 129, 130-35, 170-71, 211
Murphy, G. 117, 119
Myers, F. W. H. 90

Nash, C. B. 24, 121
Nelson, R. D. ix, xi, 2, 5, 8, 12-17, 82-85, 142-44
Nemeth, M. 175
Newbrough, J. B. 152

Osis, K. 185-86, 205

Paivio, A. 63
Palmer, J. 17-20, 66, 112, 119-22, 203, 210, 219
Paul, G. I. 189
Pearce, H. 120
Peper, E. 189-90, 193, 196
Perlstrom, J. R. 17-20
Persinger, M. A. 82, 85-90, 91-92
Pinkley, W. P. 27
Pleass, C. M. 20-23
Podmore, F. 90
Pratt, J. G. 117, 119, 120-21, 122
Price, G. 120
Prokasy, W. F. 214
Puharich, A. 53-54, 152
Puthoff, H. 217

Queiroz, E. 156-57
Query, M. R. 27
Quider, R. -P. F. ix, 180-81
Quinn, J. F. ix, 187-202

Radin, D. I. 48, 51, 93, 109-11, 138-39
Rainho, J. 182, 184
Randi, J. 32, 185, 186
Rao, K. R. 116, 119, 120-21
Raphael 152, 153
Rauscher, E. 24, 149-51, 176, 177-79
Rhine, J. B. 116-18, 119-22, 123-25, 147, 203
Rhine, L. E. 121
Riess, B. 117
Roberts, J. 152
Robinson, D. xi

Rogers, M. E. 188, 190, 197
Rogo, D. S. 148-49
Roll, W. G. 30-35, 126-29, 161-62, 163
Rose, L. 148
Rose, R. 148
Rubik, B. 149
Rubin, E. H. 60
Ruderfer, M. 122

Sai Baba, S. 186
Sammon, J. W. 58
Schaut, G. B. 85, 86, 88-90
Schechter, E. I. 6, 36-39, 73-77, 206
Schlitz, M. J. 103-06, 219
Schmeidler, G. R. 52, 63, 66, 74, 217
Schmidt, H. 136, 204
Schultz, J. W. 28
Schwartz, S. A. 24-29
Schwarz, B. E. 131
Scott, C. 120
Scriven, M. 120
Sethna, P. P. 27
Shafer, D. 48-51
Shafer, M. G. 186
Shargal, S. 51-53
Sinclair, U. 217
Slydini 183
Smith, B. M. 117, 119
Smith, J. 152
Smith, M. J. 24, 189
Soal, S. G. 120, 122
Solfvin, G. F. 101, 154-56, 217-18, 219
Sondow, N. 42-47
Spangler, D. 152, 153
Spielberger, C. D. 190, 192, 198
Spottiswoode, S. J. P. 24-29
Spradley, J. P. 103
Stanford, R. G. 51, 60, 111-15, 172-73, 205, 206, 210
Stevenson, I. 60, 90, 121, 155
Stewart, J. L. 30-35, 162-63
Stuart, C. E. 117, 119-20
Sullivan, H. S. 132

Taddonio, J. L. 203
Targ, R. 217
Tart, C. T. 40, 53-54, 55-56, 62, 90-92, 119, 145-46, 159-60, 164-65
Taves, E. 117
Taylor, A. 206
Terry, J. C. 97
Thalbourne, M. A. 186, 219
Thouless, R. H. 122, 203
Trotter, R. T. 106
Truzzi, M. 182-83

Ullman, M. 85
Utts, J. 139

Varvoglis, M. P. 205, 207
Vassy, Z. 141-42, 205
Vernon, M. 98
Vincent, W. R. 55-56
von Bertalanffy, L. 133
von Lucadou, W. 203, 219

Walker, E. H. 139-40, 204
Walter, W. G. 56-57
Warren, C. A. 56-61
Weiner, D. H. ix, xi, 111, 203-23
West, D. J. 52
White, J. 122
White, R. A. 46, 203
White, S. E. 152
Wildt, A. R. 200
Williams, D. 27
Wilson, M. 184
Wilson, S. C. 112
Winstead-Fry, P. 197
Winston, P. H. 98
Woodruff, J. L. 120
Worrall, O. 149, 150
Worth, P. 152, 153-54

Yarbro, C. Q. 152
Young, F. W. 217
Yuille, J. C. 63

Zenhausern, R. 206

SUBJECT INDEX

age, as affects children's ESP scores   51-53
altered states of consciousness   166, 168
American Journal of Obstetrics and Gynecology   26
American Psychological Association   117
American Psychologist   86
anxiety   192
"Apollo test"   124
apparitions   90, 148-49
Aquarian Gospel of Jesus the Christ   152
artifacts   65-66, 69
artificial intelligence   97, 99
AT&T Bell Laboratories   138
At the Feet of the Master   152
automatic writing   152, 153; see also channeling

Babel Inverted Group   156, 157
babesia rodhaini   217
Bell's theorem   127, 176
"blind PK"   205
BMDP Statistical Software   58
Book of Mormon   152
brain activity
   and psi   56-61
   during meditation   60
British Journal for the Philosophy of Science   133

Cambridge University   126
channeling   152-60
   as healing practice   156-57
   definition of   152
   features of discourse in   157-58
   ostensible cases of   153-54, 155, 156-57
   psychological resistance to research on   159-60
"cipher test"   122
Circular Matching Abacus Test (CMAT)   54
clairvoyance   40, 49, 52, 56-61, 71, 85-88, 122
clinical applications of parapsychology   161-62, 165-66
   ethical issues   170-71, 173-75
   legal issues   174, 175
cognitive habits, as predictor variables   42-47, 62-66

College of Marine Studies 20
competition between sexes in experiment 211-12
confidence ratings in free-response judging 40, 100, 102
conjuring see stage magic
conscious effort, as component of psi performance 45-47
"correspondence paradigm" 210
A Course in Miracles 152, 153
creativity, as predictor variable 42-43
C.R.C. Standard Mathematical Tables 57
Curandismo: Mexican American Folk Healing 106

Department of Health and Human Services 187
developmental variables and OBEs 111-15
"disobsession" therapy 156-57
displacement effects 62-77
    and attention condition of subjects 67-68, 71-72
    and cognitive style of subjects 62-66
    and target type 62-66
    and testing conditions 68, 69
    in data of single subject 71-72, 73
    in Ganzfeld data 102
    in REG-PK data 73-77
    possible artifacts in analyses of 65-66, 69
dream quality and psi performance 43-46
Duke University 18, 116-117, 203
dunaliella 20, 23

Eastern Michigan University 182
EEG recording 58, 196; see also brain activity
effortlessness and psi performance 43-47
electrical shielding
    and GESP performance 53-54, 91-92
    as measured in U.C. Davis room 55
Electroencephalography and Clinical Neurophysiology 60
electromagnetic radiation and psi 54, 78, 79-80, 82, 90, 92; see also geomagnetic activity; electrical shielding
Emory University 165
EOG recording 58
ESP 51-53, 57, 64, 67, 71, 181, 205, 214, 217; see also clairvoyance; displacement effects; free-response ESP research; Ganzfeld psi research; GESP performance; precognition; remote-viewing research; telepathy
The ESP Experience 132
ethics
    changing perspectives on 171
    clinical, in parapsychology 170-75
    of dealing with experimental subjects 172-73
ethnographic approaches to psi research 103-106
The Ethnographic Interview 103

Subject Index

European Journal of Parapsychology 56, 93, 185
event-related brain potentials 56-61
experimenter effect, psi-based 9, 10-11, 56, 150, 203-05, 216;
    see also source-of-psi problem
An Exploration of the Nature of Resonance in Psychotherapy 166
extrasensory perception see ESP
Extra-sensory Perception After Sixty Years 117, 119
extraversion and psi performance 38

Faraday cage 53-54, 92; see also electrical shielding, as measured
    in U.C. Davis room
Fate 89
fear of psi 17, 159, 164, 181
The Federalist Papers 155
feedback
    channels, function of 107-109
    dependence of state selection on 140
    lack of, and RNG-PK performance 6-12
    real-time, psychological conflict arising from 17
field investigations 148-49, 214
Foundation for Mind-Being Research 177
fraud
    by RSPK agents 31-32, 133
    experimenter 120-21, 124
    subject 120
    subject, adequacy of efforts to prevent 185-86
free-response ESP research 36-48; see also Ganzfeld psi research
    confidence ratings by judges in 40, 100, 102
    evaluation of subject performance in 97-99
    improvement of judging strategies in 41-42
    Monte Carlo method in analysis of 96
    representation of target content in 97-99
    screening of subjects for 172-73
    source of psi in 40-41
free will 127, 129
A Further Study of Visual Perception 98

Ganzfeld psi research
    analysis for displacement effects in 102
    evaluation of subject performance in 97-99
    exploratory, for predictor variables 38-39, 42-47
    Honorton-Hyman debate on 120, 121
    judging strategies to improve scoring in 100-03
    representation of target content in 41, 97-99
    types of mentation-to-target correspondence in 101
    with an automated testing system 36-37
gender, as a variable in psi tests 86, 87, 212
geomagnetic activity 78-92
    behavior of psychiatric patients and 79-80

data from tests in Faraday cage and　91-92
　　　dream telepathy-clairvoyance data and　85-88
　　　GESP performance and　90-91
　　　measurement of, in psi research　81, 85, 86, 88, 91
　　　PK data and　84-85
　　　remote-viewing data and　83-84, 90-91
　　　spontaneous psi experiences and　88-90, 91
　　　standard GMF indices and　79, 80, 82, 88
　　　statistical treatment of, in psi research　81-82, 83-84, 85, 86-87, 88-90, 92
GESP performance
　　　and electrical shielding　53-54
　　　and geomagnetic activity　90-92
goal-oriented interpretations of psi　51, 137, 139, 140

Harvard University　155
haunting　127, 162-63
healing　149, 166, 167; see also laying-on of hands, Therapeutic Touch
　　　psychic　149-50, 217-18
　　　mediumistic techniques in　156-57, 168-69
Heisenberg Uncertainty Principle　150, 178
Helix Investments, Ltd.　5
Human Dimensions　24
Human Information Processing Group, Princeton University　138
hypnotic suggestion and RSPK　30-35
hypnotizability, as predictor variable　42-43, 45, 46, 112

IAGA Bulletin　86, 88
IEEE Transactions on Computers　58
The Impact Message Inventory　134
Implications of Interpersonal Theory　132
"incline" effect　39-42
infrared spectrophotometric analysis of water　24-29
Institute for Advanced Psychology　145, 146, 176
Institute for Parapsychology　17, 66, 69, 70, 111, 116, 119, 123, 130, 136, 170, 203
Institute for Transpersonal Psychology　152
intention
　　　and mode of task instruction　4-5, 16
　　　feedback and subject's　17
　　　of operator on REG　1-5
　　　of operator on RCM　12, 16-17
　　　of Therapeutic Touch practitioner　25, 188, 194
Interactive System Model　143-44
International Brotherhood of Magicians　182
International Journal of Clinical and Experimental Hypnosis　43
Interpersonal Communication　132
Interpersonal Diagnosis of Personality　134

Subject Index

The Interpersonal Theory of Psychiatry 132
introversion and psi performance 38
Intuitive Data Sorting (IDS) model
    critical comments on 139-42
    parsimony of 142
    predictions of 138
    test of, with pseudo-REG 109-11, 138-39
    versus PK interpretations of REG data 136-43

J. B. Rhine Banquet Address ix
John E. Fetzer Foundation, Inc. 5
John F. Kennedy University 148, 154, 155, 179, 180, 182
Jonathan Livingston Seagull 152
Journal of Abnormal Psychology 135
Journal of Consulting and Clinical Psychology 63, 135
Journal of Experimental Psychology Monographs Supplement 63
Journal of Geophysical Research 81
Journal of Parapsychology ix, 37, 41, 93, 98, 116-25, 140, 159
Journal of Personality 43
Journal of Physical Chemistry 28
Journal of Psychosomatic Research 56
Journal of the American Society for Psychical Research 24, 40, 41, 46, 48, 51, 60, 62, 63, 66, 67, 68, 73, 74, 88, 94, 101, 102, 135, 140, 148, 159, 185, 186
Journal of the Optical Society of America 27, 28
Journal of Theoretical Biology 134
Journal of the Society for Psychical Research 93

Kairos Foundation 56
The Koran 152

Laurentian University 85, 88
laying-on of hands 24, 189; see also Therapeutic Touch
LISP 98

macro-PK see healing, psychic; RSPK
magic and mentalism 182-86
Magic Art Studio 182
magicians, guidelines for consulting 183, 184, 185
Maimonides Dream Laboratory 85
McDonnell Foundation 5
McGill University 24
meaning
    of experiment for subject 213-14
    role of, in psi research 203-23
    source-of-psi problem and 207-11
meditation; see also mental discipline, practice of

brain activity monitored during 60
mediumship 153-54, 156-57, 163, 168-69; <u>see also</u> channeling
<u>Memories, Dreams, and Reflections</u> 162
mental discipline, practice of 38, 39
mentalism 182-85
<u>Messages from Michael</u> 152
micro-PK 136-37; <u>see also</u> PK
Mimic Therapeutic Touch 192, 193-94
Mind Science Foundation 48, 103
miracles, religious 148
Missouri Historical Society 154
The Mobius Society 24
<u>Monte Carlo Methods</u> 94
Monte Carlo methods
   in parapsychology 93-97
   in systems research 134
multiple personality disorder 168-69
<u>The Mystery of Edwin Drood</u> 152, 155

<u>National Geographic</u> 43
National Oceanic and Atmospheric Administration 82
<u>Nature</u> 79, 134
New School for Social Research 39
New York University 197
<u>The Nine</u> 152
nonintentional psi 206-207, 216
"nonphysical" worlds 145-46

<u>Oahspe: A New Bible</u> 152
Observational Quasi-Motor Model 107-09
observational theories 11-12, 107-09, 131, 139-40, 204
The Ohrstrom Foundation 5
openness to unconscious processing 42-43, 45-47
operators <u>see</u> subject(s)
optional stopping 75
Ouija board 153
out-of-body experience (OBE) 111-115, 145-46
oxygen-hydrogen bonding in water 24, 25

"paranormal," debate over definitions of 122
Parapsychological Association ix, xi, 120, 182, 185, 186
   and clinical applications of parapsychology 174-75
Parapsychological Services Institute 30, 162, 165
parapsychology
   clinical applications of 161-62, 165-66, 170-71, 173-75
   early development of, as science 126-27
   ethical issues in 170-75
   interpersonal systems and 130-35

Subject Index

psychological needs of researchers in 164-65
research fads in 146-47
role of meaning in 203-23
use of geomagnetic data in 79-82
use of ethnographic methods in 103-06
Parapsychology Foundation, Inc. 39, 42
Parapsychology Review 60, 135
parent-child relationships and psi 132, 134
Participant Information Form (PIF) 18, 38
participants see subject[s]
PEAR Technical Report; see also Princeton Engineering Anomalies Research
   83002   12
   83003   82
   84003   2, 8, 12, 82
   85001   14
   85004   82
Perceptual and Motor Skills 86, 88
Personality and Hypnosis: A Study of Imaginative Involvement 112
personality tests see tests, personality and psychological
Physiological Reviews 79
Physiology and Behavior 61
PK 1-35, 67, 73-77, 136-43, 181, 205-06
   "blind" 205
   data and geomagnetic activity 84-85
   detectability of, in pseudo-REG experiment 110
   experimenters, phenomenology of 105-06
   in relation to task instructions 17-20
   micro- 136-37
   recurrent spontaneous 30-35, 132-34, 161, 163
   research, controversies in 121
   versus IDS interpretation of REG data 136-43
poltergeist see RSPK
possession see channeling
postmortem experiences 88-90
precognition 88-90, 140, 179
   model, IDS as 136-37, 138, 142, 143
predictor variables, in Ganzfeld subjects 38-39, 42-47
Presidential Address ix, xiii
primary-process thinking 42, 43, 47
Princeton Engineering Anomalies Research (PEAR) 1, 5, 8, 12, 82, 140, 142, 143; see also PEAR Technical Report
Princeton University 138
Proceedings of the Presented Papers of the 28th Annual Parapsychological Association Convention 139
Proceedings of the Second International Congress of Psychotronics 24
process-oriented research 121
Program Committee ix, xiii, 65
pseudorandom event generator

compared with REG as noise source 1-5
in Monte Carlo simulations 93-94
in test of IDS model 109-11, 137-39
psi; see also ESP; PK; spontaneous psi experiences
and task complexity 205
and therapeutic insight 162-63
as information-organizing principle 176
as meaningful correspondence 210
"effect size" 111
fear of 17, 159, 164, 181
in psychotherapeutic situations 131-32, 163, 166-67, 173
nonintentional 206-07, 216
source of 9-12, 40-41, 107-09; see also source-of-psi problem
Psi and Psychoanalysis 163
Psi Invaders (video game) 6, 7, 10, 73-76
PsiLab// (computerized psi-testing system) 6, 7, 10, 75, 94, 96
psi-mediated instrumental response (PMIR) 50, 51
psi source; see also source-of-psi problem
in free-response ESP 40-41
in REG research 9-12
function of 107-09
Psychical Research Foundation 10, 30, 34, 126, 161, 162
Psychic Entertainers Association 182, 183
Psychic Exploration 122
Psychic Nexus 131
The Psychic Thread 163
Psychoanalytic Quarterly 131
psychokinesis see PK
Psychological Research Foundation 30
Psychological Review 135
psychological tests see tests, personality and psychological
Psychophysical Research Laboratories 6, 10, 17, 36, 38, 73, 93, 97, 140, 141, 182, 185

RAND Corporation 63
random event generators
analyses of databases developed with 1-5, 6-7, 12, 16-17, 73-77, 84-85, 136-44
and research into nature of randomness 147
and tests of IDS model 109, 110, 141
compared with pseudo-REG as noise source 1-5
experiments with games using 6-12, 17-20; see also timing task as psi test
IDS vs. PK interpretations of research with 136-43
in Monte Carlo simulations 94, 95, 96
Interactive System Model and 143
"nonintentional psi" research with 206
sampling rate of, as variable 1, 2
selection of Ganzfeld target with 37
silent data produced with 6-12, 18-20, 73-77

Subject Index

source-of-psi problem in research with   9-12, 205
randomization tests   7, 50
Random Mechanical Cascade   12-17, 84-85
randomness, nature of   147
Rashomon   213, 215
reality, nature of   150, 176-181
recurrent spontaneous psychokinesis   see   RSPK
REG   see   random event generators
remote-viewing research   83-84, 150, 214
Research in Parapsychology (RIP)   xi, xiii, 6, 20, 24, 30, 39, 40, 62, 67, 71, 73, 75, 76, 82, 90, 91, 109, 112, 141, 182, 186
resonance between psychotherapists and clients   166-67
Revelations   152
Reviews of Geophysics and Space Physics   81
rewards in psi tests   48, 52, 211-12
RNG   see   random event generators
Rollins College   129, 171
Rosary Hill College   24
Roswell Park Cancer Hospital   24
RSPK   30-35, 132-34, 161, 163

St. John's University   111, 113, 172
St. Joseph's University   24
SAS Institute   2
Saybrook Institute   85, 168-69
Science   61, 120
Science Unlimited Research Foundation   6, 9
Scripts of Cleophas   152
Septem Sermones and Mortuos   163
Seth Speaks   152
shamanism   148-49
"signatures," in psi test data   5
Signet Handbook of Parapsychology   85
silent-data effects   6-12, 18-20, 73-77
Simplex Magic   182
Simulation and the Monte Carlo Method   96
Sioux yuwipi ceremony   149
The Skeptical Inquirer   186
Society for Psychical Research (SPR)   126, 127, 148
Society of American Magicians   182, 185
Solar Physics   81
Sonoma State University   ix
SORRAT   121
The Soul of the White Ant   135
source-of-psi problem   203-11
Space Invaders (video game)   6, 75
spectrophotometry   24-29
spontaneous psi experiences   88-90, 121, 211, 213
Spring Creek Institute   30
SRI International   55, 79, 90, 109, 136-37, 140

stage magic 182-86
Stanford University 80
The Starseed Transmissions 152
state anxiety 192
subject(s)
   believers in psi as 10, 53
   cardiovascular patients as 190, 198
   children as 51-53, 211-12
   emotional stability of 172-73
   ethical obligations to 171-73
   experienced vs. novice 38
   experimenters as 7, 11, 49
   high school students as 67, 71
   of a Ganzfeld study 100
   parapsychologists as 7, 10, 49, 71-72, 73, 103-06
   perceptions of experiment by 213-214
   psychic healer as 149-50
   RSPK focus person as 30-35
   screening of 172-73
   selected, for special ability 7, 24, 25, 29, 30-35, 57-60, 103-06, 109, 111, 138, 149-50
   Therapeutic Touch practitioners as 24, 25, 29
   university students as 18-19, 54, 63, 64, 113
   volunteers as 13, 43, 48, 49
survival, postmortem 122, 146; *see also* channeling; postmortem experiences
systems theory 126-35, 143-44
   general, and psi 130-35
   general, and RSPK 132-34
   methodological implications of, for parapsychology 130
   organismic, and psi 127-29

target(s)
   anxiety of preoperative patients as 188
   bacterial cultures as 149
   cards as 52, 54, 57, 186
   dunaliella as 20-23
   ESP symbols as 57, 67
   identification of mentation related to 97-103
   living systems as 20-23, 24, 30, 149, 188, 189, 217-18
   marine alga as 20-23
   meaningful aspect of 217
   mice as 217-18
   neurons of sea snail as 30
   number cards as 52
   objects owned by subject as 30
   "permissible" 33
   pictorial 36-38, 39, 43, 86, 97-99, 100
   piezoelectrical crystals as 30
   polystyrene balls as 13

pseudo-REG output as 1, 109, 138
REG output as 1, 6, 10, 17, 49
representation of content of 41, 97-99
type of, and displacement effects 62-66
videotapes as 36-38, 39
water as 24
words as 63
task complexity and psi 205
Tecnic Research Laboratories 149, 176, 177
telepathy 85-90, 122
tests, personality and psychological
   Barron-Welsh Art Scale 43
   Body Boundary 51-52
   Impact Message Inventory 134-35
   Independence of Judgment Scale 43
   Individual Differences Questionnaire 63
   Interpersonal Check List 134
   Myers-Briggs Type Indicator 18, 38
   STAI Form X-1 192, 198
   Stanford Hypnotic Susceptibility Scale 43
   Structural Analysis of Social Behavior 135
   Tolerance for Ambiguity Scale 43
theories
   correspondence 210
   Interactive System Model 143-44
   Intuitive Data Sorting Model 109-11, 136-43
   observational 11-12, 107-09, 131, 139-40, 204
   Observational Quasi-Motor Model 107-09
   of channeling 152
   of OBE as imaginal journey 111-15
   quantum-mechanical 140, 143
   psi-mediated instrumental response 50, 51
   systems 126-35, 143-44
Therapeutic Touch 24, 187-202
   definition of 191
   energy transfer interpretation of 187-88, 191, 197
   Mimic 192, 193-94
   procedures in 191-92
Theta 186
Time Research Institute 78
timing task as psi test 48-51

University
   of California at Berkeley 24
   of California at Davis 53, 55, 90, 92, 145, 159, 164
   of Edinburgh 100, 107
   of Idaho 62, 66
   of Illinois 56
   of Maryland 153
   of South Carolina 187

The Unobstructed Universe 152
Urantia Book 152

Virgin Mary, apparition of 148
Volition (video game) 17, 73-76

Water: A Comprehensive Treatise 24
Western science, competing traditions in 129
West Georgia College 30, 126, 161